Thinking on Thresholds

Thinking on Thresholds

The Poetics of Transitive Spaces

Edited by
Subha Mukherji

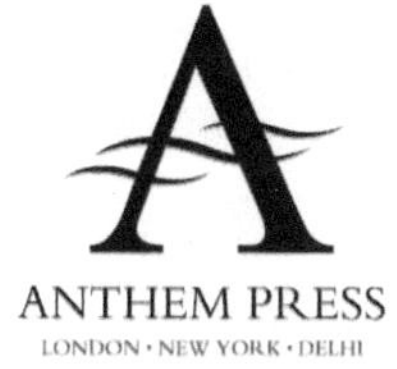

ANTHEM PRESS
LONDON • NEW YORK • DELHI

Anthem Press
An imprint of Wimbledon Publishing Company
www.anthempress.com

This edition first published in UK and USA 2013
by ANTHEM PRESS
75–76 Blackfriars Road, London SE1 8HA, UK
or PO Box 9779, London SW19 7ZG, UK
and
244 Madison Ave. #116, New York, NY 10016, USA

First published in hardback by Anthem Press in 2011

British Library Cataloguing-in-Publication Data
A catalogue record for this book is available from the British Library.

Library of Congress Cataloging-in-Publication Data
The Library of Congress has cataloged the hardcover edition as follows:
Thinking on thresholds : the poetics of transitive spaces / edited by Subha Mukherji.
p. cm.
Includes bibliographical references.
ISBN-13: 978-0-85728-665-9 (hardcover : alk. paper)
ISBN-10: 0-85728-665-X (hardcover : alk. paper)
1. Space in literature. 2. Boundaries in literature. 3. Liminality in literature.
I. Mukherji, Subha.
PN56.S667T55 2011
809'.99353–dc22
2010051141

ISBN-13: 978 1 78308 073 1 (Pbk)
ISBN-10: 1 78308 073 6 (Pbk)

This title is also available as an ebook.

In memory of Tony Nuttall –
easy inhabitant of many thresholds

ACKNOWLEDGEMENTS

I am grateful to the team of contributors to this volume for their enthusiasm for the project and their loyalty to it while it hovered on the threshold for some time. It has not only been fun, but also a privilege, to engage with their ongoing thoughts. My deepest personal debt is to Yota Batsaki, Beci Dobbin and Angela Leighton for their encouragement, their capacity for excitement and their intellectual generosity. To friends who have over time talked to me about thresholds, or offered comments, my warm thanks: they include Sukanta Chaudhuri, Mina Gorji and Nick Hammond. I am grateful, too, to Robert Douglas-Fairhurst, the series editor at Anthem, for allowing us to play with the idea. The two anonymous readers for the Press offered acute comments and invaluable suggestions: I am much beholden to them. I must finally thank Elizabeth Pender for her scrupulous copy-editing, saving us from basic errors as well as infelicities.

CONTENTS

LIST OF ILLUSTRATIONS

NOTES ON CONTRIBUTORS

Dame Gillian Beer is Professor Emeritus at the University of Cambridge and is a Fellow of the British Academy and of the Royal Society of Literature. She is Senior Research Fellow at the Yale Center for British Art for the years 2009–2011. Among her publications are *Darwin's Plots* (1983; 2000; 2009) and *Virginia Woolf: the Common Ground* (1996). She is at present finishing a study of Lewis Carroll's *Alice* books.

Terence Cave is Emeritus Professor of French Literature at the University of Oxford, Emeritus Research Fellow of St John's College, Oxford, and a Fellow of the British Academy. His published work includes *The Cornucopian Text: Problems of Writing in the French Renaissance* (OUP, 1979), *Recognitions: A Study in Poetics* (OUP, 1988) and, forthcoming from OUP in 2011, *Mignon's Afterlives: Crossing Cultures from Goethe to the Twenty-First Century*. He was the winner of the 2009 Balzan Prize for literature since 1500.

Supriya Chaudhuri is Professor and Coordinator, Centre of Advanced Study, Department of English, Jadavpur University, Kolkata, India. She works both on the European Renaissance and on 19th and 20th century India. Her recent publications include a translation of Rabindranath Tagore's novel *Jogajog/Relationships* (OUP, 2005) and essays on Shakespeare, Spenser, Renaissance translation, domestic interiors, modernism, and the films of Satyajit Ray..

Jean Chothia is Reader in Drama and Theatre in the University of Cambridge and Fellow of Selwyn College. She is the author of books on Eugene O'Neill, André Antoine, and English Drama, 1890–1940; as well as articles on English and European drama. Plays edited include a volume of 'New Woman' plays for OUP and Shaw's *Saint Joan* (New Mermaids). She is currently completing a book on the staging of crowds.

Rosita D'Amora is Lecturer of Turkish Language and Literature at the University of Salento, Lecce. Her research interests range from Ottoman social history to contemporary Turkish literature, and, most recently, the emerging investigations of gender, linguistic and cultural differences, and borders in Turkish writing. She is the editor and translator of an anthology of Mehmet Yashin's poetry, author of several articles exploring cultural exchanges between the Ottoman Empire and Europe during the 17th century and an essay on contemporary women's writing in the Middle East for the Italian Encyclopaedia *Treccani.*

Beci Dobbin is a Research Fellow at Trinity College, Cambridge. She has recently published on literary modernism and the labour-saving device and works primarily on early-to-mid twentieth century British modernism. She obtained her PhD in January 2010 – on the Business of Living in British Literary Modernism – and now divides her time between supervising modernist dissertations and writing her book.

Rick Foot is a double bassist and composer. His recent work includes *A Phenomenology of Identity*, an installation piece for the SoundLAB collective in Köln; *Twice Reflected Sun*, an album with Nancy Kerr and James Fagan; and two collections of Lorca poems set to music with singer/guitarist Keith James.

Gabriel Josipovici is a novelist, playwright and critic. He taught in the School of European Studies at the University of Sussex from 1963 to 1998. His most recent publications (all 2010) are: *Only Joking* (a novel); *Heart's Wings* (selected short fiction); and a critical and polemical book, *Whatever Happened to Modernism?*

Jonathan Lamb is the Andrew W. Mellon Professor of the Humanities at Vanderbilt University. His books include *Sterne's Fiction and the Double Principle* (1989) and *The Rhetoric of Suffering: Reading the Book of Job in the Eighteenth Century* (1995). His most recent book, *Preserving the Self in the South Seas, 1680–1840* (2001), was awarded the John Ben Snow Prize by the North American Conference on British Studies.

Jeremy Lane is Senior Lecturer in English at the University of Sussex. His publications include 'Falling Asleep in the Wake: Reading as Hypnagogic Experience' in John Brannigan et al, eds, *Re: Joyce: Text, Culture, Politics* (Basingstoke: Macmillan, 1998); and 'James Joyce's Book of laughter and Forgetting' in Manfred Pfister, ed., *A History of English Laughter: Laughter from Beowulf to Beckett and Beyond* (Amsterdam/New York: Rodopi, 2002).

Angela Leighton is Senior Research Fellow at Trinity College, Cambridge. She is the author, among others, of *Shelley and the Sublime, Victorian Women*

Poets: Writing Against the Heart, and most recently *On Form: Poetry, Aestheticism, and the Legacy of a Word*. She has also published two volumes of poetry: *A Cold Spell* and *Sea Level*.

Subha Mukherji is Lecturer in English at the University of Cambridge. She is the author of *Law and Representation in Early Modern Drama* (2006) and several articles on Shakespeare and Renaissance literature; co-editor of *Early Modern Tragicomedy* (2007) and *Fictions of Knowledge: Fact, Evidence, Doubt* (forthcoming, 2011). Her current book-project focuses on doubt and epistemology in early modern literature.

Jason Scott-Warren is a Fellow of Gonville and Caius College and Senior Lecturer in the Faculty of English, University of Cambridge. His publications include *Sir John Harington and the Book as Gift* (2001) and *Early Modern English Literature* (2005). He is currently writing a microhistorical study of Shakespeare's first documented reader.

Michael Witmore is Professor of English at the University of Wisconsin, Madison. His most recent books are *Landscapes of the Passing Strange: Reflections from Shakespeare* (with Rosamond Purcell), *Shakespearean Metaphysics* and *Pretty Creatures: Children and Fiction in the English Renaissance* (Cornell). In addition to serving as textual editor for the *Comedy of Errors* with the new *Norton Shakespeare*, he is organizer of the Working Group for Digital Inquiry, a research collective that is mapping the prose genres of Early English Books Online using techniques from bioinformatics and corpus linguistics (www.winedarksea.org).

Frontispiece. Vilhelm Hammershøi, *Interior with a Woman Standing*, 1905. Image © Bruun Rasmussen Auctioneers.

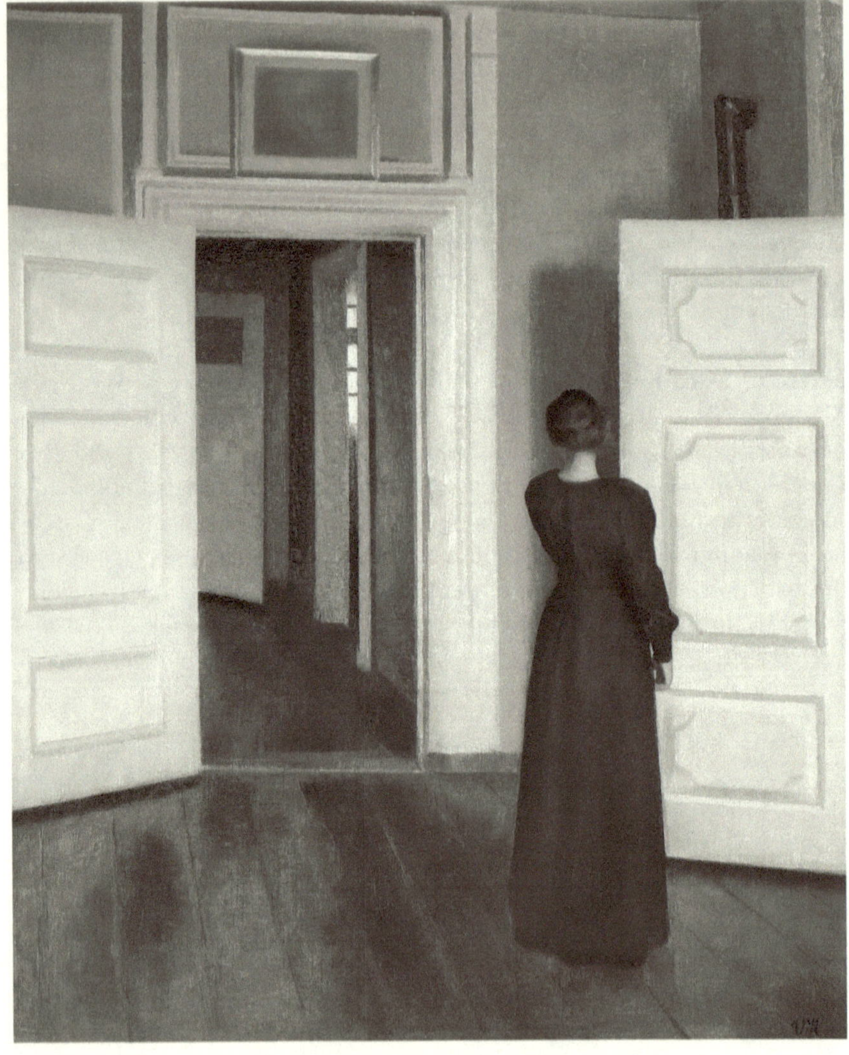

Introduction

THINKING ON THRESHOLDS

The woman in the painting on the cover of this book stands with her back to us. She is far from open to the viewer. What is half-open in the painting is the door in front of her, and indeed also the door to her right, and another door and a sliver of sun-lit window glimmering from the interior into which the central door allows us a peek. The woman's head, in keeping with the tentativeness of the doors, is half-turned towards the main door and the recess into which it opens. Her body is turned – though only partly – towards the door on the right. The positions of the human figure and the architectural figures speak to each other and build up to an image that holds a delicate, precarious, yet oddly calm and luminous sense of the uncertain, the indeterminate and the transitory. The lure of the image lies partly in the infinite possibilities of what Gaston Bachelard might have called objects that may be opened; partly in the tease of being made to pause on the brink, at the moment when clarity, definition and even interiority are just beyond grasp; partly in the fascination of transitional spaces; and partly in the risk, even unease, underlying moments of transition, and the excitement of not knowing where one might end up. It is defined by a sense of contingency, and it shapes narrative into a structure of desire. The thrill and the risk, meanwhile, are counterbalanced by the curious harmony of this tentative in-between space as, nevertheless, a cherished dwelling place, conjured up by the artist's use of light and shadow and rhythm. In fact it is an image that encapsulates the lure of the poetics of the threshold. It cannot be an accident that so many writers and artists have found in the threshold a metaphor for the creative process. As Bachelard writes, '[t]he poet speaks on the threshold of being'.[1] But it is also a condition under which, as Barthes might say, a work finds its taker. It speaks at once to the generative and the receptive imagination.

Why does the position of the threshold exert such a compelling hold on our imaginative lives? Why is it such a resonant space? Why is it so urgently the place of writing – the place where (as Derrida puts it) one may remain, avoid speaking or naming, yet speak from?[2] Through a combination of case studies and theoretical investigations, the essays in this book address these questions and speak to the imaginative power of the threshold as a productive space in literature and art. Though it engages with specialised discussions, the book begins and ends with why and how art represents, explores and negotiates threshold experience. The essays are diverse, both in terms of critical perspective and methodology, and in terms of their discursive fields, encompassing social thinking and the aesthetic imagination. In this, they reflect the multiplicity of theoretical and disciplinary approaches to the threshold. But the range itself gives meaning to the ways in which they end up being in dialogue with each other, and the consistency with which they offer a literary intervention. The essays in Part I address representations of actual, physical thresholds in literature, drama and the visual arts – the parts played by doors, windows and doorsills. Those in Part II explore thresholds of selves and worlds, both personal and political, overlapping at times with territorial borders and boundaries, and at other times, with linguistic interfaces: but the focus is always on the relation between form or medium, be it narrative or music or film or dance or historiography, and the borders being encountered or crossed or dwelt on in lived experience. Part III offers two essays, which address in different ways the object of thought in the osmotic zone that is the sensing body – that threshold between matter and mind, waking and sleeping, the worldly and the ghostly. The final group of essays, in Part IV, are explicitly concerned with the ways in which the processes of writing, reading, playing and hearing are activities that negotiate thresholds, even if in the form of a conscious effacing of demarcated boundaries.

The division of the essays into Parts is to a large extent a creation of thresholds only to sense how they may be crossed and spoken across. What emerges is the investment of all these essays, in one way or another, in the affinity between the artistic process – imagining, creating or representing – and the spatial idea of the threshold in its material and figurative manifestations. Witness Beci Dobbin's reading of doors as instruments of the management of knowledge in Nabokov's *Laughter in the Dark*, refracting in turn into narratological thresholds such as brackets which signal the uneasy epistemic balance between author and reader. Another curious feature that comes across is the capacity of the threshold as a space and a starting idea to beget yet more crossing points, to proliferate into thresholds of other kinds – cognitive, representational and even critical. This tendency is most clearly at play in Terence Cave's essay which addresses the inexhaustibly variant afterlives that are the legacy of Goethe's positioning of Mignon at multiple thresholds. There is more to this relation than simple analogy: it has to do with the issue of how categories are constructed and how they can be destabilised. The suggestive blurriness of such statements as Bachelard's is also perhaps related to this. As Jeremy Lane's essay suggests, intermediate and indeterminate states of mind are not so much fallings from us, vanishings, as a distinct state of consciousness that allows the magical thinking which makes the literary condition possible. The freedom from rational clarity enables a vigilance, a wakeful seeing. This sense of a threshold of attention is what Angela Leighton also explores, in the different context of the ear as a physical threshold of listening. Ultimately, she posits a theory of literary language itself as a productive obstacle that prevents easy meaning and forces us to listen rather than simply to hear.

The history of thinking about the threshold goes back to anthropological theory. The notion that individual as well as communal life involves a series of critical thresholds to be traversed was first theorised by Arnold van Gennep in *Les Rites de Passage* (1908), where rites of passage are divided into rites of separation (preliminal), transition (liminal), and incorporation (post-liminal). Liminality has always been a polysemous concept. In physiology and psychology, *limen* is a threshold between psychological and physical experience. What is liminal is situated at a sensory threshold, something barely perceptible; poised between the explicit and the implicit, between external and internal, and by extension, between familiar and alien. Indeed, the body itself can act as a threshold between the self and the material world. Thus, van Gennep's formulations give us a vocabulary for addressing the elusive but crucial experiences at a variety of boundaries, and offer a preliminary definition of their scope – psychic, communal, physiological, geographical, political and epistemological. Cave's essay examines the way in which literary narratives explore these transitions, both their potency and their fragility. Gabriel Josipovici's, on the other hand, sees the threshold as the porous place that most clearly marks the blurring of decisive transitions, and the joining of the individual with the larger group, in life and in narrative – be it in traditional cultures, Islamic architecture, Japanese temples, the open room of Dante's interlinked tercets, or the 'unknown, remembered gate' of Eliot.[3]

The anthropological idea of the *limen* was reconfigured by French theorists, as for example in Julia Kristeva's formulation of points of entry or insertion – an interface between concept and experience. In Derrida's work, the idea of the threshold structures the ethics of interpersonal relations, the interface between the self and the other. But it is an idea that he found productive in a variety of applications, such as his theory of hospitality – considered here in my essay on Annunciations. Sign-making is seen in Derrida's work as a threshold activity, facing in both directions, *à double sens*. The imagination itself often figures as a threshold where a rite of passage occurs between sense and sensibility.

Central to a variety of literary, critical and aesthetic applications of the threshold is the architectural imagination. Gérard Genette's notion of architextuality, and his seminal work, *Paratexts: Thresholds of Interpretation* (1987), marked an important translation of the architectural idea into textual criticism, offering a new language for thinking about the text and our experience of it. The paratext, for Genette, is not only a space of transition but of transaction; it marks as well as occupies the text's threshold, being a space which is both inside and outside – a phenomenon that Jason Scott-Warren explicitly engages with in order to show how in fact 'reading is an affair of the threshold' (158). Related to this is how narrative is implicated in its spaces – the question of frames and boundaries addressed here by both Rosita D'Amora and Cave. Genette's notion, however, was already anticipated by Derrida in *Truth in Painting*, where the paratext both frames and gives rise to the text. Derrida's critique has implications for both aesthetics and philosophy, and has had long-reaching impact on how we think about the unity of an artefact or an experience.

Unsurprisingly, the theory and history of art constitute, together, a prominent domain in which the threshold is a vital metaphor. Here too, it provides a rich resource for theoretical exploration, as in Foucault's famous analysis of *Las Meninas* in *The Order of Things*, where Velazquez, the artist who inscribes himself in his picture, is presented as someone who 'rules on the threshold of…two incompatible visibilities'.[4] This has proved a provocative – and proliferating – point of departure. As David Carroll writes, 'Foucault is interested in all such thresholds, for the threshold indicates the fragility of any perspective on the visible, including Foucault's own. The painter is said to "[*rule*] on the threshold", but, in fact, the threshold is precisely the fine line where no one and no one thing rules, where all sovereignty is undermined, where incompatible spaces, epistemes, and modes of discourse struggle for dominance'.[5] Cave's discussion of the repeated unsettling of thresholds considers such tensions around categories and boundaries. Dobbin's discussion, as well as mine, of the entwining of secrets and knowledges at the threshold tap into precisely such epistemic tussles and ambivalence. Clearly, what is merely a line in space and on the page, teems in the mind.

Yet, in paintings themselves, the threshold can intimate hinterlands – befores and afters – as much as it can delude with a false sense of access. A modern painter whose glance was riveted to doorways and windows – occasionally recalling the more portentous 'sublimity' of Kaspar David Friedrich – is Vilhelm Hammershøi, the painter of the cover-image that we started with. His works had a retrospective at the Royal Academy's exhibition, 'The Poetry of Silence' (June–September, 2008). In an acute and poetic review of it in the *Times Literary Supplement* (August 13, 2008), Josipovici comments on how, in a painting such as *Interior, Strandgade 30*, the woman we see 'is half, but only half turned towards the window and the light. We cannot tell if she is looking inwards or outwards… she is not our means of access to a vision beyond', unlike the solitary figures in Friedrich who have their backs to us. Windows and doors and their luminous materiality in Hammershøi, Josipovici feels, mark the radical contingency that is the hallmark of one kind of modernism, the kind that has freed itself of the anxiety of telos. What is evident is the mesmeric quality of the threshold, whether pregnant with signification or radiant in a presence that resists and teases hermeneutic overload; whether a juncture in a teleology, or an interruption of telos. The essays here – most prominently by Josipovici himself, but also mine – examine both textual and visual encounters with the threshold in the light of these implications, and indeed the threshold between the textual and the visual. The doors that Nabokov's Albinus faces in Dobbin's essay embody the false promise of leading somewhere, presenting only surfaces. Gillian Beer's essay, meanwhile, ponders the interplay of access and exclusion, connection and separation, at domestic thresholds in literature – in particular, windows.

Windows are made of glass. You can see through glass, and yet it 'represents the first degree of opacity', as Isobel Armstrong puts it in her gripping study of Victorian glassworks; for glass 'is both *medium and barrier*'.[6] And this is why windows are such an eloquent threshold, indeed an embodiment of some of those essential qualities and associations that make the threshold a site of poetics. Like glass, the threshold itself, though not a material medium, has nevertheless that combination of porosity and resistance that creates pressures between which the imagination thrives. Jean Chothia discusses windows on the nineteenth-century stage, underlining the paradox of illusionist theatre through the suggestion, and then complication, of a permeable surface between inner and outer worlds. Beer talks of Yeats's schoolboy image for Keats in 'Ego Dominus Tuus', 'with face and nose pressed to a sweet-shop window', 'shut out from all the luxury of the world',[7] and yet, as she points out, from that longing and deprivation, from 'that gap between the nose and the sweets, the cold glass between, comes "Luxuriant song"' (7–8). It is at the same time Yeats's comment on the condition of his own poetry – born out of the exercise of the mind in the space between glimpsing and failing to grasp or touch. The frisson of that space makes the cold glass warm with creative energy. That gap is a type of threshold, both physically and metaphorically, embodying the enticement of what lies just out of reach, the reality of the barrier as well as the possibility of stepping across, the permeable but nonetheless inalienable difference between inside and outside.

But the image of the shop-window also suggests the flâneur, gazing, window-shopping, arcade-haunting, desiring, dwelling in-between. This is Benjamin territory. In *Passagen-Werk* (or *The Arcades Project*), he not only writes about the threshold as a place at once of transitivity and intoxication, but also describes the arcade as threshold. In his larger body of work, he engages with a qualified time dialectics in addressing historical phenomena. *Passagen-Werk* is about space dialectics and its relation to temporal dialectics. Like history, the threshold is Janus-faced, looking not only in and out, but behind and ahead.[8] It is also a space that refracts into poetic intuition; more specifically, into a modern urban poetics. It is the building block of a speculative theory of culture that seeks to understand a system of relationships hovering in between 'private and public space, past and future, dream and waking'.[9] Benjamin's own description of products about to enter the world of commodities is suggestive here, for the dialectical interface at which they are located is also, for him, the point of collision or encounter of representational orders, at which the phenomenon of art generates itself:

> But they linger on the threshold. From this epoch derive the arcades and *intérieurs*, the exhibition halls and panoramas. They are residues of a dream world. The realisation of dream elements, in the course of waking up, is the paradigm of dialectical thinking.[10]

Benjamin's essay on Naples offers complementary insight into why porosity is so central to his aesthetics. 'The interlacing of street and domestic interior' that absorbs him in the First Sketches of *Passagen-Werk*[11] suffuses the architecture and activities of the entire city of Naples, where 'balcony, courtyard, window, gateway, staircase and roof' become the most fascinating sites of performance and expectation: 'porosity is the inexhaustible law of the life of this city, reappearing everywhere'.[12] The Naples café is singled out as a true laboratory of intermingling, of movement and process: 'Life is unable to sit down and stagnate in them'.[13] And where life stagnates, art freezes. The neutrality of the intermediate spaces makes them the most dynamic location, and the most fecund, as it most naturally resists settling into categories. Thus, in the overall frame of Benjamin's thought, the threshold becomes a crucial figure as a point of indifference/weakness that could turn into difference/power, a site of eventuality.[14]

In as much as Benjamin's concept of the threshold resists the doctrine of categories itself, it suggests immense possibilities for the aesthetic imagination and for genre. This sense of openness speaks precisely to the pursuit of freedom that Rick Foot identifies in improvisational jazz, to lose which is a kind of death. Hence his equation of recording with the 'death of jazz': stepping beyond the 'threshold experience' (more brink, here, than boundary) – 'the inherent process of becoming' – is to leap off the edge where music dwells, and to risk stasis (185). Foot's argument finds resonance in Jeremy Lane's idea of the creative impetus of 'hypnagogia' – the intermediate mental state between sleeping and waking in which 'an awareness of imagination as experience of and on the threshold is enabled' – and the sensuousness of that passage into freedom (143). This in turn has shades of Benjamin's 'dream elements', at the same time as it speaks to the 'dream states' to which windows provide access in the children's literature addressed in Beer's essay. Lane's examples are Montaigne, Keats and Proust, but his thesis also reminds one of Yeats on rhythm – and rhythm for Yeats was the very pulse of poetry – as a denizen of 'the threshold of sleep', where he ultimately locates 'powerful and startling life': art itself, including patterns, symbols and music.[15]

The emphasis in these essays, as in Benjamin, is on the productivity of dwelling on the threshold, recalling such diverse ideas as Keats's negative capability – the capacity to abide in uncertainties, mysteries, doubts – on the one hand, and on the other, aesthetic form as Barthes describes it – 'what is *between* the thing and its name, … what delays the name'.[16] But lingering has its aesthetic hazards, and crossing the threshold has its yield. Even Foot, for whom the process is the essence and to treat recording as a document of improvisation is a category error, admits, after Milton Babbitt, that in the context of performance, such dwelling can incur the risk of solipsism. For Beer, the threshold can offer an illusory security which is liable to dissolve or explode – as with the shattered window which Heathcliff tries to burst through to touch his dead love, hurling the reader into 'extreme fiction … a dream that will not let you go' (12). But the violence of breaking through can itself be a jolt into feeling that is productive in a creative sense, and the physical threshold here becomes the necessary obstacle that makes the bursting palpable. This in turn is in partial dialogue with Leighton's argument about the ear enforcing the labour of the mind that allows us to figure out meaning in poetry by rupturing familiar, accustomed hearing. The threshold then is not only a potential site of suspension as well as irruption, but also a place of rigour and work – the threshold between body and mind is also one between poetry and its reader, painting and its observer, music and its audience.

Several other areas have proved fertile ground for dialogue. The idea of the threshold is politically eloquent, and has had immediate and urgent application in our times in the sphere of geopolitical boundaries, their intransigencies as well as fluidities. It has been an operative metaphor as well as a sociological reality for human rights, ethnography and gender studies. Post-colonial and minority studies have been naturally drawn to its functionality. Gloria Anzaldùa's *Borderlands* influentially posits a threshold sensibility, a crossroads personhood and a new 'bastard language' in addressing the 'third space' opened up at the US-Mexican border where the 'mestiza consciousness' develops.[17] In Edward Said's thinking, a situation at the boundary between cultures is a condition of possibility for secular criticism: his example is the European humanist Erich Auerbach, for whom, he argues, writing about Europe was made possible by his 'deeply resonant and intense form of exile' across the border to Europe's other, the threshold territory of Turkey.[18] Istanbul comes to embody the literal displacement which dramatises, as it were, the tragically productive condition of proximate alienation from 'sense, nation and milieu' in which Auerbach, a refugee from European fascism, wrote *Mimesis*.[19] No wonder, then, that the threshold has provided such a charged metaphor in our times for writing out of diasporic cultural positions, as in M. G. Vassanji's 2009 Smuts lecture in Cambridge which addressed 'Writing from places in-between'.[20] It is the poetics of such writing that D'Amora and Jonathan Lamb explore in this collection, assimilating the political to an imaginative project that fuses the expository and the aesthetic. D'Amora addresses writing from, and about, hazy buffer zones – specifically the no-man's land between divided Cyprus – through a reading of the questioning of borders in the Turkish Cypriot author Mehmet Yashin's (Yaşın) fiction. She traces Yashin's rejoining of languages currently segregated by national borders and his restoration of these 'tongues' to their pre-national permeability, by fashioning an osmotic threshold of literary speech. Lamb, meanwhile, figures the beach as a threshold of cultural encounter between the indigenes and European visitors in the South Seas. He suggests that cross-cultural dancing became a form of negotiation of the differences, confusions and fantasies of this variety of no man's land, not only challenging an examination of the understanding and knowledge achieved at this boundary, but also demanding a re-examination of modern historians' access to such knowledge. Lamb's essay is also a reminder that it is not only the city, but also the coast and indeed the sea, that have come into focus in modernism's engagements with the threshold. One may recall Fredric Jameson on the sea in Conrad as 'a border and a decorative limit, but … also a highway, out of the world and in it at once.'[21] Conrad's townsfolk in Sulaco, the imaginary port on the Pacific coast of Costaguana in *Nostromo*, declare that 'under the Ocean Navigation Company's care, their lives and property were safer on the water than in their own houses on shore.'[22] The sea is the edge of land, an alternative to land as well as an interspace; but it is also a non-place between destinations. While in Conrad, the sea is distinguished from the shore, elsewhere it is the sea that defines the spatial character of the beach, and not necessarily by contrast. Feigel and Harris's collection of essays, *Modernism on Sea*, signposts the sea-shore as a liminal site of modernist culture in Britain.[23] Lamb takes the conversation further afield, and brings the Pacific coast into imaginative dialogue with another kind of beach, the one that separates the present from the past, and at which cultural history operates.

The threshold has acquired increasing potency in thinking about the body and the world in medical and anthropological research, with ramifications in literary and cultural studies on the body, the skin, and the psyche. Like Lane,

Michael Witmore also addresses several of these interfaces, at the same time raising questions about history and its relation to the boundaries of self and consciousness. The threshold here is what is breached when bodies touch and sensation happens; and the ghost in *Hamlet* is shown to make the very idea paradoxical and problematic. But the intertwining of flesh, voice and memory that so troubles Hamlet ultimately provides the threshold at which we touch the past and are touched by it. It is interesting that the spectral has been seen as an operative category in literature, in as much as it raises questions about boundaries: T. J. Lustig, for example, in his book on 'the ghostly' in Henry James, sees it as a threshold experience which focuses heightened attention to the aesthetic moment and its physiological accounts. From Defoe's Mrs. Veal to Shakespeare's Old Hamlet, ghosts are said to have become a 'touchstone' in understanding the perceptual functions of fiction.[24] In its very different context, my essay also apprehends a phenomenological threshold in its reading of the way in which poems and paintings grasp as well as demand an experience at 'the edges of our flesh', on the brink between mind and muscle.[25]

Finally, a prominent context for thinking of thresholds has turned out to be the investigation of domestic space across disciplines and periods. Important historicist work on spatial perceptions and the gendering of the domestic interior includes Lena Orlin's on the early modern household, Michael McKeon's on the history of domesticity in the eighteenth century, Milette Shamir's on architecture, gender and privacy in Antebellum American Literature, and critical studies of domestic œconomies in relation to literary genres such as late sixteenth- and early seventeenth-century domestic drama.[26] The threshold of the house emerges as a significant affective space in such studies, as well as in the literary treatments some of them engage with. Its containing nature and its transgressive temptations are vividly spelt out, for example, in the anonymous 1590s domestic tragedy, *A Warning for Fair Women*, based on a contemporary scandal, and juggling providentialism and sensationalism as such plays often did. Here, Mistress Sanders, a city merchant's wife living a hum-drum life, encounters her prospective seducer as she sits on the threshold of her marital home: the result is adultery, murder and execution.[27] The creation of other in-between spaces inside the house, such as hallways and corridors, with changes in architectural trends, has been traced both in the seventeenth and eighteenth centuries, suggesting shifts in the experience of privacy and its limits. Chiara Briganti and Kathy Mezei's comprehensive project, *The Domestic Space Reader* (in progress for Toronto University Press), will gather together some of the most significant writing on domestic space across times, cultures and disciplines, from anthropology to fiction, and devote an entire section to 'Liminal Spaces' – domestic thresholds such as doors, windows, porch and garden. Supriya Chaudhuri's essay in our volume takes part in, and feeds into, this burgeoning interest, directly exploring as it does the gendered interface between the home and the world in nineteenth- and early twentieth century India, with special reference to Rabindranath Tagore's great novel *The Home and the World*, and its cinematic treatment by Satyajit Ray – arousing thoughts in turn of the threshold between media. And yet, such a temporally and culturally specific exploration is, at the same time, in dialogue with Gillian Beer's reflections on Woolf's Clarissa Dalloway's sense of being left out, or left in, when she is not invited to a lunch party at which her husband is a guest. As Clarissa walks up the stairs slowly, as if she had just left a party, she pauses by the open staircase window. As Beer puts it, the window 'becomes the focal point of feeling' as it does at other moments to other characters (14). The curious link is the organic connection between physical thresholds of the house and the animated liminal functions of thought and imagination that come alive at these apertures, the chiaroscuro at play at these boundaries that can open out or close in. Both this conjunction, and the way in which it cuts across societies and times despite highly specific nuances, are part of the story.

This book, then, thinks of the threshold not only as a space or a metaphor but also as a constitutive term, a category of experience that organizes thinking and feeling, in lived reality and in art. It aims to do so in a language that gets across some of the pleasure and play of the artworks in question, something of their feel; and which demonstrates as well as reflects on the regenerative threshold between representation and aesthetics. What is it in narrative and mimetic art that prompts the expansion of the idea of the threshold in art theory? What is it in life that leads anthropological theorists to seize on this spatial concept? What is it in literary texts that draws critics to think in abstract and theoretical terms about this space? From Keats's 'charmed magic casements', and the 'burden of the mystery' that enwraps him as he stands 'in a mist' at the threshold of the many doors that are set open on all sides of the 'Chamber of Maiden Thoughts', to the door that swings open in the middle of Isa's reverie in Woolf's *Between the Acts*, through which Mrs. Swithins marches reality into Isa's fantasy, from the porch and the doorways in Annunciation paintings of the fifteenth century to the windows on the late nineteenth-century stage, thresholds pervade and provoke. Poetic form itself can be a kind of threshold, the 'constructed space' of W. S. Graham, '[so] that somehow something may move across / The caught habits of language…'[28] Speaking aslant, 'lines that cut through time or cross it withershins',[29] seem to capture and create something intrinsic to the grain of poetry. It is the texture of such thresholds, and the power of such movements across, that this book seeks to communicate – Beer and Leighton's essays capture these elusive but profoundly affective functions, while Josipovici's both enacts and muses on them. The volume also brings into dialogue, uniquely, the theoretical uses of the idea and what Keats would call 'a sense of real things' – entities that can suffer an unfortunate divorce in critical practice. For it is part of its aim to unite the discursive and the affective, domains which the threshold seems naturally to straddle. To that end, the essays here are thoughts in process – 'essays' in the original sense of the term, attempts at working out, and through, an idea, opening up rather than sealing off fields of thought, probing rather than resolving the enticing insecurity of dwelling on thresholds – both those represented in art, and those at which works of imagination are in touch with their self-effecting pulse. For it is at the mobile threshold between these two senses that the idea of 'thresholds' finds its life in art, and indeed in criticism.

Subha Mukherji

Notes

1 Gaston Bachelard, *The Poetics of Space*, trans. Maria Jolas, introd. John Stilgoe (Boston, Mass.: Beacon, 1994), xvi.

2 Jacques Derrida, 'How to Avoid Speaking: Denials', trans. Ken Friedren, in *Derrida and Negative Theology*, ed. Harold Coward and Toby Foshay (Albany: State University of New York Press, 1992), 73–142 (96–122, especially 96 and 121; see also 94).

3 T. S. Eliot, 'Little Gidding', in *Collected Poems 1909–1962* (London: Faber and Faber, 1974, repr. 2002), 201–209 (209).

4 Michel Foucault, *The Order of Things: An Archaeology of the Human Science* (London: Tavistock Publications, 1970), 3.

5 David Carroll, *Paraesthetics: Foucault, Lyotard, Derrida* (New York: Methuen, 1987), 62–3.

6 Isobel Armstrong, *Victorian Glassworks: Glass Culture and the Imagination 1830–1880* (Oxford: Oxford University Press, 2008), 7.

7 W. B. Yeats, 'Ego Dominus Tuus', in *The Collected Poems of W. B. Yeats* (London: Macmillan, 1950), 180–183 (182).

8 See Walter Benjamin, *The Arcades Project*, trans. Howard Eiland and Kevin McLaughlin (Cambridge, Mass.: Harvard University Press, 1999, repr. 2002), 14, epigraph from Maxime du Camp.

9 Jan Mieszkowski, 'Art Forms', in David S. Ferris, ed., *The Cambridge Companion to Walter Benjamin* (Cambridge: Cambridge University Press, 2004), 35–53 (49).

10 Benjamin, *Arcades*, 13.

11 Ibid., 861.

12 Walter Benjamin, 'Naples', in *Reflections: Essays, Aphorisms, Autobiographical Writings*, ed. Peter Demetz (New York: Schocken, 1987), 163–173 (167 and 168).

13 Ibid., 172.

14 I am grateful to Michele del Prete for an illuminating conversation about Benjamin's dialectics, and for directing me to Winfried Menninghaus's excellent discussion in *Schwellenkunde: Walter Benjamin's Passage des Mythos* (Frankfurt am Main: Suhrkamp, 1986).

15 W. B. Yeats, 'The Symbolism of Poetry', in *Essays and Introductions* (London: Macmillan, 1961), 153–164 (160).

16 Roland Barthes, *The Responsibility of Forms: Critical Essays on Music, Art, and Representation*, trans. Richard Howard (Oxford: Blackwell, 1986), 234.

17 Gloria Andalzùa, *Borderlands/La Frontera: The New Mestiza* (San Francisco: Aunt Lute, 1987).

18 Edward Said, 'Secular Criticism', in *The World, Text and the Critic* (Cambridge, Mass.: Harvard University Press, 1983), 1–30 (6).

19 Ibid., especially 5–9 (6). See also Erich Auerbach, *Mimesis: The Representation of Reality in Western Literature*, trans. Willard R. Trask (Princeton, N. J.: Princeton University Press, 1953), 557, for Auerbach's own comment on the conditions under which he reached 'the point of writing' in Istanbul.

20 See also the works of Amitav Ghosh – especially *Shadow Lines* (1988) and *In an Antique Land* (1992) – which combine fiction with anthropology and ethnography to negotiate both the artificiality and the dialogic potential of 'shadow lines' between cultures, nations, histories and disciplines.

21 Fredric Jameson, *The Political Unconscious* (1981; London: Routledge, 2002), 198. For Jameson's Conrad, this sense of its being 'out of the world and in it at once' lends the sea the deceptive allure of an oasis from capitalism; it carries forward not only the world's trade but also its fantasies.

22 Joseph Conrad, *Nostromo: A Tale of the Seaboard*, ed. Jacques Berthould and Mara Kalnins (Oxford: Oxford University Press, 2007), 9.

23 Lara Feigel and Alexandra Harris, eds, *Modernism on Sea: Art and Culture at the British Seaside* (Oxford: Peter Lang, 2005).

24 T. J. Lustig, *Henry James and the Ghostly* (Cambridge: Cambridge University Press, 1994), Ch. 1, 'The Threshold', 10–49 (34).

25 W. B. Yeats, *Discoveries: A Volume of Essays* (Dundrum: Dunn Emer Press, 1907), 38.

26 See, for example, Lena Cowen Orlin, *Private Matters and Public Culture in post-Reformation England* (Ithaca: Cornell University Press, 1994); Michael McKeon, *The Secret History of Domesticity: Public, Private and the Division of Knowledge* (Baltimore: Johns Hopkins University Press, 2005); and Milette Shamir, *Inexpressible Privacy: The Interior Life of Antebellum American Literature* (Philadelphia: University of Pennsylvania Press, 2006).

27 *A Warning for Fair Women*, ed. Charles Dale Cannon (The Hague: Mouton, 1975).

28 W. S. Graham, 'The Constructed Space', in *New Collected Poems*, ed. Matthew Francis (London: Faber and Faber, 2004), 161–2 (162).

29 W. B. Yeats, 'Coole Park, 1929' in *Selected Poetry*, 169–70 (170).

Part One

DOORS, WINDOWS, ENTRIES

Chapter One

WINDOWS: LOOKING IN, LOOKING OUT, BREAKING THROUGH

Gillian Beer

Windows: all about us, unremarkable; or remarkable mainly in their scientific extensions, as microscopes, telescopes, X-rays, CAT scans. Here it is the *unremarked* I want to examine: domestic windows, and some of their meanings in literature.[1]

What is a window? framed space? A liminal connection between inner and outer? an aperture that reveals a scene beyond, or a scene within? an impermeable membrane? security against weather and intruders? or the source of replenishing light? Doors police the threshold, windows relate the outside world to the interior. But windows, particularly in cinema, as often suggest spying and seclusion as they do an opening into the contingent world outside the self. Hitchcock's *Rear Window* is the classic example. The act of photography funnels sight through an aperture upon a scene at once distanced and held, beyond the power of touch. Paintings may present themselves as windows into a landscape, as we experience in Corot or in Bruegel, or the figures in them may crowd forward, bulging out of the frame towards us, as if emerging through a window. That effect is found in Pre-Raphaelite work, for example, in Rossetti's picture in the Fitzwilliam Museum of a girl peering out of a lattice window. My materials and my argument here, though, are concerned not so much with visual art as with literature and with the *unframed* images that writing conjures in the reader's mind.

The window may affirm connection but equally it may assert exclusion. When a window is mentioned the viewpoint most often implied is of the person looking out: though, I shall suggest, looking in is as powerful an experience. I wrote this essay on a programme called 'windows' and the framed screen suggests access to the interior of my thoughts, made manifest though not quite material, on the screen's surface. It suggests also access through the computer to further tools and potentialities: 'windows' as a brand name heightens our expectations of enlightenment. That idea of 'enlightenment' was brought to a crisis long ago in Mary Shelley's *Frankenstein*. One of the most poignant examples of the window as figuring both access and exclusion occurs in the monster's story. The creature tells how the panes of the windows in his hovel 'had been filled up with wood':

> In one of these was a small and almost imperceptible chink, through which the eye could just penetrate. Through this crevice a small room was visible, whitewashed and clean, but very bare of furniture.[2]

The monster spends the winter as a benign secret observer of the gentle family, gradually learning through his growing affection for them how relationships work and how language can be used. His pleasure in silent learning is disrupted when in an experience of looking, out of doors, he discovers himself reflected in a pond, and starts back, an anti-Narcissus, shamed and horrified:

> I had admired the perfect forms of my cottagers – their grace, beauty, and delicate complexions: but how was I terrified, when I viewed myself in a transparent pool! At first I started back, unable to believe that it was indeed I who was reflected in the mirror; and when I became fully convinced that I was in reality the monster that I am, I was filled with the bitterest sensations of despondence and mortification.[3]

The monster has learnt to judge himself by the measure of the human, first through his window-crack out into benign enlightenment, and then through the reflecting pool that allows him no escape from himself and his difference. Window and mirror are the two poles of his experience here.

The monster's window was covered by wood, not glass, so sight was almost baffled. Nowadays, the idea of a window in a building brings with it the suggestion of glass: of sight without touch. Glass privileges sight and subdues the haptic (in which sight realises itself as touch). But windows originally, and above all, let in light and air and were often open spaces covered only by shutters or curtains. Even after glass came into use casement windows swung open entire, leaving no barrier between inner and framed outer air: as Keats wrote in 'To a Nightingale': 'magic casements, opening on the foam/Of perilous seas'. Then came sash windows with their obdurate, and doubled, layer of glass when the window is fully open, set like a sash around the middle. Though a less metaphorical source for the word is claimed as being the French 'chassis' or frame.

All the materials set into a window frame – whether horn, mica, or glass – seal the passage between outer and inner, inner and outer. Often in the past they offered a blurred translucency rather than full vision. What did St. Paul mean when he said that now we see as *through* a glass, darkly? Or did he mean *in* a glass, dimly? Different translations suggest that he meant either a window or a mirror. Perhaps, he meant not so much a looking glass as the swirling surface of green glass such as the Romans often produced, or the thick knotted surfaces of glass such as George Herbert evokes in his poem of the 1630s, 'The Elixir':

> A man that looks on glasse,
> On it may stay his eye;
> Or if he pleaseth, through it passe,
> And then the heav'n espie.[4]

The eye, that is, may dwell on the material substance of the glass or may pass through it to what – more glorious – lies beyond. Elsewhere, in a poem called 'The Windows' Herbert writes of 'brittle, crazy glass': *crazing* (irregular cracking) detains the eye, making it dwell on the surface instead of reaching further. So the soul is hampered by the materiality of the world, Herbert implies. The eye itself was traditionally held to be the window between the soul (or, sometimes, the heart or mind) and the outer world, vouching for the inner qualities of the person in their gaze upon the world: 'Behold the window of my heart, mine eie', a character in Shakespeare's *Love's Labours Lost* offers as assurance.

But rather than mount an argument to track historical change in the functions of windows – a vast field in itself – I here take some examples of the different meanings that windows have borne in literature depending on whether the viewpoint is from within or from without. Doors manifestly control threshold spaces, but windows do so too. I shall examine some of the taboos that have gathered around the presence of windows and their association with revolutionary or catastrophic change. The social changes expressed in the material actuality of windows cannot, of course, be ignored: in Britain windows were blocked up as a result of window taxes but are still structurally apparent on some old houses (a theme that the sculptor Rachel Whiteread took up in her sculpture, 'House', where all the interior elements of an actual abandoned house – fireplaces, lintels, doors, windows – were expressed on the exterior of the building, so that the whole seemed inside out, and blind). Now, since the coming of plate glass, strengthened glass, one-way glass, entire buildings may be great palaces of window space.

The window registers connection and difference between interior and exterior. It allows us to be in two scenes at once. It affirms the presence of other ways of being, other patterns of objects, just beyond the concentrated space of the observer. The earliest poem that we have from the pen of the

American poet Elizabeth Bishop (aged 16, and published in the Walnut Hill School magazine in 1927) is a singularly harmonious imagining of such encounter. As so often, the presence of a tree marks the trajectory to and fro between inner and outer, its leaves tracing the air they share.

To a Tree

Oh, tree outside my window, we are kin,
For you ask nothing of a friend but this:
To lean against the window and peer in
And watch me move about! Sufficient bliss

For me, who stand behind its framework stout,
Full of my tiny tragedies and grotesque grieves,
To lean against the window and peer out,
Admitting infintes'mal leaves.[5]

That exquisite mingling of inner and outer has an erotic aspect too. The window is the passage way for lovers, romantically in *Romeo and Juliet*, with chilling energy in Julien's exploits in Stendhal's *Le Rouge et le Noir*, and absurdly in *The Marriage of Figaro* where Cherubino escaping out of the window lands among the gardener's prize plants. In this comic instance the erotic symbolism of entering the mistress's bedroom through a window orifice is less potent than the humiliation of the window as a point of flight from discovery.

When I was a child at school all the classroom windows were set at a height where it was impossible for a child to look out of them. This was supposed to aid concentration, and the enclosure certainly re-enforced the authority of the teacher as the dominant presence. Even now, in many new office buildings, windows have been done away with in the interiors, replaced by diffused lighting and air-conditioning. Yet rooms entirely without windows have been traditionally understood as sinister or subjected, and remain at least disagreeable. The presence of windows brings the light of the outside world to bear on what is happening within the room. Their absence subdues. Few managing directors lack windows in their offices. The window in its presence or absence is, then, very much part of the language of class, especially in the nineteenth century.

In a particularly affecting scene in Elizabeth Gaskell's *Mary Barton* (1848), a novel that explores the conditions of the working classes in England in the 1840's, the worker John Barton and his friend climb down into a noxious cellar where a family, starving and sick, are just surviving. The smell is foetid; the darkness all encompassing; the children at death's door; the mother on the point of starvation. John Barton goes to get medicine at a pharmacy, or what the narrative here calls a 'druggist's'. The narrator intervenes with a comradely address to the middle-class reader, a solidarity that is alluring and then firmly debarred:

> It is a pretty sight to walk through a street with lighted shops; the gas is so brilliant, the display of goods so much more vividly shown than by day, and of all shops a druggist's looks the most like the tales of our childhood, from Aladdin's garden of enchanted fruits to the charming Rosamond with her purple jar. No such associations had Barton; yet he felt the contrast between the well-filled, well-lighted shops and the dim gloomy cellar, and it made him moody that such contrasts should exist.[6]

First we readers are invited to step outside the frame of John's urgent errand, to delight as flaneurs and window-shoppers in the brightness of the windows and especially the glow of the jars in the apothecary's window. We are invited, too, to share the cultural privilege of a childhood stocked with storybooks of Aladdin and Rosamond, themselves windows into other worlds. Then, abruptly, the whole is silenced: 'No such associations had Barton'. He is troubled by the contrast between the wealth that lies openly displayed yet reserved inside the shops and the subterranean life of the very poor. He looks into the windows, but may enter only on the urgent mission to save life, rather than relishing aesthetic display. Yet there also is a residue of aesthetic pleasure trafficked between writer and reader in the description of the glowing shops, which has the effect of isolating John Barton further.

The idea of the excluded poor gazing in at elaborate window displays of wealth is a powerful image of class conflict that occurs also in Dickens and in Hans Andersen ('The Little Match Girl'). Indeed, it only begins to shift with the coming of open access to the big department stores at the beginning of the twentieth century, as Rachel Bowlby illuminatingly shows in *Just Looking* (1985). The emphasis on appetite forever unsatisfied, on a need that declares itself as greed because it is so voracious, is the ground of W. B. Yeats's self-argument in 'Ego Dominus Tuus'. The figure he adopts for understanding vehement longing is the excluded child 'with face and nose pressed to a sweet-shop window'. Yeats argues with his alter ego about creativity and happiness: are they possible together? 'Those that love the world serve it in action', and 'art / is but a vision of reality'.

> *Hic.* And yet
> No one denies to Keats love of the world;
> Remember his deliberate happiness.

Ille. His art is happy, but who know his mind?
I see a schoolboy when I think of him,
With face and nose pressed to a sweet-shop window,
For certainly he sank into his grave
His senses and his heart unsatisfied,
And made – being poor, ailing, and ignorant,
Shut out from all the luxury of the world,
The coarse-bred son of a livery-stable keeper –
Luxuriant song.[7]

Again the rank class image, here condescendingly of a schoolboy at a sweet shop window – yet then the turn: out of that exclusion, that poverty, that lack of satisfaction, that greed of the eyes, that gap between the nose and the sweets, the cold glass between, comes 'Luxuriant song'. The poet cannot cross the threshold but his singing can. The window affords sight, but not the intimacy of touch or taste. The poet makes all these senses into sound. Rather, the *poets* make them (for both Keats and Yeats are being praised here, in a language that at once depresses and heightens the senses).

Both the examples I have given, from Gaskell and from Yeats, emphasise separation. They use the window, with its display within, to measure the absolute exclusion of the observer, enticed to cross the transparent threshold of the glass, yet denied entry. The hard surface cannot be penetrated, despite the dream-like intensity of the desired objects that the window shields.

The window and – even more – the looking-glass have both been understood as indications of wealth. Windows are usually permanent structures; not so looking-glasses: reflective surfaces of every kind can be called into service. A body of water may give the eye access to objects beneath its surface; more often it gives back glancing lights and, when calm, its surface tension poises reflections of scenery and faces: as Narcissus discovered, to his cost. The window guides sight outward, or inward. But the one act impossible with a mirror is looking through the medium of its glass. Instead, delusive scenes are played back from the world by which we are already surrounded. In Tennyson's poem 'The Lady of Shallott' discovers the contrast to her cost and, with that cost, finds her freedom. So long as she looks in the mirror she can see only the back of the tapestry she is working on and reflections of the outer world. Once she looks out of the window she sees Sir Launcelot, embodied, care-free, only air between herself and her desire.

Thomas Hardy, describing the life of the rural poor in the later nineteenth-century, describes the frequent removals that families were obliged to undertake in search of work, with all their goods on a cart. The passage moves through the precious possessions loaded onto the waggon (first the infant, then the clock, and the looking glass) to a reminiscence of how working men shaved themselves: the body at risk without an external reflector is capable of inducing something *like* sight entirely through touch:

> The other object of solicitude is the looking-glass, usually held in the lap of the eldest girl. It is emphatically spoken of as *the* looking-glass, there being but one in the house, except possibly a small shaving-glass for the husband. But labouring men are not much dependent upon mirrors for a clean chin. I have seen many men shaving in the chimney corner, looking into the fire; or, in the summer, in the garden, with their eyes fixed upon a gooseberry-bush, gazing as steadfastly as if there were a perfect reflection of their image – from which it would seem that the concentrated look of shavers in general was originally demanded rather by the mind than by the eye. On the other hand, I knew a man who used to walk about the room all the time he was engaged in the operation, and how he escaped cutting himself was a marvel. Certain luxurious dandies of the furrow, who could not do without a reflected image of themselves when using the razor, obtained it till quite recently by placing the crown of an old hat outside the window-pane, then confronting it inside the room and falling to – a contrivance which formed a very clear reflection of a face in high light.[8]

Hardy gives an affectionate review of the enterprise with which people keep what is precious to them and improvise comforts, even in the midst of dearth (the hat in the window-pane). There is gentle sexual allusion in the looking glass being kept in the lap of the (generic) eldest girl. Hardy realises, too, the degree to which the mind structures the body in space, so that the men can shave by an inner bodily map. The somatic intensity of Hardy's observation expands the social realism of his description to take in the force of desire. It moves towards a kind of dreaming.

When the realist separation of inner and outer yields, the suggestion is of dream: windows can figure the access to dream states (as they quite often do in literature for children: Peter Pan and Mary Poppins for example). Alice goes *through* the looking-glass and finds that the surface melts away and that the world beyond does not replicate ours. In Freud's extraordinary account of 'The Wolfman' the young child, in a dream, sees seven white wolves seated motionless in the tree outside his bedroom. Freud's patient, giving an account of this terrifying dream many years later, observes to Freud:

> The only action in the dream was *the opening of the window, for the wolves were sitting quite still* in the branches of the tree, to the right and left of the tree trunk, not moving at all, and looking right at me. (my italics)[9]

Over several years of brooding on this dream, Freud became convinced that the inversion of movement and stasis signified a refusal to recall the primal scene. Be that as it may, the uncanny stillness of the creatures and the window's action in opening by itself shows animate and inanimate chillingly reversed. Inside and outside are not kept securely apart. The securing function of the window is dissolved with dream inevitability. The unconscious becomes manifest in that curiously passive threat of the outside world stilled while dream motion is concentrated in the independent action of the casement window.

Robert Frost's poem 'After Apple-Picking' literalises the dissolve on the threshold between wake and sleep by drawing on the strangeness of what is seen through a sheet of ice:

> But I am done with apple-picking now.
> Essence of winter sleep is on the night,
> The scent of apples: I am drowsing off.
> I cannot rub the strangeness from my sight
> I got from looking through a pane of glass
> I skimmed this morning from the drinking trough
> And held against the world of hoary grass.
> It melted, and I let it fall and break.
> But I was well
> Upon my way to sleep before it fell,
> And I could tell
> What form my dreaming was about to take.[10]

The ice, like seventeenth century glass, buckles the scene it gives access to. Time warps, too, in this description. The ice leaves a residue of distortion, like the residue of exhaustion in the muscles and body of the apple-picker:

> My instep arch not only keeps the ache,
> It keeps the pressure of a ladder-round.

Water made hard, as ice, yields something other than reflection, something as unstable as its own condition. The approach of dream after physical exhaustion here bears excess meanings, meanings blurred by their own profusion. The framed image, already held in memory not presence, is at once intensified and made more mysterious.

So far my examples have shown the window either as access outward or as an excluding surface that denies participation. They have suggested also that windows can become reflecting looking glass, dwelling on the self rather than the scene beyond, and that, in the case of the Frost poem, the transient medium of ice as a window onto familiar things is a way of dreaming memory. But in all these cases, whether social realist or dream state, the window remains the stable medium of transition. Yet, this stability can be as deceptive as the boundary marked by any threshold. In *Wuthering Heights*, however, something much more eerie and at the same time more physical occurs, something that breaks through the separation inherent in the idea of the window in a way that changed the novel as a form. Much of Emily Bronte's book is recounted by Lockwood. Lockwood is the bourgeois town-dweller who is unfortunate enough to have rented a house in this remote place of which the surly Heathcliff is landlord. Lockwood on his arrival goes to Heathcliff's house, Wuthering Heights, to make arrangements. He is brought to the ground by Heathcliff's dogs, suffers faintness and a nose-bleed, and is obliged to stay overnight in a room assigned to him by a new housekeeper who remarks that Mr. Heathcliff does not willingly let people lodge in this room. Within the room is 'a large oak case, with squares cut out near the top resembling coach windows.' Inside this is the bed, and on the window sill is a name scratched many times in different forms: 'Catherine Earnshaw, Catherine Heathcliff, Catherine Linton.' – a girl's possible identities. He leafs through old books and some of this girl's diaries, and he sleeps. He dreams. He is woken by the branch of a fir tree touching the lattice window, the wind 'rattled its dry cones against the panes'. This is his description of what happens next:

> I thought, I rose and endeavoured to unhasp the casement. The hook was soldered into the staple…
>
> 'I must stop it nevertheless!' I muttered, knocking my knuckles through the glass, and stretching an arm out to seize the importunate branch; instead of which my fingers closed on the fingers of a little, ice-cold hand.
>
> The intense horror of nightmare came over me; I tried to draw back my arm, but the hand clung to it, and a most melancholy voice sobbed – 'let me in, let me in!' 'Who are you?' I asked, struggling, meanwhile, to disengage myself.
>
> 'Catherine Linton', it replied shiveringly… 'I'm come home: I'd lost my way on the moor!'
>
> As it spoke, I discerned, obscurely, a child's face looking through the window. Terror made me cruel; and, finding it useless to attempt to shake the creature off, I pulled its wrist on to the broken pane, and rubbed it to and fro till the blood ran down and soaked the bedclothes.[11]

The shock is that the violence does not stay inside the dream. All the indications that this is nightmare are denied by the blood in actuality pouring down and soaking the bedclothes. Reality is reinforced by the terrible detail, such as his 'rubbing' the wrist 'to and fro' on the broken glass (something domestic, even cosy, in that word 'rubbing' brings the experience very close in). Touch returns with a vengeance and the reader shares the action of the narrator as well as the torment of the child. The window, that ordinarily permits sight without touch, is here shattered back into its dangerous physical elements. It shows itself to be a precarious threshold, with material as well as uncanny possibilities of dissolution and explosion. The serene surface becomes jagged shards of harm, splinters of glass that obliterate the boundary between nightmare and waking. The passage opens matter-of-factly enough (though with that equivocating 'I thought'). Lockwood gets up to stop the branch tapping against the pane, but then with dreamlike ease he knocks his knuckles through the glass, significantly, without blood. This is surely dream, isn't it? But the very assertion of nightmare horror as the child grips his fingers removes the certainty that this is dream. The child's voice and her appeal 'let me in, let me in' suggest something between dream and waking. Then, hideously, 'terror made me cruel' and the material actuality of broken glass, and blood soaking the bedclothes, breaks through the taboo of separation between inner and outer, dream and actuality, powerful and excluded, that I have argued is ordinarily enacted in the idea of the window.

Emily Bronte, like Bunuel, refuses to allow the reader secure residence outside the frame of her pictured world. She lacerates. She forces us into passional extremes where judgement founders in identification. When Lockwood leaves the room Heathcliff 'wrenched open the lattice, bursting as he pulled at it, into an uncontrollable passion of tears.' (This is the same lattice window where the hook was *soldered* into the staple). 'Bursting' is the key word here: bursting open, bursting out, bursting into.

> 'Come in! come in!' he sobbed, 'Cathy, do come! oh! do – *once* more. Oh, my heart's darling! hear me *this* time, Catherine, at last.'[12]

The window is the membrane between life and death, burst through. Heathcliff in his reckless need has no qualms in conjuring the dead beloved to return. The shock of discovering desperate cruelty inside the urbane Mr. Lockwood is matched by that of hearing the desperate longing inside the curmudgeonly Heathcliff. Bronte hurls us into a world of emotion and over the brink of feeling. The shattering of the window and the hand invading becomes the means of shattering the reader's reserves. This is extreme fiction. This is a dream that will not let you go.

So the shattering of the window and the re-assertion of touch – here in its most violent form – act out some of the rage felt by the excluded. Bronte's novel has often been claimed by Marxist commentators as a symbolic depiction of class ruptures, with the orphaned and abandoned Heathcliff at the centre of interpretation (is he gypsy, bastard, black, Irish? suggestions have been made to identify him with all these groups – in any case he is the outsider). The scene with the window and the abandoned child wailing suggests other exclusions, too, not solely based on class or ethnic origins: the dead, the needy, subjugated infant appetites.

So what about 'breaking through'? The breaking of windows is the sign of riot, even of revolution. The suffragettes broke windows, but this is no guarantee of virtuous rebellion. The violation of thresholds may also signify oppression on the march. In Gunter Grass's *The Tin Drum* Oscar uses the extreme high pitch of his voice to bore holes in shop windows in order that the poor can reach and seize the goods inside. This seems good: no longer are the poor excluded from the wealth of the window displays. But two chapters later we reach 'Kristallnacht' (the night of broken glass) in 1938. Synagogues are burned and the windows of hundreds of shops owned by Jews are shattered. This actual terrible event presaged the final coming of Nazism.

My last example of reserve and breaking through is from that subtle exploration of connection and separation, Virginia Woolf's novel *Mrs Dalloway* (remember too that the first book of *To the Lighthouse* is called 'The Window'). In narrative terms the two principal figures of the book – Clarissa Dalloway and Septimus Smith – are closely connected, yet in social terms they have almost nothing in common and never meet. Their contacts – their lack of contact – are expressed through a third figure: the elderly woman into whose room Clarissa persistently half-sees as evening draws on:

> And she watched out of the window the old lady opposite climbing upstairs. Let her climb upstairs if she wanted to; let her stop; then let her, as Clarissa had often seen her, gain her bedroom, part her curtains, and disappear again into the background. Somehow one respected that – that old woman looking out of the window, quite unconscious that she was being watched.[13]

Clarissa Dalloway is a privileged society hostess, Septimus Smith an impoverished lower-middle-class survivor from fighting in the first world war, his health both mental and physical wrecked by his experiences. They share being alive in London on a day in 1925. Clarissa Dalloway experiences the sense of being left out – or left in – much earlier in the novel when she is not included in a lunch party to which her husband is invited. The occasion may seem slight; the emotions are not so and Woolf invokes, in an extended musing sentence, a mixture of enlarged metaphor and impressionist description to conjure Clarissa's experience at that moment:

> She began to go slowly upstairs, with her hand on the banisters, as if she had left a party, where now this friend now that had flashed back her face, her voice; had shut the door and gone out and stood alone, a single figure against the appalling night, or rather, to be accurate, against the stare of this matter-of-fact June morning; soft with the glow of rose-petals for some, she knew, and felt it, as she paused by the open staircase window which let in blinds flapping, dogs barking, let in, she thought, feeling herself suddenly shrivelled, aged, breastless, the grinding, blowing, flowering of the day, out of doors, out of the window, out of her body and brain which now failed, since Lady Bruton, whose lunch parties were said to be extraordinarily amusing, had not invited her.[14]

The whimsical shifts of scale between passionate isolation, abandonment, and the trivial social occasion set the novel on its course, wayward and intimate, and full of grief for the horrors of war and peace.

The window again becomes the focal point of feeling, but this time as an expression of contingency and detachment in extremis, when Septimus Smith, pursued by doctors, his mental anguish ignored, hears the doctor approaching up the stairs to take him away:

> Getting up rather unsteadily, hopping indeed from foot to foot, he considered Mrs. Filmer's nice clean bread-knife with "Bread" carved on the handle. Ah, but one mustn't spoil that. The gas fire? But it was too late now. Holmes was coming. Razors he might have got, but Rezia, who always did that sort of thing, had packed them. There remained only the window, the large Bloomsbury lodging-house window; the tiresome, the troublesome, and rather melodramatic business of opening the window and throwing himself out… Holmes was at the door. 'I'll give it you!' he cried, and flung himself vigorously, violently down on to Mrs. Filmer's area railings.[15]

Septimus, so punctilious that he shrinks from dirtying Mrs Filmer's nice clean bread knife by his death, is impaled. Again, the *horror* of the window breaks through: the window here is a void, a height, an inducement to falling.

That night, shocked to hear of the death of a young man she did not know – or, more, shocked by the intrusion of death into her party – Clarissa retreats for a little while to her room. She feels in her body the pain of the unknown man:

> Always her body went through it, when she was told, first, suddenly, of an accident; her dress flamed, her body burnt. He had thrown himself from a

> window. Up had flashed the ground; through him, blundering, bruising, went the rusty spikes.[16]

Mrs. Dalloway makes a somatic identification with Septimus, despite their social distance. She does not pity him. Instead:

> She parted the curtains; she looked. Oh, but how surprising! – in the room opposite the old lady stared straight at her! She was going to bed… It was fascinating to watch her, moving about, that old lady, crossing the room, coming to the window. Could she see her? It was fascinating, with people still laughing and shouting in the drawing-room, to watch that old woman, quite quietly, going to bed alone. She pulled the blind now. The clock began striking. The young man had killed himself; but she did not pity him; with the clock striking the hour, one, two, three, she did not pity him, with all this going on. There! the old lady had put out her light! the whole house was dark now with this going on, she repeated, and the words came to her, Fear no more the heat of the sun. She must go back to them.[17]

This extraordinary passage, which I have nevertheless had to abbreviate for quotation, withholds judgment on behaviour, so that like Clarissa Dalloway we peer into the obscurity of other lives, curiously comforted, yet in mourning. Clarissa in the early part of the day did not recognise herself in the old woman, though we as readers and listeners can hear the same words chiming for them both; now she recognises herself in Septimus and also in the gaze of the other woman looking back at her, separated by their two windows, even now only doubtfully answering Clarissa's gaze. The reserve of the window is retained here; an expression of connection both profound and contingent.

The window can express in literary works the social reality of privilege and exclusion; it can also give access to the often violent levelling of all hierarchies in dream experience. Looking out, looking in, breaking through: the impermeable pages of paper, once overwritten with the words of poets and novelists, change their state. They cease to be opaque. They swing open. The frame of the page dissolves. The images and happenings released make free in the interior of our experience. They have entered through (shall we call it the window?) of the page as we read, but they escape its confines to explore at large what lies within us. Perhaps that paradox also helps to explain the power of windows as a presence in literature, a potent figure for the threshold as a protective or a terrifying space which might harden or dissolve, open out or close in, at any time.

Notes

1 An earlier version of this essay was given as a plenary paper at the 2004 'Synapsis Comparative Literature Symposium' at Siena and was then published in Italian in the proceedings of that conference.
2 Mary Shelley, *Frankenstein: or, The Modern Prometheus* (London: Colburn and Bentley, 1831), 91.
3 Shelley, *Frankenstein*, 97.
4 George Herbert, 'The Elixir', in *The Works of George Herbert*, ed. F. E. Hutchinson (Oxford: Clarendon Press, 1941), 184.
5 Elizabeth Bishop, *The Complete Poems 1927–1979* (London: Chatto and Windus, 1983), 212.
6 Elizabeth Gaskell, *Mary Barton* (The Knutsford Edition: London: Smith, Elder, 1906), 69.
7 W. B. Yeats, 'Ego Dominus Tuus', in *The Collected Poems of W. B. Yeats* (London: Macmillan, 1950), 180–183 (182).
8 Thomas Hardy, 'The Dorsetshire Labourer', *Longman's Magazine*, July 1883, 252–69, collected in *Thomas Hardy's Personal Writings*, ed. Harold Orel (London: Macmillan, 1967), 178–9.
9 Sigmund Freud, *'The Wolfman' and Other Cases*, ed. Gillian Beer (London: Penguin, 2003), 227.
10 Robert Frost, 'After Apple-Picking', in *Collected Poems, Prose, and Plays*, sel. Richard Poirier and Mark Richardson (New York: The Library of America, 1995), 70–1 (70).
11 Emily Bronte, *Wuthering Heights*, ed. Hilda Marsden (Oxford: Clarendon Press, 1976), 30–1.
12 Bronte, *Wuthering Heights*, 35.
13 Virginia Woolf, *Mrs. Dalloway* (London: Chatto and Windus, 1968), 139–40.
14 Ibid., 35.
15 Ibid., 164.
16 Ibid., 202.
17 Ibid., 204.

Chapter Two

'ZERO…ZERO…AND ZERO': PERMEABLE WALLS AND OFF-STAGE SPACES

Jean Chothia

The characteristic setting of late nineteenth century realist theatre is the room, a domestic space enclosed by walls on three sides of the stage, and often by a ceiling too, with the fourth side open to the auditorium. The fundamental conceit of illusionist staging is that the audience look in on another, self-contained, world. The actors cross the threshold from the real private space of the dressing room into the public space of the stage as if they were entering the private space of a domestic room from the public world outside. The practice of darkening the auditorium, widespread by the end of the century, helped concentrate audience attention on a facsimile world, parallel to, rather than directly interactive with, their own. The proscenium arch framing the stage figured as an imaginary barrier between stage and auditorium. It was, in Jean Jullien's words, 'a fourth wall, transparent for the public, opaque for the actor'.[1] Jullien was writing in response to the stagings at André Antoine's *Théâtre Libre*, in Paris, but the phrase was quickly appropriated as a general shorthand for the new realistic theatre that emerged throughout Europe in response to Zola's polemics, Ibsen's plays and reports of Antoine's stagings.[2] This imaginary barrier, not-quite-wall and not-quite-window, is fundamental to the achievement as well as the contradictions inherent in illusionist theatre.

In illusionist theatre, the set, a temporary structure, must appear permanent, its walls seem solid, and the actors who appear within it must seem to *be* the characters they impersonate. These characters speak previously-composed words as if they are spontaneous; their movements and gestures are carefully rehearsed to appear unstudied. They enter and exit not from the wings but through doorways whose frames are sufficiently solid that they can be slammed without a tell-tale shake to remind the audience of their ephemerality. Attention to verisimilitude and to details of domestic interiors that were developed on the *avant garde* stages of European realism,[3] helped create belief in the lives to be disturbed or damaged by the action of the play. The door, through which Ibsen's Nora left her dolls' house was offstage, but the sound of its slamming would probably not have reverberated so loudly throughout Europe had the room in which the audience encountered her seemed less realistic.

Practicable doors and windows contributed to the verisimilitude sought by the late nineteenth century realists but also to the dramatic expressiveness of their plays. Windows, whose solid frames with glazed insets replaced the old canvas backdrops on which both frames and a scene beyond might have been painted, had a particular significance since they offered a source for natural-seeming light. Side- or back-lighting could replace the footlights, the signature of all that was artificial about the earlier nineteenth century stage. Changing light, as if from the sky beyond the window, could provide a measure of passing time and, indeed, of weather. A character gazing away from the room out through the window as, for example, Pinero directs that Paula Tanqueray, ill at ease in her husband's country home, should, could suggest longing or melancholy.[4]

Illusionist theatre can be read as the response to the emergence of fully developed characters and detailed descriptions of place of nineteenth century realist novels with their interest in the relationship between appearance and interiority and their concern with the interaction between environment and the individual. But any such reading must acknowledge the difference between words on the page and words in performance. The live presence of actors, *embodying* the fiction in the same space and time as the audience, offers an experience different in kind from that of the word on the page. The three-dimensional mode meant that environment could be more evidently realised on stage than in the verbal descriptions of prose fiction but, by the same token, it was also more fixed.

Built walls marked the confines of the stage space more clearly than open wings. The doors that pierced them functioned as a threshold between the stage and the world beyond the room. The plays of late nineteenth century realism might well claim to present what Jean Jullien, rephrasing Zola's rather more poetic '*lambeau d'existence*' [shred of existence], was the first to label '*une tranche de vie*' [a slice of life],[5] but writers and stage directors remained alert to the ways in which the shaping imagination could supply dramatic power to their supposedly unvarnished truths. The effectiveness, for example, not just of a door slammed but of a character framed still in a doorway, especially if lit from behind, was soon realised. A contemporary wrote of the

Théâtre Libre production of *Jacques Damour*, adapted from a Zola story of an old communard returned after the amnesty to find that his wife, believing him drowned, had remarried:

> the vision of Antoine on the threshold nailed me to my seat. I will always remember the life-likeness of his slow arrival. I recall that the silences were held a long time.[6]

The paradox inherent in realist theatre, which must use ever more skilful artifice to conceal the necessary construction of the theatrical event, was already acknowledged in one of its founding documents. Strindberg commented in his Preface to *Miss Julie*, the consciously-Naturalist play written in response to news of Antoine's innovations in staging:

> [W]hen one has only one set, one is entitled to demand that it be realistic – though nothing is more difficult than to make a room which looks like a room, however skilful the artist may be at creating fire-spouting volcanoes and waterfalls. Even if the walls have to be of canvas, it is surely time to stop painting them with shelves and kitchen utensils. We have so many other stage conventions in which we are expected to believe that we may as well avoid overstraining our imagination by asking it to believe in painted saucepans.[7]

Even as he demands realistic staging, Strindberg acknowledges the multiple assumptions and subterfuges of theatrical performance and its necessary dependence on audience imagination.

On-stage space in most theatres is finite, bounded by the back wall of the stage, but it is infinitely extensible in audience imagination, prompted by references in the dialogue. Labelling the visible, on-stage space 'mimetic' and other, described, spaces 'diegetic', Michael Issacharoff differentiates the essentially static architectural spaces of theatre and stage from the more elusive 'dramatic spaces' evinced through dialogue.[8] These diegetic spaces, reformulated by Hanna Scolnicov as 'conceived' to be set against 'perceived' spaces,[9] have a different dynamic from those realised on stage. They expand the dimensions of the on-stage action through their evocation of other times, places, people and images. Although the activity of realist plays takes place within enclosed on-stage mimetic rooms, diegetic, conceived, spaces exist here too. The dialogue constantly has recourse to times, places, persons and events that have impacted on, coexist with or might be shaped by the on-stage activity. Jacques Damour's telling of the sufferings of his long banishment; the servant Jean's of his childhood admiration of Miss Julie and his recognition of her impossible distance from him; Paula Tanqueray's memories of the apartment she once shared with her lover, and his seduction of her; Osvald Alving's of the joyful life in the warm south in Ibsen's *Ghosts*, are all offered for audience imagining in the dialogue,[10] as are Miss Julie's humiliation of and by her former fiancé, Paula's innocent girlhood or the misery of the Alving marriage.

It is the case that objects serving as metonymic prompts to audience' imagining can occur in any play but they tend to be more frequent in realist stagings where, along with elements of the set, they function as another kind of threshold between the perceived and the conceived. The marquis's boots that Jean must polish and the bell pull to whose summons he must respond, visible throughout the action of *Miss Julie*, are a constant reminder that Julie has a father and a social position and Jean a master to whom he is subservient. They are reminders, too, of power relationships in society at large. A portrait of Napoleon dominating the General's study in the first scene of *The Death of the Duke of Enghien*, Léon Hennique's French history play, is a reminder of ultimate authority, much as is the portrait of General Gabler that dominates the living room of his daughter's marital home in Ibsen's *Hedda Gabler*.[11]

Increasingly realistic figuring of on-stage space and, indeed, on-stage time, in illusionist theatre meant that the conceived world beyond the perceived stage space could be more literally identified and stabilised. This was particularly true of immediately contingent spaces. The implication of the fictional world's continuation beyond the stage space was, of course, already fragmentarily evident in English Renaissance theatre, despite its generally presentational nature, as its multiple off-stage sounds – trumpets, striking clocks, knockings at doors, and '*shouts without*' – attest. Even on these unlocalised stages, the off-stage area beyond the doors to the stage could on occasion be more specifically populated. In *Hamlet*, Laertes pounds on the door of Claudius' Court and is allowed in, while off-stage cries register the presence of his waiting supporters. In the First Folio version of the play, Laertes even instructs 'Stand you all without'.[12] Properties and costume could also suggest immediately adjacent activity, as with *The Tempest* direction that reads '*Enter Mariners wet*'.[13] The gallery, or the 'above', figuring briefly as a window or balcony, might act as threshold between the visible space of the stage, for the moment representing a street, garden or courtyard, and a 'within', understood to be the house. This, frequently, is figured as a secluded female space from which, imprisoned by jealous husbands or anxious fathers, women view the outside world; are courted, like Celia in Jonson's *Volpone*, by those with nefarious designs on their chastity, or, like Shakespeare's Jessica in *The Merchant of Venice*, conspire escape and throw down a dowry to a lover waiting below.[14] When Juliet, talking to Romeo from her balcony, interrupts herself to say:

> I heare some noyse within deare Love, adue:
>
> *Cals within.*
>
> Anon good Nurse, sweet Mountague be true:[15]

the audience has little problem identifying the different respondents and assuming the presence of the nurse in Juliet's chamber beyond the balcony.

These identifications are brief and shifting. The change in the late nineteenth century – and much of the theatre that has succeeded it – is the consistency with which the illusion of the fictional world's continuation into the adjoining side- and back-stage spaces is maintained and the way in which repeated reference in the dialogue, as well as much-increased use of off-stage sound, demands audience participation in the fabrication. In making their exits and entrances, actors quickly learned to maintain the fiction that each door led consistently to the same location, another specified room, or a stairway, or perhaps to the garden or a street. The conceived world beyond the stage space might be further attested by sights or sounds seen through a door or, with more continuous presence, through the window. Whenever the door is opened, in Strindberg's *The Dance of Death*, a soldier is glimpsed standing as if on guard outside.[16] In Act 1 of Chekhov's *The Cherry Orchard*, Varya, throwing open the window, cries

> The sun's up now and it's not cold. Look mother, what marvellous trees! And the air is glorious. The starlings are singing'.[17]

And, through the window, and for the rest of the scene, the audience indeed have a view of profusely blossoming cherry trees.

Such examples are legion. The stage direction for W. B. Yeats' verse play *The Green Helmet* reads '*through the window one can see nothing but the sea*'.[18] Antoine's practice of building sets forward of the stage's back wall to create a usable passage that permitted characters to be glimpsed passing the window before they entered, was soon imitated. Strindberg directed that his set for *Miss Julie* should run diagonally across the stage, as if to show a corner of a larger room that continued beyond the visible stage. Not only were some pieces of furniture to be placed partly off the stage but, since the diagonal arrangement left a larger than usual area behind the set, he asked for the inclusion of:

> three quarters of a big, arched exit porch, with twin glass doors, through which can be seen a fountain with a statue of Cupid, lilac bushes in bloom, and tall Lombardy poplars[19]

The country folk, whose ribald singing, already heard off-stage, drives Miss Julie to her desperate retreat into Jean's bedroom, are seen invading the garden before they enter through Strindberg's twin glass doors. The dubious moral quality of Hugh, in *The Second Mrs Tanqueray,* is registered well before he is revealed as Paula's former lover by his entrance through the French window, instead of announced properly at the front door. The potential of windows as an extension of the acting space and a convenient hiding place, particularly when heavily curtained, was a gift to *fin de siècle* farce. Successive characters in Pinero's *The Magistrate* not only hide behind the curtain but, at a salient moment, a loud crash signals the collapse of the overloaded balcony to which the miscreants had retreated.[20]

Besides this kind of practical function, what could be seen or heard through the window offered formative possibilities for mood and meaning. The inherent metaphorical presence of windows – the word traced in the OED to the Old Norse words for 'wind' and 'eye', and present in common usage to reference insight into the mind or soul – could serve to extend and deepen audience response. The impression of elemental forces beyond the control of the characters or, more frequently and often with intense irony, *indifferent* to them, could be indicated by changes in lighting or by weather effects, be they gloom, teeming rain or sudden sunshine.

Darkening or brightening skies measure the passing of time, but also shape the fabric of feeling of a play. In the first scene of *Ghosts*, characters enter wet, as do the mariners in *The Tempest*, but the persistent rain, louring skies and grey countryside beyond the windows of Ibsen's Norwegian room are a continuous presence in the set. They are repeatedly referenced in the dialogue in Osvald's contrasting the gloomy north with the joy of life in Paris and the warm south as well as in the wet clothes and the umbrellas as successive characters enter. In the closing moments of the play, as Osvald's cry 'Mother, give me the sun' signals his descent into insanity, beams of the sunlight for which he has longed stream in, in a powerful scenic image that has frequently been echoed by later dramatists.[21] An off-stage rain effect, incessant through the first scene of Hennique's *The Death of the Duke of Enghien,* is intensified in the silence at the end of the scene. As the duke's fortunes darken in Scene 2, the day brightens through windows at the back of the stage and, as Enghien raises his glass to toast the *soi-disant* Louis XVIII, the noise of advancing Republican soldiers is heard off-stage, first seemingly distant but then increasingly close. In the final scene the duke, following a hugger-mugger trial, is led out to execution. The audience can interpret the dim sounds from outside but it is only when the duke's wife, who has entered having found his cell empty, opens the window, that the off-stage sounds clarify into a reading of the death sentence and the report of the firing squad's guns. Both the sounds and the princess's silence are felt by the audience. Henry James, who saw the production in London,

> found a strong impression in it – an impression of the hurried, extemporised cross-examination, by night, of an impatient and mystified prisoner, whose dreadful fate had been determined in advance, who was to be shot, high-handedly, in the dismal dawn. The arrangement didn't worry and distract me: it was simplifying, intensifying. It gave, what a judicious *mise en scène* should always do, the essence of the matter, and left the embroidery to the actors.[22]

Audience interpretation of off-stage sound and space is often crucial to 'the essence of the matter'. As with Hennique's play, much of the action of the final scene of Hauptmann's *The Weavers*, which recreates the 1844 Silesian weavers' uprising, takes place off-stage.[23] Already in Act IV, the family of the master, Dreissiger, responded first with bravado and then with growing panic, to off-stage sounds of the advance of the rioting weavers. In the *Théâtre Libre* production the first sounds of the riot began with a small group of supers placed deep in the theatre. The sounds of singing and marching footsteps were joined by others posted closer and closer to the stage. Following the retreat of the Dreissigers, the stage was held empty for a moment, as if to establish a threat to the audience too, before the angry, drunken weavers, bursting through all available doors and windows, invaded the stage space. The threshold is crossed rather differently in the final act of the play. Here Hilse, an elderly weaver, preaches resignation despite pleas from his family that he join the uprising. The noise of the main body of the crowd passing by sounds from off-stage and various friends call for Hilse to join them. Left alone, he reiterates his trust in God and, returning doggedly to his loom by the window, takes up his weaving again. Martial music and the sound of disciplined marching footsteps signal the arrival of the military. When off-stage gunfire and cries from the crowd follow, it seems that Hauptmann has endorsed quietism until, in the final moments of the play, the window is shattered and Old Hilse, caught by a stray bullet, falls dead at his loom.

James found the *mise en scène* of Hennique's play 'simplifying, intensifying', and Francisque Sarcey, the leading French critic of the day, usually sceptical of realist drama, found the ending of *The Weavers* 'overwhelm[ed] the imagination and grip[ped] the heart'.[24] But the risk was always that the ingenuity of the device would distract from the reality it was intended to imitate. As the conservative critic Emile Faguet commented of Antoine's practice, 'alarm, gunshots, drumrolls. These things happen in the corridors. On stage – nothing!'[25]

The Weavers, with *Ghosts* and Tolstoi's *Power of Darkness*, quickly came to figure as a classic of late nineteenth century *avant garde* realism. In the Inter War years of the twentieth century, Sean O'Casey's plays demonstrate a remarkable engaging with questions of illusion and theatrical artifice as he revisits many of the strategies of the earlier period. He contrives at once to tantalise and to hold the balance. The tenement activity of O'Casey's early plays offers a recognisably realist representation of the financial scrimping and gossip of the urban poor.[26] Hawkers dropping in selling coal-blocks or sewing machines; a young man lying late in bed; a landlord demanding rent, and neighbours borrowing milk, taking in others' parcels, minding others' children and learning one another's business, all contribute to the impression of closely-observed, realistic activity. But the frequent comings and goings enabled by the doors and windows of the tenement or the public house settings also chime with the traditional comic pattern of successive entrances and exits and accompanying deceptions, misunderstandings and mounting confusion of such works as Ben Jonson's *The Alchemist* or, more recently, Feydeau's farces or Pinero's *Magistrate*. Theatrical artifice and the playfulness of theatre are present within the realistic texture.

The set, similarly, may present the characteristic enclosed space of the realist domestic stage but it is also an evident source for an expansive scenic imagination in which windows, always prominent in O'Casey's stage directions, are significant. In the simplest version, in *The Shadow of a Gunman*, the opening directions require '*large windows*' that '*occupy practically the whole of the back wall space*'.[27] Although a woman's figure briefly '*appears at the window*' (119) and moonlight shines through to light Act II, the signals from outside are otherwise mainly aural: the cries of a passing newsboy announce the ambush of the Republican Maguire; shouts and shots from the street register the arrest and death of the credulous Minnie. A more complex development comes in *Juno and the Paycock* when, the Boyles' raucous party having been interrupted by the funeral of Tancred, an Irish Republican neighbour, they first, looking offstage through the window, comment on the event, then *exeunt* to view it, leaving a cowering Johnny alone on stage. A Republican Mobilizer then enters with a summons that, revealing Johnny as the betrayer of Tancred, draws from him the cry, 'I've lost me arm, an' me hip's desthroyed so I'll never be able to walk agen! Good God, haven't I done enough for Ireland?' The Mobilizer's response, 'Boyle, no man can do enough for Ireland',[28] announcing Johnny's doom, ends the act, while through the window come the murmured 'Hail Mary's of the crowd, mourning the slaughtered Tancred (77). This particular threshold has become a significant enabling device of moral complexity.

Such simultaneity of perception, demanding audience attention and discriminatory listening, is extended in *The Plough and the Stars*, O'Casey's next play, set in 1916. In Act I, Mrs Govan, watching from the window, provides a running commentary on the assembling for parade of the Citizen Army, while the other characters are absorbed in their own concerns. Peter busies himself accumulating an ostentatious costume in which he plans to parade while, at the front of the stage, the Covey and Fluther wage an absurd argument about the origin of the universe.[29] The technique gathers force in Act II, where now '*three fourths of the back is occupied by a tall, wide, two-paned window*' (43) and *The Shadow of a Gunman*'s brief figuring of a woman beyond the window is reworked when the back view of a Republican orator is silhouetted against the window and he is heard rousing an unseen crowd. The attention of the audience is transfixed by the silhouette and the oratory but also by the strange reflection of themselves in the supposed presence of the crowd, listening beyond the stage space. The fragile barrier between inside and outside world is penetrated literally in another of O'Casey's complex endings when Bessie, like Old Hilse in *The Weavers* supposedly safe from the fighting, is killed by the mischance of a bullet through the window. The ironies and implications here are understood by the audience, not the characters, when the intruding British soldiers sit for their cup of tea amid the chaos and catastrophe and casually comment, 'there gows the general attack on the Powst Office' (136). The decisive moment in the collapse of the Dublin Easter Rising is registered in the deepening red flares, visible through the window, while the homesick soldiers sing 'Keep the Home Fires Burning' (137). This vital element of O'Casey's theatrical vocabulary, the window, re-emerges with newly compelling presence in his subsequent work. Act II of *The Silver Tassie*, set in the First World War, not only features a stained glass window, which places a vividly-lit Virgin Mary in ironic juxtaposition with existence in the war zone, but:

> *At back a lost wall and window are indicated by an arched piece of broken coping pointing from the left to the right, and a similar piece of masonry pointing from the right to the left. Between these two lacerated fingers of stone can be seen the country...*[30]

Broken, the membrane no longer provides privacy, security or separation.

The presence of windows in realist settings, then, contributes to the verisimilitude of location while extending the playing area. They enable the public world to penetrate the private, functioning as permeable membranes between the perceived and the conceived, through which the off-stage noise of the outside world can sound realistically. They enable the construction of powerful scenic images, when figures are framed by, seen beyond, or silhouetted against a window. While serving to intensify the illusion that the audience looks into an actual room, they contribute significantly to the development of dramatic plots. They permit age-old theatrical devices, such as over-hearing and surprise entrances, to seem less artificially contrived. They provide more natural-seeming opportunities for the concealments and collapses of farce.

Their very presence underlines the paradox that is illusionist theatre, with its claim to present the real. The ingenuity of their uses admits consciousness of the essential artifice of the dramatic event; of the shaping role of the dramatist, the stage manager and the designer; of distinction between the on-stage, fictional world of the characters and the back-stage reality of corridors, dressing rooms and actors. Even while serving to intensify the illusion that the audience looks into an actual room, they threaten to subvert its self-contained nature.

A teasing recognition of this surfaces in Samuel Beckett's work. Where O'Casey's theatrical ingenuity might have brought consciousness of artifice, with Beckett, the consciousness is ingrained in the texture of the play and acknowledged as such in the dialogue. The setting of *Endgame* is again a room and there are windows in the back wall but they are high up so the audience knows what is beyond only by report. From one window, a deserted earth is reported, from the other, in an echo of Yeats' play, a grey unmoving sea. Life beyond the room is further shut out by the stage direction that the one picture hanging has its face to the wall.[31] The play opens with Clov, with much business, climbing a ladder to look in turn out of each of the windows and, before long, what he saw – or didn't see – is registered:

> HAMM: What time is it?
> CLOV: The same as usual.
> HAMM: (*Gesture towards window right.*) Have you looked?
> CLOV: Yes.
> HAMM: Well?
> CLOV: Zero.
> HAMM: It'd need to rain.
> CLOV: It won't rain. (13)

At about the mid-point of the play, ordered to look out with the telescope, Clov, having first dropped it, '*picks up the telescope, turns it on auditorium*' and, notoriously, announces 'I see…a multitude…in transports…of joy.' His words, and his further comment, 'That's what I call a magnifier' (25), acknowledge that it is not a wall nor even a transparent window that stands between stage and audience but rather a theatrical convention. This is reasserted when, immediately afterwards, having climbed his ladder again and saying 'Let's see', Clov turns the telescope on what the direction, now tellingly using stage language, calls '*the without*', and:

> (*He looks, moving the telescope.*) Zero…(*he looks*)…zero (*he looks*)…and zero.
> HAMM: Nothing stirs. All is -
> CLOV: Zer -

HAMM: (*Violently*.) Wait till you're spoken to! (*Normal voice*.) All is...all is...all is what? (*Violently*.) All is what?
CLOV: What all is? In a word? Is that what you want to know? Just a moment. (*He turns the telescope on the without, looks, lowers the telescope, turns towards Hamm*.) Corpsed.[32] (25)

Somewhat later in the play, Beckett focuses on the convention of off-stage sound when Hamm asks Clov to open the window. The exchange runs:

HAMM: Open the window.
CLOV: What for?
HAMM: I want to hear the sea.
CLOV: You wouldn't hear it.
HAMM: Even if you opened the window?
CLOV: No. (42–3)

Clov, under orders, opens the window for Hamm to hear the sea. No evident sound is heard.

Notes

1 Jean Jullien, *Le Théâtre vivant* (Paris: Charpentier, 1892), 11. Translations from French are my own.
2 The classic texts here are: Emile Zola, 'Naturalisme au théâtre', in *Le Roman Experimental* (Paris: Charpentier, 1880), 107–156; Henrik Ibsen, most particularly *A Doll's House* (1879) and *Ghosts* (1882), and André Antoine's manifestos: *Le Théâtre Libre* (Paris: 1887; 1887–90; May 1890; Oct 1891; 1893–4) and *Mes Souvenirs sur le Théâtre Libre* 1887–93 (Paris: Fayard, 1921).
3 These included the *Théâtre Libre* and *Théâtre Antoine* in Paris; the *Freie Bühne* (Berlin); the Art Theatre (Moscow); the Independent Theatre and the Barker and Vedrenne seasons at the Court Theatre (London).
4 Arthur Wing Pinero, *The Second Mrs Tanqueray* (1893), in *Arthur Wing Pinero: Three Plays*, ed. Stephen Wyatt (London: Methuen, 1985), 82–156, Act II, passim.
5 Zola, 'Naturalisme', 124; Jullien, *Le Théâtre*, 17.
6 Charles Mosnier, *André Antoine*, 7 vols (ms, in the Bibliothèque de l'Arsenal, Paris, n.d.), 1:35. *Jacques Damour* by Léon Hennique was premièred on 30 March 1887.
7 August Strindberg, 'Preface to *Miss Julie*', (1888), in *Strindberg Plays: One*, trans. Michael Meyer (London: Methuen, 1976), 91–103 (101–2).
8 Michael Issacharoff, *Discourse as Performance* (Stanford: Stanford University Press, 1989), 55; originally published as *Le Spectacle du discours* (Paris: Librairie José Corti, 1985).
9 Hanna Scolnicov, *Women's Theatrical Space* (Cambridge: Cambridge University Press, 1994), 92.
10 Léon Hennique, *Jacques Damour* (Paris: Charpentier, 1887); August Strindberg, *Miss Julie*, in *Plays: One*, 105–146 (118–19, 109); Pinero, *Mrs Tanqueray*, 135–6; Henrik Ibsen, *Ghosts* (1882), Act II, passim.

11 Léon Hennique, *La Mort du Duc d'Enghien*, written 1873, produced at the *Théâtre Libre* on 10 December 1888 and subsequently toured through Europe, including to London in 1889; Henrik Ibsen, *Hedda Gabler*, written 1890, premièred in Munich in January 1891 and then, in April, in English translation at the Vaudeville Theatre, London.

12 *Hamlet* [IV.v.96–118, 114]. Quotations from Shakespeare are from William Shakespeare, *The First Folio: Norton Facsimile* (New York: Hamlyn, 1968).

13 *The Tempest* [I.i.59]. See Alan C. Dessen and Leslie Thomson, *A Dictionary of Stage Directions in English Drama, 1580–1642* (Cambridge: Cambridge University Press, 1999) for further examples of stage directions.

14 Scolnicov offers a detailed analysis of this *topos* in *Women's Theatrical Space*, Ch. 5.

15 *Romeo and Juliet* [II.ii.140–1].

16 August Strindberg, *The Dance of Death* (1900), Part I, passim.

17 Anton Chekhov, *The Cherry Orchard*, in *The Oxford Chekhov*, ed. and trans. Ronald Hingley, 9 vols (London: Oxford University Press, 1964–80), 3 (1964): 141–198 (157).

18 W. B. Yeats, *The Green Helmet* (1910), in *Plays in Prose and Verse* (London: Macmillan, 1922), 303–327 (305).

19 *Strindberg Plays: One*, 107.

20 Arthur Wing Pinero, *The Magistrate* (1885), Act II, Scene i, in *Three Plays*, 5–75 (48). Notable farces of the period include Brandon Thomas, *Charley's Aunt* (1892) and Georges Feydeau, *Le Dindon* (*Sauce for the Goose*, 1896).

21 Henrik Ibsen, *Ghosts*, Act III, in *Ghosts and Two Other Plays by Henrik Ibsen*, trans. and ed. R. Farquharson Sharp (London: Dent, 1911), 67–141 (141). See the final moments of Eugene O'Neill, *Days Without End* (1934) and of Arthur Miller, *The Crucible* (1953) for echoes of this effect.

22 Henry James, 'After the Play' (1889), reprinted in *Henry James: The Scenic Art*, ed. Allan Wade (London: Hart-Davis, 1949), 226–242 (241). James saw the *Théâtre Libre* production when it played at the Royalty Theatre, London, in February 1889.

23 *Premièred* at the Berlin *Freie Bühne* in 1893, Gerhart Hauptmann's play was produced in quick succession by the independent theatres of Berlin and Paris and banned as quickly in London, New York, Moscow and St Petersburg, among others.

24 *Le Temps*, 5 June 1893, reprinted in Francisque Sarcey, *Quarante ans de théâtre: Feuilletons dramatiques*, 8 vols (Paris: Bibliothèque des Annales Politiques et Littéraires, 1900–02), 8 (1902): 384–94 (385).

25 Emile Faguet, *Notes sur le théâtre contemporain*, 2nd ser. (Paris: Lecène et Oudin, 1890), 112 (25 March 1889).

26 Known as the 'Dublin Plays', these include *The Shadow of a Gunman* (1923); *Juno and the Paycock* (1924) and *The Plough and the Stars* (1926). They are set among the city's tenement dwellers in the context of very recent Irish political events, respectively, the Independence War, the Civil War and then the Easter Rising.

27 Sean O'Casey, *The Shadow of a Gunman*, in *Two Plays: Juno and The Paycock and The Shadow of a Gunman* (London: Macmillan, 1925), 115–199 (117).

28 Sean O'Casey, *Juno and The Paycock*, in *Two Plays*, 1–113 (77).

29 Sean O'Casey, *The Plough and the Stars* (London: Macmillan, 1926), 15–18.

30 Sean O'Casey, *The Silver Tassie* (London: Macmillan, 1928), 41.

31 Samuel Beckett, *Endgame* (London: Faber and Faber, 1958, repr. 1964), 11.

32 '*corpse: actors' slang*. To confuse or "put out" (an actor) in the performance of his part; to spoil (a scene or piece of acting) by some blunder' (OED).

Chapter Three

'THE QUEER PART DOORS PLAY' IN NABOKOV'S *LAUGHTER IN THE DARK*

Beci Dobbin

Two thirds of the way through *Laughter in the Dark*, when the protagonist Albinus becomes convinced that his mistress Margot is drowning behind the bathroom door, Nabokov parenthetically confides that Albinus is 'quite unconscious of the queer part doors played in his and her life.'[1] In this instance, the closed door, along with the sound of rushing water, conceal Margot's infidelity; she and her lover Axel Rex canoodle in the room adjoining the bathroom, on the other side to that in which Albinus panics. Albinus is thus 'unconscious' of the bathroom door's implication in the sense that he mis-suspects it of harbouring tragedy. Although unconscious of its actual implication, he suspects it of meaning something.[2]

One way of reading Albinus's misconstruction is as a kind of displaced critical acuity. No, the bathroom door does not signify death, but doors do consistently anticipate change in the novel. '[N]o sooner had she crossed the threshold than she yielded with pleasure and zest to [her] fate', writes Nabokov of Margot's double seduction by her first lover's flat and the lifestyle it seems to foreshadow.[3] More bleakly, Albinus opens the door of his family home to find that his wife has discovered his affair and left him; he opens the 'creaky' (from 'croak') nursery door to find his daughter's dead body; and ultimately, he expects to 'unlock the door of his blindness' by killing his faithless mistress.[4] Albinus *is* conscious of the meaning of doors as harbingers of loss. However, his premonition is more important than the specific form it takes. For Nabokov is less concerned in this novel with the consequences of transition than with the doorway as inter-space; a locus of imaginative activity in its own right. Hovering outside his front door on the morning of Margot's heedless love letter, he reflects: 'now he had to open his door, walk in, and see… What would he see?… Would it not be best, perhaps, not to enter at all – just to leave everything as it was, to desert, vanish?'[5] The limit in which this and other thresholds consist is uniquely generative. Characters think most (and best) in the company of doors.

'Doors were always against [Albinus]', says Nabokov, punning on 'against', but the joke has a serious side: Albinus spends much of the novel in states of suspension, waiting behind literal and metaphorical closed doors for surprises he rarely wants.[6] In this respect, *Laughter in Dark* contrasts with other novels by Nabokov, in which doors symbolise (as well as instrumentalise) passage. Leona Toker writes that 'one of the most important images in the Nabokov *oeuvre* is that of a nonhermetic partition, a door that has come ajar', the open crack envisaging either escape, (mis)adventure or death.[7] In *Lolita*, Humbert's 'raped little table with its open drawer' holds no such promise or portent, but it does inscribe forms of tres*passing*; upon the desk, upon Lolita and between present and future, thus muddying Humbert's meaning (for only Lolita's rape deserves outrage).[8] In *King, Queen, Knave*, doors not only suggest opportunities, as Toker argues; they also focus the impatience at the novel's centre: 'Damn this key', explodes Franz, 'Always starts by behaving as if it had never been in this lock before.'[9] Among the obstacles that encumber his path are a tenacious mistress, an indomitable uncle whose death would enrich him and the daily grind of his poverty; like a cornered chess-piece, he aspires to jump. In *The Enchanter*, another impatient protagonist loses his way in a labyrinthine hotel and rouses himself in vain to pounce on a pre-adolescent girl: 'He found the right door, licked his chops, grabbed the doorknob, was about to – '[10] In discovering his 'vulgar mistake' he deflates like an anticlimactic fairytale wolf – but the locked door retains its implication of passage. 'Wrong room, eh?' queries the irritated occupant, 'Well, next time find the right room. There's somebody in here…trying to train a young person, that somebody is being interrupted.'[11] Literal passage is symbolically twined with a rite of passage, neither of which is performed at all smoothly by the protagonist, who pleads to his lover-in-training as he prematurely ejaculates: 'Be quiet, it's nothing bad, it's just a kind of game, it happens sometimes…'[12]

As Will Norman and Duncan White argue, 'transition…is integral to Nabokov's art just as it was imposed on him in life.'[13] Mobility is as fundamental to his plots (and style)[14] as it was to his émigré existence. Doors mean passage because life meant passage. However another way of experiencing Nabokov's exilic doors is in terms of limbo. In *Mary*, when the philosophical Alfyorov is asked by Ganin to explain 'what is symbolic' about their being stuck in a lift, he replies:

> 'Well, the fact that we've stopped, motionless, in this darkness. And that we're waiting. At lunch today that man – what's his name – oh yes, Podtyagin – was arguing with me about the sense of this émigré life of ours, the perpetual waiting.'[15]

'Sense' cuts three ways; it implies the feel of émigré life, its nonsensicality and, implicitly, its association with a particular kind of reflective rationality. Alfyorov philosophises because he has nothing better to do. The lift's closed steel door simultaneously invokes departure as an argument against making himself at home and blocks his escape. Albinus is likewise perennially stuck between destinations, deliberating. His 'walk up and down the long, whitewashed, white-enamelled passage' in the hospital where his daughter is born,[16] symbolises his epistemological position through much of the novel as an unenlightened worrier. His unconsciousness is a form of consciousness: it is why he thinks.

Albinus differs from Alfyorov in the sense that he is not explicitly an immigrant (though his Berlin home and Latin surname hint at his family's Italian provenance), and that he is no philosopher. If, as Simon Blackburn writes, 'it is to the philosophical tradition that we have to look if we want to know what is required to be sensible, or what the order of reason might be', Albinus is the last place we should look for philosophy.[17] Where Alfyorov meditates on his intermediate state, Albinus fastidiously examines details, either in his capacity as connoisseur of art and female beauty, or as helpless victim of change; a sort of post-adolescent teenager. Surfaces matter in part because he understands nothing else ('As a child he never built things like other boys'),[18] and in part because surfaces are the idler's familiar terrain. Thus, the white-washed, white-enamelled walls of the hospital are comprehensively known to him, the telephone over which he 'mounts guard' familiarly 'gleam[s] and [is] mute,'[19] and the front door of his family home 'upon which his scholarly name gleamed sedately' is easily summoned from memory.[20] Barbara Straumann traces Nabokov's investment in details and the 'patterns' that connect them to 'the need of the exile to recreate a world in and through language after an entire geocultural home and homeland have been lost ...'[21] Yet the details that preoccupy Albinus are precisely the furnishings of exile: the way the world looks to an existential nomad awaiting his fate.

Albinus spends the bulk of the novel as an outcast; Margot drops him, his wife Elisabeth abandons him, his friends' wives keep their distance, and when later he loses his vision, Margot and Rex imprison him behind a 'barricade of boxes and trunks'. [22] Exile begins as a sentence remotely prescribed to a philanderer and ends, paradoxically, as a mode of cohabitation. Albinus goes from examining the surfaces of doors and telephones to collecting a small change of authentic smells and sounds from a world otherwise fabricated by his enemies. Blank but knowable surfaces are replaced by an intrinsic 'door': a 'solid darkness that was like a part of himself.'[23] Another contemporary for whom exile not only meant the loss of a home but the immediacy of a trap is suggested on the novel's opening page by the fictional author Udo Conrad's story of a 'conjuror who spirited himself away at his farewell performance', later entitled *The Vanishing Trick*.[24] Adam Phillips writes of Harry Houdini (née Erik Weisz), the escapologist who was buried in the box intended for a disappearing trick: 'he would devote his life to the performance of a violent parody of assimilation. He would be the man who could adapt to anything AND escape from it.'[25] If Houdini was a violent parody of assimilation, Albinus parodies Houdini not just in his helpless bewilderment before one closed door after another but also in his limply compliant adaptation to alien encumbrances. 'How wise she is', he muses 'tenderly', in recalling that Margot 'locked [her door] at night [so that] he was shut in.'[26]

Sir Arthur Conan Doyle describes Houdini as 'picking off [a] locked padlock as one picks a plum from a tree' and slipping through handcuffs as though they were 'made of jelly':[27] yet the spectacle with which he became synonymous was not of a man effortlessly surmounting obstacles but of one confronting them in all their lethal potential. It took him over an hour to emerge, sweaty, tousled and gagging for air, from a nailed coffin in Boston in 1907. 'All the time I was in there I was thinking of death', he said: escape was as much an encounter with the body's limits as with the *idea* of mortality.[28] Where Albinus contemplates doors whose desertion would be cowardly ('Would it not be best to .. vanish?'), Houdini pondered enclosures whose desertion would be celebrated as heroism or magic; yet they were both in their own ways grappling with death. 'This future', Albinus reflects, when his daughter's funeral raises the possibility of a return to Elisabeth, '[was] like one of those long dusty passages where one finds a nailed-up coffin…'[29] Nailed-up, presumably, because the un-nailed coffin affords an irrational hope. To return to the predictability of marital life would somehow be to concede to death, while his relationship with Margot is a kind of un-nailed coffin: it is just as indissoluble as marriage but seems by its non-formality to promise the chance of escape – Rex is right to suspect that he has no intention of marrying her. After the nailed-up coffin of marital life and the un-nailed coffin of his affair with Margot comes the 'impenetrable black shroud' of blindness, elsewhere configured as an 'impenetrable wall' and a 'locked door.'[30] The toll for attempting to shirk his mortality, it seems, is a version of a death in life or enshrouded life; he 'panics' in his sightlessness like 'one who wakes to find himself in his grave.'[31] Moreover, where Elisabeth survives her appendicitis (as Houdini did not),[32] Albinus's entombment in his own mind anticipates his premature death in the room where he was certain of trapping and killing Margot. His dying words are, 'I can't breathe.'[33] The desire to escape thus eventually leads him to a permanent prison, but one that at least differs from a world of blank surfaces in its comprehensibility. 'Now I know everything', he says.

If Albinus may be read as a parody of Houdini in his hopeless but repetitive and pensive imprisonment, Margot is an escapologist in her own right who spares little consideration for anything, let alone the strictly temporary constraints upon her body and aspirations. She is mobile in the conventional Nabokovian sense, as defined by Norman and White; nothing can hold her. Her father was a locksmith, then a porter. Doors are a family specialism, and the only aspect of her history of subsequent use. 'The past was safe in its cage', she muses, in passing her old neighbourhood; her escape retrospectively feels like the past's entrapment, so definitive is her triumph over it.[34] Indeed, the entrapment of her prisoners becomes a calling card. Before she meets Albinus, Rex traps the pimp who loaned her out to him in the lavatory, just as later she locks up Albinus, while seeming herself to be stuck somewhere in his house. On both the occasions when Albinus plans to shoot her, he engineers a trap and is trapped himself. By closing the door behind them in the hotel room and dragging the table to the doorway in the novel's concluding scene, he constructs a hermetic space; a nailed-down coffin, complemented by 'the seven compressed deaths' in 'the treasure house' of his gun.[35] Absolute confinement *is* death. Yet, in the first instance, her protests persuade him to whisk her away in a car which he cannot drive, and crashes (Udo Conrad's reference to the bus as a 'moving prison' is obliquely prophetic),[36] and in the second instance he becomes entangled in a chair, thereby allowing her to disarm and shoot him. The 'wide open' door of his death scene is simultaneously the symbol of her escape and of his entrapment because just as the entrapment of others is her criminal signature, her freedom is always the trace of another's defeat.[37] The only apparent cost of successes like these is a perennial naivety (despite her worldliness), which Nabokov finds contemptible. 'The water is wet', she 'cries', surprised.[38] Like the cat which Albinus's step-brother sees 'slither[ing] between the bars of the garden railings' after her seemingly miraculous disappearance from his house, she is conscious of her surroundings only to the extent that they obstruct or accommodate her passage through them.[39] Doors might as well be railings – more gap than surface – for all the attention she pays.

Margot's naivety is the by-product of movement, while Albinus's 'unconsciousness' or inability to determine the implications of his experience is an effect of his liminal status. Although both are always in transition, only Albinus conceives of himself as an exile. At the beginning of the novel, in reflecting on an idea for a new style of cartoon he borrows from Udo Conrad, he seems to 'ma[ke] it his own by liking it, playing with it, letting it grow upon him, [which] goes to make lawful property in the free city of the mind.'[40]

In the free city of the mind, origins and endings lose definition; all ideas are fair game because ownership is a matter of appropriation. Albinus's idea is to adapt for animated film a Dutch painting of a pot-house, with hens 'beginning to peck on the threshold' – a version of his marriage to Elisabeth, who flicks through magazines while he 'pecks at her with little kisses…'[41] Neither the idea nor the Dutch painting will be his own, just as his marriage is someone else's doing: 'a remarkably athletic female cousin who, thank God, finally sprained her ankle in Pontresina, was chiefly responsible for their union.'[42] Elisabeth is a proxy for her cousin; his desire for someone else is at once the basis of his marriage and its intrinsic disclaimer. Origin operates paradoxically as an index of *in*authenticity.

The idea that Albinus inhabits a world of fakes is developed in relation to his gallery, which the professional counterfeiter Rex finds to be sprinkled with his own work; in relation to his immediate visual impressions and memories, which he mentally (mis)attributes to the Old Masters; and in relation to Margot and Rex, whose platonic relationship veils an amorous history of which Albinus is unaware. Even when seeming to invest in origins, he undermines them; the hats he labels with his name so that artists stop stealing them at parties anticipate a topsy-turvy version of his gallery of fakes, in which painters sport the mis-signed headwear of art collectors. Nor is he more than superficially interested in Margot's history. Where in Nabokov's *Mary*, exile implies a blend of nostalgia and a whimsical engagement with the rootless present, and while for Houdini exilic life meant a parodic adaptation to life in America in the early Twentieth century (according to Phillips), in *Laughter in the Dark*, Albinus's exile is a form of amnesia. There are no origins to be haunted by, even when he becomes blind: 'He was horrified to realize how little he had used his eyes – for [the] colours [he remembers] moved across too vague a background…' Edward Said describes the 'beginning' of a book as 'the main entrance to what it offers';[43] Albinus's life seems full of new beginnings, thresholds promising much but leading nowhere. The entry to the bathroom never reveals a misbehaving Margot, the door behind which he expects to 'see' the dissolution of his marriage leads him only to an empty house, and the nursery he enters so tentatively shows him just 'a vague glimpse of [the] little dead face' of his daughter before 'dimness' intervenes. Change happens, but Albinus seems unable to encounter it head-on. Whether doors open or not, he can only see surfaces; images with no ostensible origin or future. Margot nags him as he drives her away from the hotel and Rex, 'I shall be thankful when we get *somewhere*.'[44] He crashes the car.

Authenticity is meaningless to Albinus, but crucial to Rex, whose meticulously dated drawing of Margot functions both as evidence of their earlier dalliance and as a guarantee of his affection. She expects the door through which he slips 'something crinkly' to slam but its pneumatic slowness allows him to withdraw in his own time, and she expects the scrap to be a banknote but finds instead 'the back view of a girl, bare-shouldered, bare-legged, on a bed, with her face to the wall.'[45] Both the pneumatic door and the picture deprive her of the upper hand by conceding to Rex the dignity of retreat, from the conversation and from their relationship. The image is inscribed 'first in pencil, then overwritten in ink – [with] the day, month, and year when he had left her.'[46] These controlled departures point to his reliance on a semblance of authenticity for success; he leaves 'presently', having 'stood there, pull[ing] at his lower lip' like a demented Hamlet in Ophelia's chamber (whose amorous compositions are returned to him),[47] and the specificity and inking of the date lend his spontaneous decision the inherent legitimacy of fate. If authenticity is beyond Albinus's grasp, it is Rex's industry. The counterfeiter understands the value of apparent genuineness, just as the caricaturist knows the value of essences. Max Beerbohm once joked that he aimed to 'boil a man down to the essentials.'[48] Rex's drawing of Margot is 'bare' in the double sense of naked and economically summed up. Already vicariously endowed with credibility by its association with a banknote (whose value likewise depends on its authoritative markings), the picture achieves its impact by the precision with which it invokes the only aspect of her origins that matters to Margot, and promotes it to a fated romance; minting it in the act of emphasis.

Doors and openings consistently feature as props in Rex's (re)presentation of himself to others in part because of their ability to confer significance onto ordinary actions. His snow-drenched arrival in Albinus's doorway for a party and his flamboyant first appearance at Frau Levandovsky's, dressed entirely in blue, are rendered meaningful by his dramatic enhancement of the door's assimilative function – the element of its meaning most conducive to subtle romanticising. Where the melodramatic Margot habitually slams doors, her more efficient co-conspirator waits for them to open: he recognises their *intrinsic* drama. In response to the news of Albinus's daughter's death he recounts the story of a boy who 'cut himself while opening a tin of preserved peaches – you know, the large, soft, slippery kind that plap in the mouth and slither down. He died a few days later of blood poisoning.'[49] Rex's ostensible point is to establish death's 'fatuousness' for a grieving Albinus, yet the boy dies because he takes the business of entrance for granted in a way that Rex, who knows the exact sensation of swallowing a peach, would never do. Rex's familiarity with the mechanics of assimilation enables him to control the processes whereby novelty is introduced. When down on his luck, he tellingly imagines that 'the *hinges* of his luck had got stuck.'[50] His first name Axel suggests axle, the central revolving rod connecting one wheel to another in a car. By name and nature, he controls turning mechanisms. The slowly closing pneumatic door is in league with him.

It is only when Albinus's step-brother appears, flushed in 'amazement', behind the glass door of the room in which he keeps him hostage, that Rex is outmanoeuvred. For far from controlling the door's revelatory capacity here, he is caught off guard, and as Ellen Pifer puts it, 'the inhuman artist discovers himself in the ethical world.'[51] His uniquely vivid appreciation of the significance of beginnings, both in the sense of origins and openings – in the passive and active senses, as Said understands them[52] – is ultimately undermined by his unreadiness. Nabokov ends his story by reducing him to a flimsy cartoon of the postlapsarian Adam, by subjecting him to a mythical beginning he cannot control: 'like Adam after the Fall, Rex, cowering by the white wall and grinning wanly, covered his nakedness with his hand.' This engineer of illusory beginnings is finally reducible to a sketch in part because he has no authentic existence on which to fall back. Although native to Germany, he seems to come from nowhere; out of the blue, as his blue suit suggests when he first appears on Frau Levandovsky's doorstep, with a powdered face and wig-like hair ('his lustreless black hair…was certainly not a wig, although it looked uncommonly like one.')[53] He reminds Margot of a lynx.

The lynx compares to the cat that 'slithers between the bars of the garden railings' in its ability to see in the dark, a skill which Margot also demonstrates at the beginning of the novel in the 'velvety darkness' of the cinema, where she stands at the exit waiting to navigate customers to their seats.[54] Nabokov's association between cinematic darkness and pairs of gleaming eyes is reinforced by the cinema's name, Argus – after the many eyed monster and/or the Eurasian butterfly with eyelike patterning – and by the resemblance of one of Margot's brother's friends to the German actor Conrad Veidt, whose 'pale face and deep-set eyes predestined him for phantasmagoric parts in films of the uncanny.'[55] Among Veidt's roles in the late 1920s was that of a circus freak whose face had been cut into a permanent smile, so that only his eyes expressed his emotional experience. *The Man Who Laughs* not only shares its titular mirth and emphasis on staring eyes with Nabokov's novel, but also its conception of the body as mask or screen. The protagonist mediates his emotions through the contours of his grimace. Despite its appeal as a spectacle, his face is thus as vacant as the eyes of his blind girlfriend. Between them they compose one fully expressive or one entirely blank face. Soppily, they are one another's other halves. Significantly, Nabokov's sense of the body as screen is introduced by his depiction of a glass door as a version of the cinema from which Margot has just departed when Albinus first propositions her: 'She smiled at him through the glass pane and then ran down the dim passage towards the back yard.'[56] The smile is intimate and yet impenetrable. Albinus can only follow her with his eyes.

Barbara Wyllie reads Margot as the 'incarnation of a [cinematic] romantic ideal', with her 'pale, sulky, painfully beautiful face', but the feline heroine's supporting role in a film produced by Albinus's business associates establishes not just her incompetence as an actress, as Wyllie concedes, but also her comic as opposed to romantic screen presence.[57] In *Flesh and the Devil*, another late 1920s film which Nabokov's wife remembers watching with him,[58] Greta Garbo's queenliness is offset by Barbara Kent's jerky desperation in pursuit of a man who loves her only platonically. Margot's 'stuffy, clumsy, angular gestures' on camera, combined with her dark hair, petiteness, youth and abandonment by her lover in favour of a husky voiced rival with 'exquisite shoulders', distance her as much from Garbo as they liken her to Kent. Thus, what cinema brings to the novel is not a model of star-struck infatuation. Rather, it contextualises Nabokov's conception of Margot as an endlessly examinable image whose intentions remain concealed; as an image on a screen. The Russian novelist Fedor Sepun wrote in *Theatre and Cinema* in 1932 that 'film [was] able to show things that [were] otherwise invisible…but…ha[d] no inner relationship with the visible.'[59] Margot's film appearance renders her body visible in a way that surprises and unsettles her, exposing her every absentminded gesture to an amused audience; yet it fails to show the sincerity of her ambition to succeed as an actress. Like Veidt's character in *The Man Who Laughs*, she is comic in spite of herself. However, the visibility that counts against her here works in her favour elsewhere. When Albinus, stationed at the door of their hotel room, mentally girds himself to shoot her for her amorous truancy, he becomes transfixed by her 'glossy black head', 'the bluish shade on her neck where the hair had been shaved' and 'the sore place just above her heel [where] the blood had soaked through her white sock.'[60] What the camera and his gaze expose is nuance; the shade on her neck and the stain in her sock. What his gaze fails to show is her panicked scheming: '('…if I were to rush to the door,' she thought, I might just manage to run out. Then I'd scream…')'[61] One kind of invisibility is exposed while another remains unfathomable, and in Sepun's words, there is no 'inner relationship' between the two. The subtlety of Albinus's observations of Margot is out of sync with his insensitivity to her perspective. His position at the room's threshold configures both his indecision and liminal vantage point: he can only see so far.

Andrew Field understands Albinus's predecessor's 'framing' by the entrance in *Camera Obscura* as a reference to 'the spiritual doorway of the *camera obscura* that is the novel.'[62] The camera obscura was used by artists before the invention of photography to reproduce traceable images. It worked like the human eye, transferring visual information from a small hole onto a screen.

Albinus compares to the camera obscura and to cinema in the arbitrary narrowness of his perspective ('He was horrified to realize how little he had used his eyes'), in his awareness of certain kinds of 'invisibility' and blindness to others and in his reliance on light. Where Margot 'smoothly' traverses the cinema's darkness, he 'shuffles' and 'gropes' his way to his seat.[63] Moreover, just as the temporality of the cinematic image is a recorded present with no intrinsic consciousness of past or future, Albinus is constitutionally incapable either of taking the future into account (because forward planning would suggest 'one of those long, dusty passages where one finds a nailed-up box'), or of bringing the past to bear on his reasoning – except in the vague sense of anticipating scenes of crisis behind closed doors. When he arrives in the cinema where Margot works, the film whose ending he catches mirrors his experience in the double sense that its story is his own, as Stuart Dabney observes,[64] and that it is composed of images without context. The events which he 'could not understand since he had not seen their beginning' are implicitly descriptive of the cinema as a medium whose exclusive reference to the present restricts it to unfolding its narratives moment by moment, unlike the classical paintings in Albinus's gallery which invoke mythical and historical trajectories.[65] Albinus shares with film an innate susceptibility to disorientation.

Albinus's only chance of understanding his experience is to track the storyline that matters to him as closely as possible (focussing on Margot rather than Elisabeth), a process which is undermined by his gullible acceptance of Margot and Rex's lies, his overhasty assumptions and his inability to know what he cannot see at first hand. Waiting to shoot Margot when she opens the door of their room, 'his mind [goes] out to track her.'[66] He imagines her entry into the hotel and journey in the lift and listens out for the 'click of her heels along the corridor', but misses his cue because she is wearing tennis shoes. The film in his mind and the film outside it have come adrift. The 'white closed door' he confronts as Margot patters into his hearing range thus suggests a blank screen whose impending revelations he is as helpless to foreknow or remember as the cinema goer who arrives after a film has started. Similarly, in his death scene, although his back is turned to a closed door in the hope of blocking Margot's escape, his engagement with the unfolding drama is helplessly reactive. The room he 'sees distinctly' in his mind's eye is irrelevant to its existence in real time.[67] Again, he confronts a blankness; the white closed door is succeeded by his blindness. Nabokov's 'dark' joke is to place the man least equipped to reason *contextually* – an exile with no sense of history, who collects art of dubious origin and sets out to forget his past and mortality, living for as well as in the moment, like a film – in the position of having to act as a man whose fortune depends on his genius for reasoning contextually;

the premeditative murderer. *Despair*'s Hermann kicks himself for forgetting to retrieve his victim's walking stick, while Albinus fails to anticipate even the most predictable of Margot's movements. Of course she is wearing tennis shoes; he knows she was playing tennis.

Nevertheless, where Margot is insensible to all but the most conventional forms of pleasure, and Rex fetishistically fixates on the mechanics of manipulation – on 'hinges' – Albinus is able to luxuriate in the 'stripes of sunshine cross[ing] and recross[ing]' Margot's body or the way an old painting's beauty gradually emerges through the smoke of old varnish when it is restored.[68] To Albinus, beauty means 'ripples of light on the inner curve of a bridge';[69] it is a quality of the liminal space, only perceptible by those who devote their lives to examining it. Thus, miserable as his ending is, his numerous beginnings, hovering over one ominous surface after another, are at least of interest to him. Although Margot's slipperiness frustrates him in the closing scene, her 'warmth tinged with…perfume' and the sense of her 'trembling like the air above sand on a very hot day' engage his imagination.[70] There is something to be gained just by existing on the threshold. '[D]etail is always welcome', says Nabokov, having given away the plot of his novel on the opening page.[71]

Nabokov's brackets, as liminal moments in their own right, routinely take this welcome for granted, pausing to note the resemblance between the 'inside' of a cat's ear and 'dark pink blotting paper, much used', or with a curiosity that imitates Albinus, the 'fine down between [Margot's] pretty shoulders.'[72] Typographically, they configure openings in the body of the text, as Nabokov foregrounds in the line: '(A window opened in the fourth storey, but it was too late.)'[73] Yet nothing *useful* is ever disclosed: the dappled inside of a cat's ear does not even benefit the cat. Brackets are windows that open *too late.* Or they en-suite bathrooms like that between Rex and Albinus's bedrooms, in which the water over-runs while Rex and Margot frolic unsuspected. An anomaly in the layout of the hotel where they are staying, the bathroom connects Albinus to their secret while barring him from its discovery. By disclosing the bath's overflow it categorises the sort of secret it is limited to telling – the superfluous one. The novel's brackets are superfluous in the double sense that their content is intrinsically supplementary, and that their tone resists assimilation into the narrative. It is not just that the narrator undermines his characters, as in the line: '([Albinus] was quite unconscious of the queer part doors played in his and her life.)' The irony also undermines its own premise; Albinus's nervousness on Margot's behalf betrays a memory of the negative implications of doors thus far in the novel, but his full recognition of a door theme would disturb the conceit that he believes his existence to be real. His unconsciousness is appropriate. What the brackets reveal, then, is an ambivalence at the heart of Nabokov's self-presentation. Fredric Jameson associates the work of the 'great European exiles – Nabokov and Chandler fully as much as Hitchcock', with a unique capacity for the 'disassemblage' of ordinary experience.[74] The term 'disassemblage' is immediately suggestive of the Nabokovian parenthesis whose function is to split hairs inconsequentially, whether in relation to fictional objects or meta-fictionally, as an ambivalence of authorial tone. Superfluous to the story, his brackets are meaningful only as compelling distractions, like the bridge's up-lit underbelly. Yet such detail is crucial to Albinus, who spends his life in the company of doors and screens, and to the novel's full implication. Doubtful irony is one of the subtlest ways in which it laughs.

In *Literature and the Taste of Knowledge*, Michael Wood draws attention in passing to a door in *The Life of Sebastian Knight* which troubles the story's credibility by staging an unimaginable exchange. 'V…can scarcely, in any intelligible universe, have introduced himself as so-and-so', he writes of an encounter between the narrator, V, and Pahl Pahlovitch Rechnoy – who gives his full name – at an open door.[75] As Wood suggests, Nabokov's main intention here is to disrupt a realist convention, yet there is also a sense in which Pahl is exploiting an opportunity for role play which V humours. 'Come in' Pahl enthuses, 'as if he had been expecting me', V then introduces himself as 'so-and-so' and Pahl 'guffaw[s] heartily' in making his long-winded reply, 'as if it were a good joke.'[76] *Laughter in the Dark* shares with this moment in *The Life of Sebastian Knight* and the lift scene in *Mary* its conception of the threshold as a dynamic space, whether characters venture beyond it or not. To pause at a doorway is to grapple with one's mortality, like Houdini or Albinus, to manipulate the 'hinges' of disclosure, like Rex, to become preoccupied by intricate surfaces, like Albinus or Nabokov, or to engage imaginatively with a text composed of details. Even Margot, who spends the novel slipping through the bars of ineffectual cages, dreams of an ever-suspended moment of arrival: 'there was always that vision of herself…being helped out of a gorgeous car by a gorgeous hotel porter…'[77] Her ambition is to be surrounded by gorgeousness on her way to a door that never opens.

Notes

1 Vladimir Nabokov, *Laughter in the Dark* (London: Penguin, 2001; first published in Russian as *Kamera Obskura*, 1933), 132.

2 *Laughter in the Dark* is the story of an art collector's infatuation with a young cinema attendant. The discovery of his affair ends his marriage and leads to his cohabitation with his mistress, who conceals her own affair with his confidant. The suspicion of her infidelity culminates in a car crash, as a result of which he loses his vision. While

nursing him, she and her lover continue their dalliance at his expense. When their betrayal is exposed, he plots to trap and kill her, but dies himself in the scuffle.

3 Ibid., 23.

4 Ibid., 112 and 181.

5 Ibid., 55.

6 Ibid., 186.

7 Leona Toker, *Nabokov: The Mystery of Literary Structures* (Ithaca: Cornell University Press, 1989), 60.

8 Vladimir Nabokov, *Lolita* (1959; Harmondsworth: Penguin, 2000), 96.

9 Vladimir Nabokov, *King, Queen, Knave* (London: Harmondsworth, 2001; first published in Russian, 1928), 120.

10 Vladimir Nabokov, *The Enchanter* (1986; London: Penguin, 2009), 52.

11 Ibid., 53.

12 Ibid., 57.

13 Will Norman and Duncan White, *Transitional Nabokov* (Oxford: Peter Lang, 2009), 2.

14 Norman and White define Nabokov's style as 'the inked simulacrum of the agile consciousness *in process*.' (2)

15 Vladimir Nabokov, *Mary* (London: Penguin, 2009; first published in Russian, 1926), 3.

16 Nabokov, *Laughter in the Dark*, 12.

17 Simon Blackburn, *Truth* (London: Penguin, 2006), ix.

18 Nabokov, *Laughter in the Dark*, 149.

19 Ibid., 48.

20 Ibid., 55.

21 Barbara Straumann, *Figurations of Exile in Hitchcock and Nabokov* (Edinburgh: Edinburgh University Press, 2008), 49.

22 Nabokov, *Laughter in the Dark*, 167.

23 Ibid., 157.

24 Ibid., 5 and 86.

25 Adam Phillips, *Houdini's Box: On the Arts of Escape* (London: Faber and Faber, 2002), 8.

26 Nabokov, *Laughter in the Dark*, 171.

27 Sir Arthur Conan Doyle, *The Edge of the Unknown* (London: John Murray, 1930), 25 and 24.

28 William Kalush and Larry Sloman, *The Secret Life of Houdini: The Making of America's first Superhero* (New York: Atria Books, 2006), 190.

29 Nabokov, *Laughter in the Dark*, 115.

30 Ibid., 157 and 181.

31 Ibid., 157.

32 'Elisabeth proved to have a tender little scar – the result of appendicitis.' (11)

33 Nabokov, *Laughter in the Dark*, 187.

34 Ibid., 127.

35 Ibid., 181.

36 Ibid., 137.

37 Ibid., 187.

38 Ibid., 73.

39 Ibid., 46.

40 Ibid., 5.

41 Ibid., 15.

42 Ibid., 10–11.

43 Edward Said, *Beginnings* (London: Granta, 1998), 3.
44 Nabokov, *Laughter in the Dark*, 151.
45 Ibid., 88.
46 Ibid., 88.
47 'I did repel his letters, and denied / His access to me.' William Shakespeare, *The Tragedy of Hamlet, Prince of Denmark*, in *The Riverside Shakespeare*, ed. G. Blakemore Evans (Boston: Houghton Mifflin, 1974), II.i.106–7.
48 N. J. Hall, *Max Beerbohm: A Kind of Life* (New Haven: Yale University Press, 2002), 186.
49 Nabokov, *Laughter in the Dark*, 117.
50 Ibid., 90.
51 Ellen Pifer, *Nabokov and the Novel* (Massachusetts: Harvard University Press, 1980), 161.
52 Said, *Beginnings*, 6.
53 Nabokov, *Laughter in the Dark*, 21.
54 Ibid., 13.
55 *The BFI Companion to German Cinema*, ed. Thomas Elsaesser (London: British Film Institute, 1999), 241.
56 Nabokov, *Laughter in the Dark*, 29.
57 Barbara Wyllie, *Nabokov at the Movies* (Jefferson: McFarland and Co., 2003), 74–75.
58 Alfred Appel, *Nabokov's Dark Cinema* (New York: Oxford University Press, 1974), 41.
59 Quoted in Sabine Hake, *The Cinema's Weird Machine: Writing on Film in Germany, 1907–1933* (Lincoln: University of Nebraska Press, 1993), 159.
60 Nabokov, *Laughter in the Dark*, 145.
61 Ibid., 146.
62 Andrew Field, *Nabokov: His Life and Art* (London: Hodder and Stoughton Ltd, 1967), 163.
63 Nabokov, *Laughter in the Dark*, 13.
64 Stuart Dabney, *Nabokov: The Dimensions of Parody* (Baton Rouge: Louisiana State University Press, 1978), 93.
65 Nabokov, *Laughter in the Dark*, 13.
66 Ibid., 144.
67 Ibid., 185.
68 Ibid., 74 and 60.
69 Ibid., 10.
70 Ibid., 185.
71 Ibid., 5.
72 Ibid., 20 and 19.
73 Nabokov, *Laughter in the Dark*, 183.
74 Fredric Jameson, *Signatures of the Visible* (New York: Routledge, 1992, 2007), 143.
75 Michael Wood, *Literature and the Taste of Knowledge* (Cambridge: Cambridge University Press, 2005), 115.
76 Vladimir Nabokov, *The Real Life of Sebastian Knight* (1941; London: Penguin, 2001), 118.
77 Nabokov, *Laughter in the Dark*, 19.

Chapter Four

'INVASION FROM OUTER SPACE'[1]: THE THRESHOLD OF ANNUNCIATIONS[2]

Subha Mukherji

In Lino Mannocci's inkjet monotype sequence on the theme of the Annunciation (2009),[3] we are faced with a set of five somewhat uncanny images – familiar yet strange; or the familiar rendered alien.[4] 'I am the Lord's servant', the first in the series (Figure 1), is immediately recognisable not only because of the traditional configuration of the angel and Mary facing each other, but also because the angel is Domenico Veneziano's Gabriel, made by cutting out a stencilled image of Veneziano's famous painting of the Annunciation in the Fitzwilliam Museum (Figure 2), around which Mannocci has organised his exhibition of (mainly) Renaissance engravings of the Annunciation, running parallelly.[5] But it is also eerie because, instead of the neat symmetry of that painting, and the clear sense of Gabriel entering Mary's space both in Veneziano and in the pictorial tradition more widely, here we have Mary's tentative half-entry into a frame which is occupied firmly by the angel and his world, including an embryonic cloud floating purposefully down towards Mary, and what looks like a sickle moon peeping out of clouds instead of the harmonious light suffusing Veneziano's canvas. In fact, Mary's kneeling body is half out of the frame, and half in, a position brought to life here by Mannocci's manipulation of his specific craft: using an etching press, paper and a plate, he places Mary's inkjet figure *across* the plate-mark, rather than within it, before printing, to play with the boundaries. Her arms, outstretched behind her, and her feet, are not inhabitants of this space; her body hovers on the threshold, making her figure look somehow precarious, not yet fully or surely belonging to the main frame. And unlike Veneziano's Mary, her fragile head is bowed lower than the angel's, almost laid down for the cloud to descend on. The next monotype, 'May it be as you have said' (Figure 3), depicts the next moment – the sky is dark, the cloud looks ominous

Figure 1. Lino Mannocci, *I am the Lord's Servant*, 2009. Monotype. © Lino Mannocci. Image © Fitzwilliam Museum, University of Cambridge.

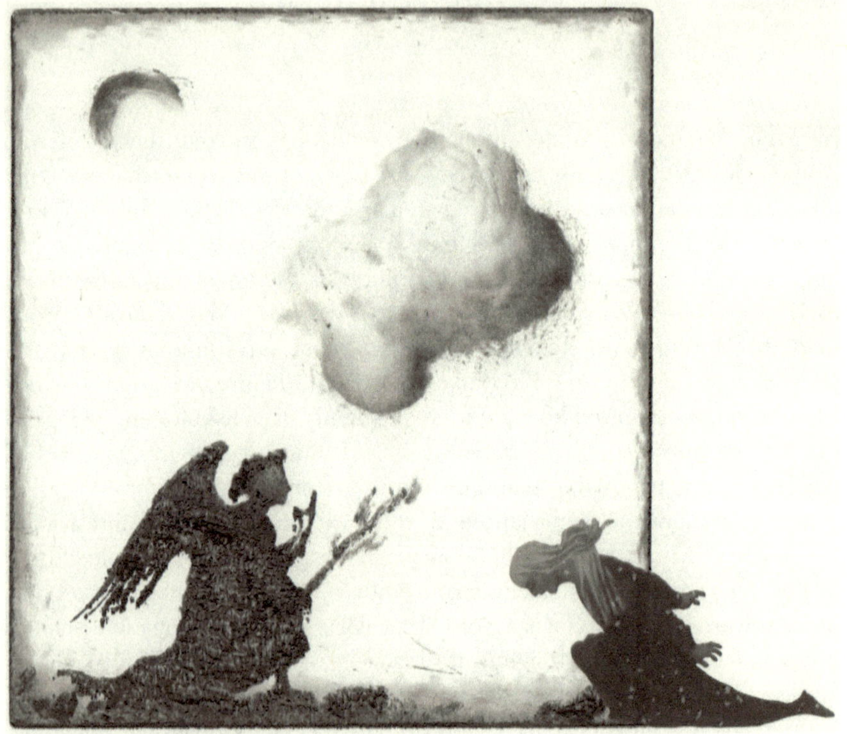

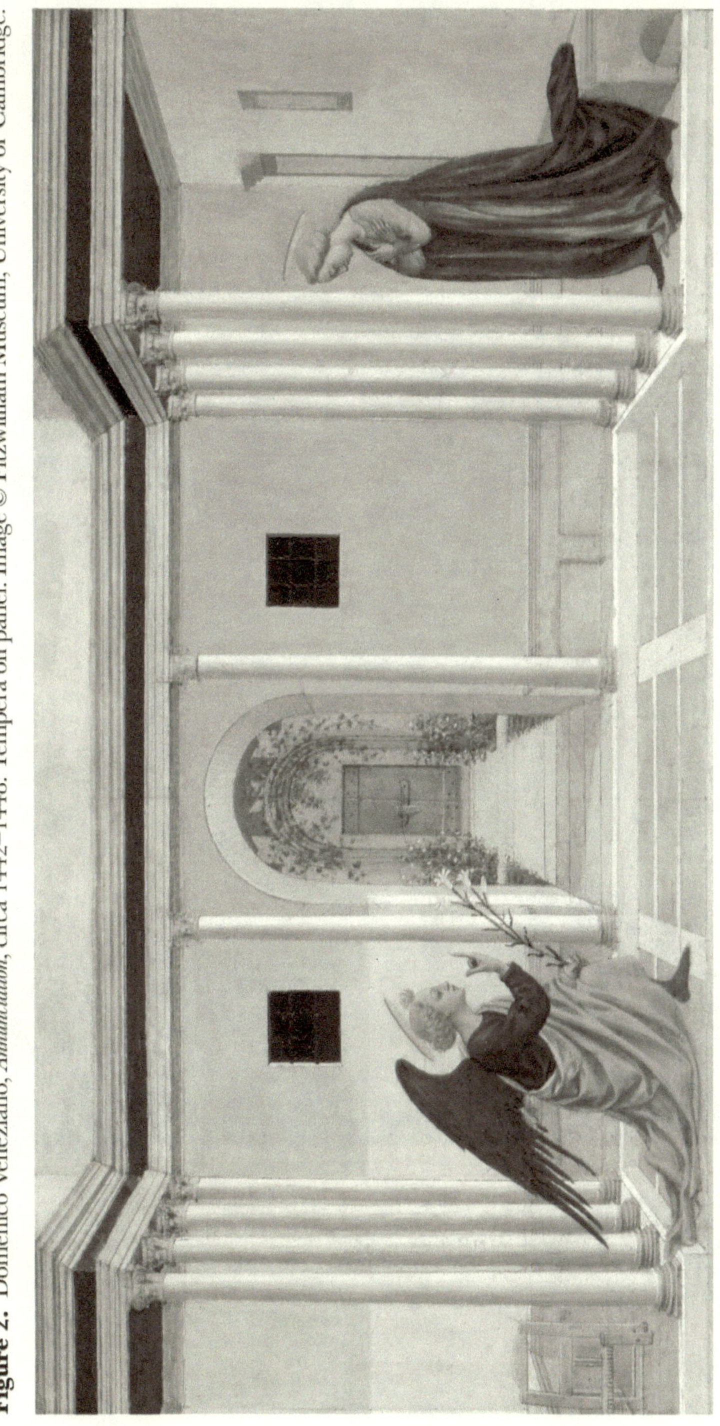

Figure 2. Domenico Veneziano, *Annunciation*, circa 1442–1448. Tempera on panel. Image © Fitzwilliam Museum, University of Cambridge.

Figure 3. Lino Mannocci, *May it be as you have said*, 2009. Monotype. © Lino Mannocci. Image © Fitzwilliam Museum, University of Cambridge.

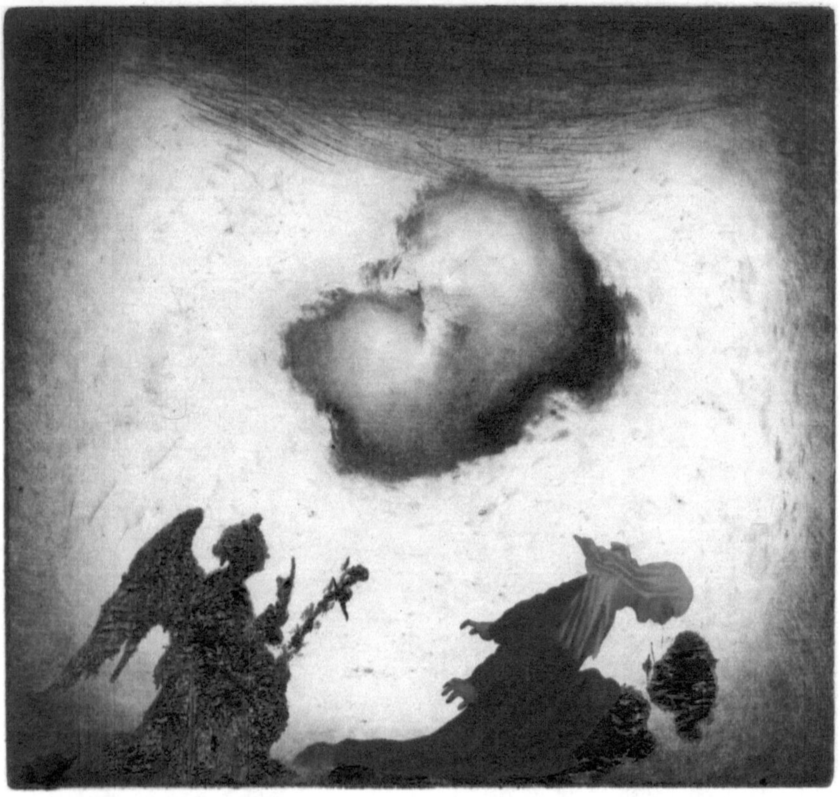

Figure 4. Domenico Veneziano, *St. Zenobius performs a miracle*, circa 1442–1448. Tempera on panel. Image © Fitzwilliam Museum, University of Cambridge.

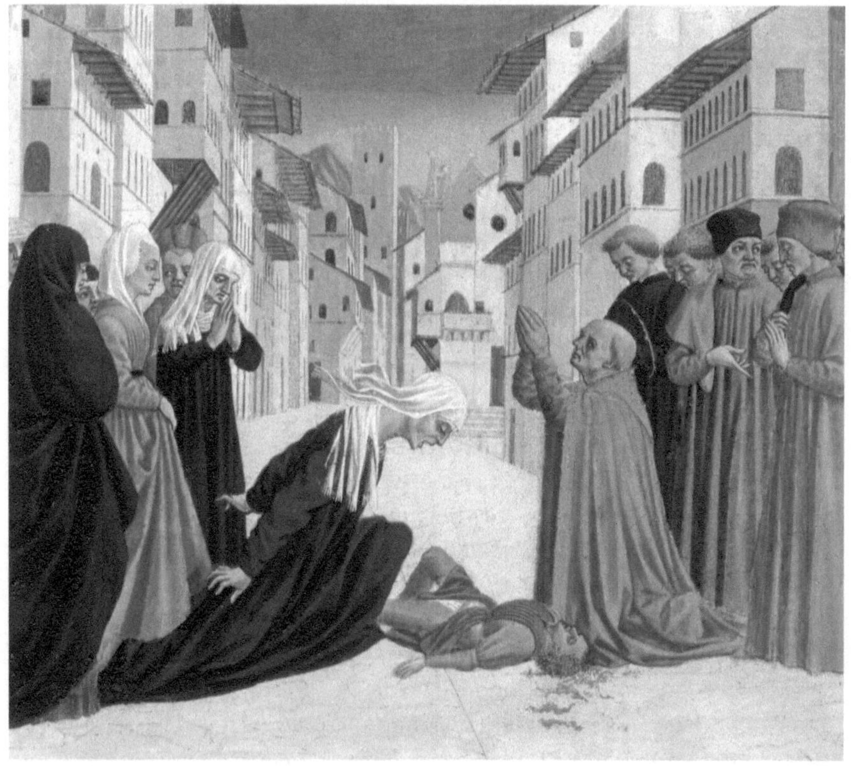

and brooding, and Mary, now repositioned into the frame, has her back turned firmly to the angel still static in Veneziano's pose. Her head is bowed low, but facing away, and seemingly gazing into a little dark piece fallen off, as it were, from the cloud; her arms stretched out behind her, before Gabriel, in resigned obeisance or terrified surrender, but suggesting declination too. She is nothing like Veneziano's gracefully acquiescent Mary, but turns out, in fact, to be a redeployment of the wailing mother grieving over her dead son's body – no son of God, he – in Veneziano's 'St. Zenobius performs a miracle' (Figure 4), also at the Fitzwilliam. The third image is the frightening, desolate 'Then the angel left her'. Here, Mary has progressed to the left side of the frame where Gabriel had been; inescapably placed, scripted and left alone in the space that was never hers to begin with, bowing to a blindingly bright cloudy tower of smoke vanishing like a flame. Unexpectedly, it reminded me of the devastating disorientation in Pasolini's semi-allegorical film *Teorema*, once the magnetic, mysterious surprise-visitor, imagined as an angel (or devil?) sent from God, leaves just as suddenly the family he infiltrates, after seducing and possessing each one of its members.[6]

The Biblical moment, canonised in religion and art, which Mannocci emplots into narrative in these prints is the angel Gabriel's announcement of the news of the virginal conception to Mary.[7] The range of affective and generic possibilities written into Mannocci's variations on this event may seem to be anachronistic. But myth, by its very nature, invites reinterpretation at different moments in history, and across genres, even while it embodies an essential component of symbolic narrative that persists – like the timeless and unchanging Gabriel who has survived into the Mannocci prints from Veneziano (as opposed to the wavering, endlessly readjusted positions Mary occupies). Besides, how unthinkable were such variations at the time when the events flourished most abundantly as a theme of art? I want to look at some key examples in the representational history of the annunciation across time and genres, taking the idea of entry or crossing as a starting point. No earlier representation that I know of reverses the agency of entrance as Mannocci's first image does. It reimagines the point of entry to arrest a site of vigilance, to constitute a punctum – poised to catch the meaning of the fugitive, and its relation to what remains, what lies behind and ahead.[8] No wonder Mannocci also creates an image of Apollo and Daphne, capturing (after Bernini) the moment of Ovidian metamorphosis – the threshold between two media and two life forms, and the working of a divine process which corresponds to the agency of generation as well as fiction, of birth as well as of metaphor. Most depictions of the annunciation, however, do share a related feature: the mythical moment is realised at a threshold. Whether physically demarcated or poetically figured, the point of crossing functions as an interruption that either accentuates the continuum or its rupture. In either case, it focuses on a passage.

Among the many possibilities of 'passage' that the moment encapsulates is the event of invitation, which is also the event of arrival. The ambiguities that Mannocci's sequence pick up on are inherent to it: who owns which space? is the angel welcome? who is crossing over? The annunciation brings alive the generic potentials of hospitality, and its reversals and violations, located as it is at the threshold between invitation and invasion, hospitality and occupation. The uncanny (*das unheimlich* – literally, 'not knowing') is not only a function of the mixture of recognition and surprise in the reception of artefacts of Annunciation, as with Mannocci's first image, but is built into the structure of the event itself. The dialectic of meanings in *unheimlich* straddles what is unhomely or unfamiliar and what is revealed, penetrated, or made known when it should have been concealed. What is revealed was, by implication, hidden not only from others but also from the self – while the first meaning of *heimlich* is 'familiar' or 'agreeable', the second is 'secret' or 'unknown'. Hence the association of the uncanny, in Freud, with the return of repressed knowledge.[9] The uncanny thus provides a curious location where knowledge and unknowing, the understood and the mysterious, the quotidian and the weird, either conjoin, or tensely confront each other. It is about the tremor we feel when we have an unexpected visitor at our own, familiar doorstep. It can be a space of enchantment, and also of terror. To that extent, the uncanny is also often a boundary between categories of experience, and therefore, potentially, of genres. The annunciation is a repository of all these possibilities. Some representations use its central threshold to convey the miraculous fecundity and beatitude of the moment. Others, more unusual, can suggest surprise, unease, even fear. It is the latter I will focus on. I will reflect, in the process, on the gendering of hospitality and entry, and what that helps us recuperate of a certain kind of tragic experience at the threshold between genres – not the one sung in heroic mode but a strand that runs through the dominant tragic discourses like a plaintiff lament, an articulation of loss, incomprehension and passive suffering. The discussion will also intimate, however, the curious propensity of the physical threshold as an object of representation to refract into yet more thresholds – metaphorical, epistemic, formal, phenomenological, and even critical.

Possibly the most delicate rendering of the Annunciation in visual art is, to my mind, Fra Angelico's rendering (Figure 5), the one that suddenly gleams upon the visitor in the little museum of San Marco in Florence, as s/he turns the corner at the top of the winding stair leading straight to this painting. And even its poster reproduction in my study surprises me with harmony and serenity. Gabriel has stepped into Mary's balcony, their space is symmetrically divided as well as joined up by the central pillar, the two figures are united in their gesture of cross-armed, reverent bowing. They are caught up in the same world of colours, his wings picking up the green of her cloak, her hair-band reflecting the pink of his robe, and her green uniting the indoor space with the grass beyond the balcony, the enveloping zone which shades off into the outer space from which the angel has appeared. That world and hers seem to be in the process of generative continuum, not in opposition. The threshold at which this encounter happens is figured as a space of union. Mary's reception of the word seems beatific, accepting, and instinct with the numinous in this moment. The angel is clearly bent in the posture of salutation. It is a picture one wants to live with. The peace it breathes, however, is conditional upon what Derrida would call 'absolute hospitality': '*The* law of unlimited hospitality', which displaces and overrides 'the law*s*...which are conditioned and conditional...across family, civil society, and the State'.[10] It is premised, in other words, on a 'strange hierarchy', but it is visually translated into symmetry.

Look now at another Annunciation (Figure 6) – an image one would hesitate to invite into the habitable fantasy of one's living space precisely because of its flagrant denial of this peace. Its vivid and visual acknowledgement of the incipient violence of absolute hospitality, with the muscular Gabriel (and his troop of sturdy little winged angels) breaking through the fragile roof of Mary's abode, places this image in a counter-beatific tradition of representing the moment of arrival. This is Tintoretto's *Annunciation*, bleeding through the darkly luminous surface of the Scuola Grande di San Rocco in Venice, a vast canvas that bursts upon the guest, the visitor, the stranger, surprising her not with the harmony and containment of Beato Angelico's vision, but with Dionysiac ravagement. There is a subtle transference here: the violence of the 'foreigner' is turned upon the observer who has come in from outside to partake of the moment of approach; the visitor, or foreigner, at the Scuola who, expecting consummation, finds confrontation. For 'crossing the threshold is entering, and not only approaching or coming' (*Of Hospitality*, 123). It does more than acknowledge, and does something more violent; it questions the very process of entry. It is, of course, the very first canvas facing one as one enters the Scuola.

Derrida offers a suggestive exploration of the ambivalence of hospitality, a crucial theme at stake in representations of the Annunciation. For him, it is at once a profoundly emotive and political metaphor, and one which, like the threshold the guest steps across, is Janus-faced:

> ...there is no politics without...an open hospitality to the guest as *ghost*, whom one holds, just as he holds us, hostage.[11]

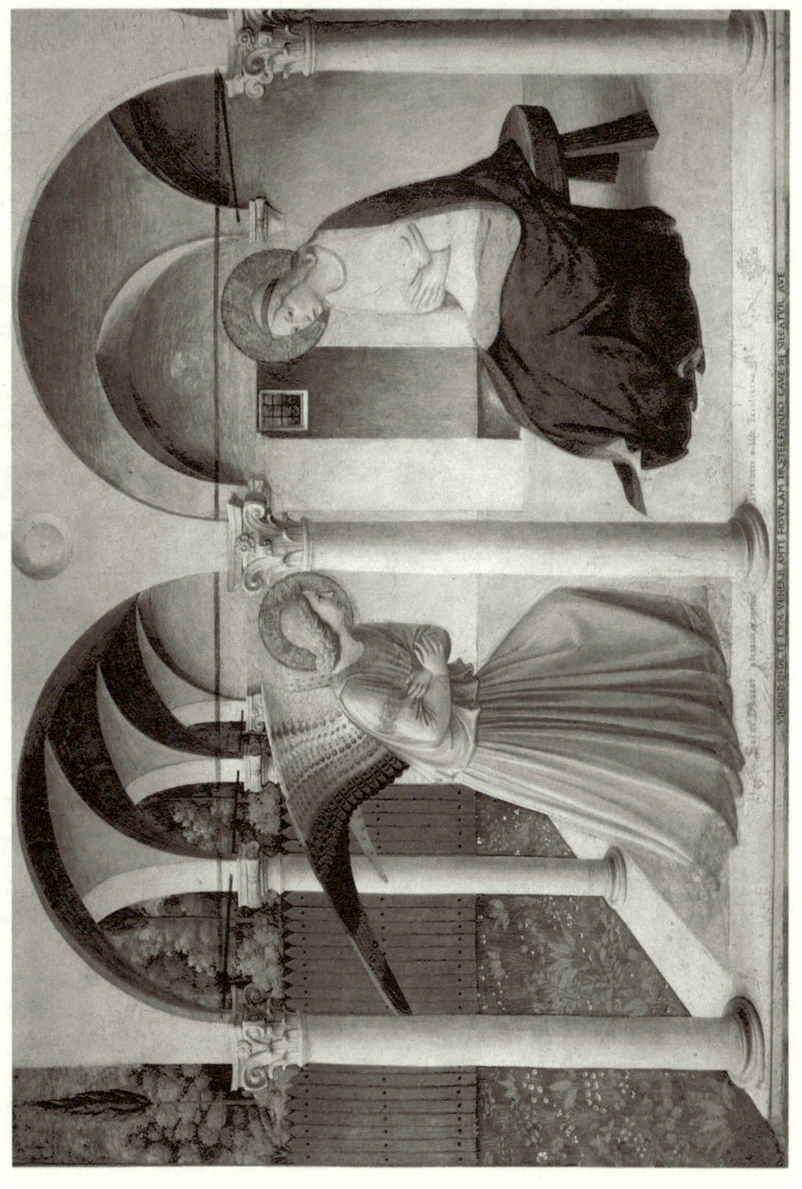

Figure 5. Beato Angelico, *Annunciation*, circa 1438–1445. Image © A. Quattrone.

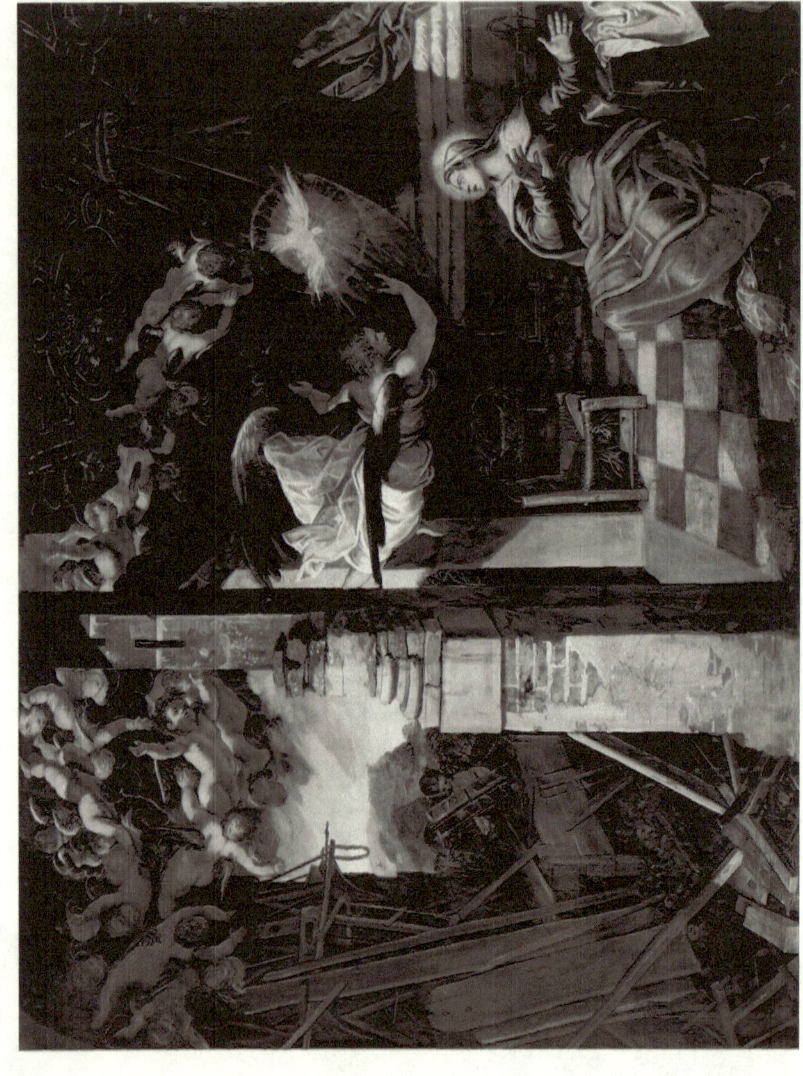

Figure 6. Jacopo Tintoretto, *Annunciation*, 1581/2. Image © Cameraphoto.

The first, more obvious implication is that of the power of the host. This power and the ceremony through which it is tempered and controlled, when abused, can cause a tragic rupture in nature: witness how, in Shakespeare's *Macbeth*, the Macbeths betray the unspoken bond and *hold* Duncan in their castle inescapably – inescapably both for Duncan and, as they will realise, for themselves. But the even more painful betrayal is the one in which the host takes over, and defies the understood relation. When Tarquin turns rapaciously upon Lucrece in Shakespeare's *Lucrece*, or Iachimo in *Cymbeline*, in a differently sinister way, upon Imogen who has housed him with grace, we have examples of this. The idea of ingratitude and betrayal implicit here finds a painful extension in Lear's image of his Pelican daughters (3.4.71), and an equally vivid expression in the all-licensed fool's jingle:

> For you know, nuncle,
> The hedge-sparrow fed the cuckoo so long
> That it's had it head bit off by it young;
> So out went the candle, and we were left darkling.
>
> (*King Lear*, Folio, 1.4.188–91)

In the same play, the guests in Gloucester's house, Cornwall and Goneril, gradually become trespassers: first they order him to shut up his doors – a command that *could* be protective, but verges on the tyrannical; then the sisters have him blinded and 'thrust him out at gates' – his own gate, the threshold of his own house, becomes the site of tragic reversal (3.7.93). As Heather Dubrow, in a recent article on land law and Lear puts it, 'The guest taking over the house, effecting a Bakhtinian reversal of roles, is of course a familiar and transcultural comedic turn. But to Shakespeare's audience the situation would also have signaled the insecurity of dwelling places in their own historical moment.'[12] Dubrow offers a rigorously historicist interrogation of what becomes, in the play, a tragic insecurity and dispossession, rather than a comedic topsy-turvydom.

What Shakespeare dramatises and Dubrow historicises, Derrida theorises. But crucially, Derrida is engaged with both sides of the fragile equation, though one takes the other over as his imagination progresses. He does not simply conceptualise the unconditionality of letting the guest in, but dwells, himself, on the threshold between addressing 'the violence of the power of hospitality' – and this belongs to the patriarch, the familial despot, the father, the spouse (149) – and the subtle reversal through which 'the guest becomes the host's host' (125); and from host to hostage is one small step for the inviting host, as from guest to parasite (59). That threshold is where the *peripeteia* – or reversal – of the social, political or divine plot occurs; when the invited foreigner to whom we open our doors, be it in an act of invitation or asylum, but on whom we hope to retain our mastery, takes us over. It is also the site where the conflation of invader, liberator and foreigner, as between guest and host, is made possible. After all, the Latin *hostis*, which means 'guest', also means 'enemy' – the double sense Derrida is playing on when he reflects on the 'paradoxical filiation of the *hostis*' (21). On the one hand, he speaks of the desire to be entered, to be occupied. On the other,

> It is *as if* the stranger or foreigner held the keys. This is always the situation of the foreigner, in politics too, that of coming as a legislator to lay down the law and liberate the people or the nation by coming from outside, by entering into the nation or the house, into the home that lets him enter after having appealed to him… So it is indeed the master, the one who invites, the inviting host, who becomes hostage – and who really always has been. And the guest, the invited hostage, becomes the one who invites the one who invites, the master of the host…

This is a paradox easily identifiable in contemporary international politics, in vexed and controversial examples in the realms of political asylum and acts of terror, and of war and occupation.[13] The balance keeps getting disturbed, and the ineffable symmetry of powers which maintains the equilibrium of political as well as domestic life is proved to be tragically vulnerable.

The tension between the householder's mastery and the need, even desire, to abandon all claims to ownership, on which Derrida's notion of 'impossible' hospitality pivots, is precisely the tension that is not allowed its delicate poise by Tintoretto. In his painting, the *hostis* tears through the fabric of Mary's bedchamber, even as the holy dove pierces the surprised and passive 'hollow of [her] ear', and divinity penetrates her womb, that very little room. The 'door and windows' – the point of entry into the interior that defines Derridian hospitality (61) – crumble and dissolve into a whirl of wings, great and small, fluttering frighteningly into Mary's chamber; the wood lies in a pile of wreckage around it, leaving only a broken pillar stripped of its paint and with the bricks showing. This is a pillar which, unlike Fra Angelico's, marks the roughness of the crossing of the threshold, not the assimilation of the other. It sharply separates the divine space and Mary's bedroom, contributing to the dominance of vertical movement which replaces the horizontal symmetry of Fra Angelico's painting with Gabriel and Mary facing each other; here, Gabriel and his angelic cascade burst in from above. Light itself becomes an invader from outer space, as it infiltrates the shady afternoon world where Mary has been knitting and reading. It is captured at the moment of transition, and not seen through to what van

Gennep calls the 'post-liminal' stage.[14] The light that streams in also lights up Mary's face, with its look of absolute startlement and terror: she has jumped out of her skin, which has made her book (the Bible) fall on her lap, her knitting to her feet. Gabriel's face and posture, on the other hand, have the certainty of knowledge and of mission.

This vision of a violent annunciation finds its closest echo in the poetry of the twentieth century – in Yeats – though, after him, several poets have addressed this moment, most notably Geoffrey Hill and Charles Tomlinson. But Yeats knew the terror of wings viscerally, as viewers of Hitchcock's *Birds* do, as Tintoretto, and perhaps Mary, did. He also knew of the peculiar pain of asymmetrical knowledge. The most explicit treatment of the Annunciation is his poem, 'The Mother of God', which opens with the three-fold terror of love', and ends as Mary's interrogation of what Tomlinson calls 'this gratuitous occasion/Of unchaptered gospel':

The threefold terror of love; a fallen flare
Through the hollow of an ear;
Wings beating about the room;
The terror of all terrors that I bore
The Heavens in my womb.

Had I not found content among the shows
Every common woman knows,
Chimney corner, garden walk,
Or rocky cistern where we tread the clothes
And gather all the talk?

What is this flesh I purchased with my pains,
This fallen star my milk sustains,
This love that makes my heart's blood stop
Or strikes a sudden chill into my bones
And bids my hair stand up?

The ear becomes the receptacle as the word, entering, becomes flesh at the very moment the angel enters the room, and the Heavens occupy a human womb, with annunciation coinciding with conception – at once evoking and questioning all those Byzantine mosaic depictions of the ray of light striking Mary's ear (either through the dove or directly from above) as though there were a continuum between heaven and its purpose, divinity and its human, female agent.[15] The multiple entry is apprehended only in terms of disjointed sensations – till retrospect allows Mary the recognition of what actually happened, in the final line of the first stanza. The conceptual follows the corporeal, just as the stanza progresses from snapshots or semiotic impressions to the structured sense and settled rhythm of lines 4–5. The second stanza is Mary's wistful remembrance of the bliss of her ordinary past, the common 'shows/That every woman knows', the shared, communal and specifically female activities of washing, housework, and of gathering 'talk' as though it were an extension of the gentle materiality of the cloth they trod and gathered – a world away from the brilliant invasion of light and word and divine flesh. 'Had [she] not found content' among these – perhaps 'cóntent' as well as 'contént'? Had she asked for the terrible burden of distinction that she now bears? 'What is this flesh I purchased with my pain?' she asks in the third stanza, having paid her price and gained the child and the doomed temptation to maternal love that it brings – 'this fallen star my milk sustains…?' The 'uncanny' is not only embodied in her response, but gendered. The verse juxtaposes the intimate, the familiar and the feminine with the alien, the strange, and the incomprehensible, till the 'love' she feels is itself made strange by the chill it strikes into her bones, by stopping her heart's blood. It becomes, in other words, something like death. Here is yet another version of materialisation, as 'word' registers across the threshold of the body in flesh, bone and blood. Can cognition happen without the intervention of matter? And what is it that 'bids her hair stand up' so – is it the knowledge of her child's future? Could she have known of it when she opened her doors to the divine visitor? Is Yeats remembering that barely audible yet distinct voice within the corpus of medieval religious lyrics, a thin but discernible strand, where Mary complains to Jesus that she was never told?

> A! dere sone, that is a heavy cas.
> When Gabrell knelt before my face
> And said, "Heille! Lady, full of grace",
> He never told me nothing of this.[16]

Tintoretto's Mary is a harshly interrupted reader of the Bible. But perhaps such depictions interrupt traditional readings of the Bible on more planes than one; or at least create thresholds in the reading process that make us pause. We stop hearing and start listening, as Angela Leighton might say; looking turns to watching, or even watching out.[17] Meanwhile, Mannocci's transposition of Veneziano's grieving mother in place of the beatified Mary makes sense afresh, foreshortening the future into the present, intimating the Crucifixion in the moment of the Annunciation in a far from typological way. His Mary has already turned her back on Gabriel's greeting, as it were, to face its consequence, her dead child.

The tenor of annunciation pictures and poems is fundamental to Christian experience but not limited to it. It is the stuff of myth in the sense in which, according to Lévi-Strauss, myth functions as a vehicle for accommodating disparate kinds of knowledge occupying the same cultural space, and for tracing the underlying structure of relations between elements of a story across separate domains.[18] Yeats was, of course, steeped in mythology; but what does he do with it? The idea of ravishment that hovers over the 'Mother of God' is more explicit in Yeats's 'Leda and the Swan', which opens, like the later, more theological poem, *in medias res*, with 'the great wings beating still/ Above the staggering girl'.

> A sudden blow: the great wings beating still 1
> Above the staggering girl, her thighs caressed
> By the dark webs, her nape caught in his bill,
> He holds her helpless breast upon his breast.
>
> How can those terrified vague fingers push 5
> The feathered glory from her loosening thighs,
> And how can body, laid in that white rush,
> But feel the strange heart beating where it lies?
>
> A shudder in the loins engenders there 9
> The broken wall, the burning roof and tower
> And Agamemnon dead.
> Being so caught up, 11
> So mastered by the brute blood of the air,
> Did she put on his knowledge with his power
> Before the indifferent beak could let her drop? 14

'Leda' is apparently unconcerned with Christianity, and focused on the Pagan myth of Zeus and Leda. Zeus appears to Leda in the form of a swan. They have consensual, or non-consensual, sex – depending on particular narrative versions of the myth – and out of this union are born Helen and Clytemnestra, and Polydeucis and Castor, hatched from two eggs laid by Leda.[19] And so, in Yeats's version, 'the shudder in the loins engenders there/The broken wall, the burning roof and tower/And Agamemnon dead'; it engenders, in the same act, the *Oresteia*, the first great Western tragic cycle, and *The Iliad*, the first great epic. But significance, and cultural capital, are only born in retrospect, unless one is a God. Jove might have known the larger, more significant narrative already written, and Leda's mere instrumentality in that plot; so the swan's beaks could be 'indifferent' to the human agent and 'let her drop' after the violent consummation was over. But could Leda have known? Could she even have intimated the glamour of the moment?

> So mastered by the brute blood of the air,
> Did she put on his knowledge with his power?

The narrator's question is precisely about the asymmetry of knowledge, once the poem has shot out of the immediate, almost stelled present of that past moment – with the great wings beating '*still*' – into the future through the act, and verb, of '[engendering]', and the violent break in the verse at l. 11, and thence to the present in which that 'future' has become history. He is aware from his temporal position of the momentousness of that point in history when Leda bore the divine guest, and her thighs loosened, whether through overwhelming force, or through irresistible response, or through the narrator's eye. But when the wrestle ended and the ejaculatory shudder of the divine beast shot into her womb through her broken wall, that fragile *limen*, did she, in wearing divinity, also wear his knowledge?[20] Behind the relatively specific allusion to the Trojan future, there gleams a more obscure idea of divine gnosis mysteriously intersecting with human frailty. In fact the phrase 'put on' recalls Horace's Europa Ode (*Odes*, III.xxvii). Jove, inflamed by her beauty, came to Europa as a bull and as she caressed him and put garlands round his neck and climbed on his back, he ran off with her across the sea to Crete. As Europa laments whatever has happened between her and the bull – rape or submission (or sex in a dream!) – Venus appears, smiling treacherously, and says:

> uxor invincti Iovis esse nescis:
> mitte singultus, bene ferre magnam
> disce fortunam…
> [You do not know that you are the bride of unconquered Jove; stop sobbing and learn to *carry*/to *wear* your good fortune]

This could almost seem to be a variation on Elisabeth's greeting to Mary: 'Blessed art thou among women, and blessed is the fruit of thy womb' (Luke I.42). The idea of 'putting on' the magnitude and benediction of the divine body evokes the Biblical image of transfiguration: the divinisation of a human body expressed in terms of wearing a freshly laundered garment (Mark, I. 2–3). Yet Leda, like Mary, has been transfigured by an alien coupling: 'how can body, laid in that white rush,/But feel the strange heart beating where it lies?' But could she feel – or value – the historical consequence of her suffering? Could she have known that Jove was descending on her with the full gravity of Western epic and tragedy? And if she were told, would she sing the Magnificat, as in Luke, or would she, like Yeats's Mother of God, feel her heart's blood stop and a chill spread up her spine, and turn a question back upon the symbolic order and religious metaphor itself? For what is the immaculate conception if not the ultimate metaphor, one in which Annunciation is a necessary component, as word turns into flesh and 'soul purples itself'?[21] The mysterious, godly penetration has resulted nonetheless in an intrinsically human, physical experience. The rape of Lucrece by Tarquin is hailed by the historian Livy as a felicitous event, as it led to a popular uprise against the dynasty of the Tarquins and ushered in the republic. But what is momentous, and therefore historically and politically happy, becomes, in Shakespeare's poem, the theme for the tragedy of a woman who has had no agency in it; like Hecuba, like the Trojan women, like the women in J. M. Synge's twentieth-century poetic play *Riders to the Sea* where the men have all left, one by one, and gone to the sea, never to return. The vision of Good Friday is the retrospective vision of all mankind; when it is an anticipated event in Mary's life, what can the Crucifixion do but 'bid [her] hair stand up'? The cost she pays is more mundane, less symbolic, than the price paid by Christ upon the hill.

> Alas! Dere son, sorrow now is my happe
> To see my child that souks my pappe
> So ruthfully taken out of my lappe.[22]

The power of the uncanny suffuses 'Leda' too, not only in the conjoining of 'feathered glory' and 'staggering girl', but re-enacted at the threshold between rhyme or metrical speech and organic rhythm. Yeats described his own verse as 'contrapuntal', '[combining] the past and the present' by crossing 'traditional metres' with the rhythm of 'vivid speech'. The former he calls a 'ghostly voice, an invariable possibility, an unconscious norm', and the latter the cadence of passionate speech that 'has no laws except that it must not exorcise the ghostly voice'.[23] Adelyn Dougherty was the first to read Yeats's verse, after Yeats, as an interplay between verse-line or metrical unit, and a 'stretch of speech… bounded by pause-punctuation' or 'textual pauses' (17). The rhythmic structure of one is artificial and abstract, and that of the other 'natural' (17, n. 12).[24] Building on her reading of the 'tension between the speech-unit and the verse line', Michael Golston offers an intricate and tempting reading of the poem which posits an ultimate coincidence of the two, conveying a thematically meaningful merger of the divine and the mortal rhythms.[25] The initial 'rhythmic confusion', he writes, expresses Leda's disorientation but gives way to synchrony and restored metre as 'the mortal…actually sees [the swan]' (l. 4), leading to the engendering of 'Great Literature' – the offspring of the shuddering act of union, which is also a joining of 'traditional Unity of being and modern, mortal speech'; the body laid in the 'white rush' is said to be the page itself, writing the history of the race 'dictated by the rhythms of its blood' (188). Yet this is to ignore the specificity of images – how can the mortal see the beast when her nape is caught in his bills? – and the sound of the verse as it progresses, as well as its vocal, tonal and perspectival shifts. It is to gloss over the poem's refusal of thematic and formal neatness, and its own organic knowledge which teeters on that discrepancy between historical or divine knowledge and human incomprehension which its content intimates. The clustering of primary stresses in 'greát wíngs beáting', which crosses the continuous blank verse in the first quatrain with speech-rhythm, does not end there; it reappears in both the following quatrains ('stránge heart beáting'; 'só caúght úp'; 'the brúte bloód'). And Yeats does something he hardly ever does elsewhere – break the iambic pentameter line with force, making it impossible for us to read l. 11 as a verse-unit, or indeed a sense unit, even if we shift stresses here and there. It is as if the speaker, now distanced from the spell of the event, emerged from its mesmerising diversion, is finally able to slip into, or regain, a speech-rhythm; only, this is a different use of uncertainty from the first quatrain's. The formal echo of the bewildering close-up camera-shots in that stanza, close to capturing Leda's viewing position, now gives way to a voice that has acquired a separate position enabling a reflection on her subjectivity. It has 'caught up', from having been at one with Leda's absorption: its caught-upness was perhaps always haunted by the sense of catching up, enmeshing knowledges absent with those shut away but liable to return as uncanny spectres. Indeed, the poem's final question even raises the possibility of Leda's own phenomenological intuition, poised on the edge of consciousness: the kind of awareness she may or may not have had, or caught up with, even in the moment when she was 'caught up' by beak and web – akin to the way poetry knows, as opposed to the oracular knowledge of myth.

Dougherty's admittedly sketchy model is far more illuminating here than Golston's, as are Yeats's own remarks. The poem oscillates between the ghost of the archetypal or mythic embodied in the overarching meter, and 'those wavering, meditative, organic rhythms' which, here, belong not so much with timeless myth as with the beat our pulses can feel, the body that we can all relate to – Leda's, the poet's and the reader's.[26] This is the body in which the heart-beat must be felt, and therefore must seem 'strange', just as the 'greát wíngs beáting stíll' are strange to the larger iambic pentametric structure – the insistent, patterned, mythic drive of that metre resumes and rises to a climax from lines 9 to 11.5, but also breaks at the very same moment: a moment generated by the shudder which translates from assured metric stride and masculine power to tentative rhythm and female body. Briefly united with the ghostly bird, Leda's body had almost lost its human, gendered, known identity in the abstract noun, floating without the mooring of possessive pronoun or definite article – 'how can body…' But the overwhelming indistinction of that moment past, the threshold crossed and the wall broken, 'body' regains attributes of person and gender. The crossing, however, is demarcated by the coincidence of violence and beauty in the rupture after 'Agamemnon dead' – roughing up the predictable, reassuring threshold of line-ending. Time also shifts here from the mythical back to the momentuous and the sensory. '[S]mitten even in the presence of the most high beauty by knowledge of our solitude, our rhythm shudders'.[27] 'Our rhythm' – poetic voice as well as reader's ear – takes over from the determined shudder of the avian/divine penis and, 'caught up' with Leda's post-coital consciousness, transmutes into the shudder of solitude; it becomes itself a bodily register of uncertainty, ending the poem with a question that is keenly audible in the thud of the last, unexpected hexametric iamb of 'her dróp', persisting against the grain of the larger iambic pentameter and defying a sense of closure. The incomplete consonance in the off-rhyme of 'up' and 'drop' not only creates unease but alerts us aurally to the ruthless rapidity with which the two opposite movements have played themselves out in Leda's mind and body. 'Indifferent beak' gives both physicality and affect to 'caught up' and 'mastered', just as it gives 'drop' the ring of human hurt and intensifies its abrupt desolation. The strain of compressing stresses to make 'the indifferent beak' two iambic units – for that is what it would take to fit this line into the metre – is the ear's resistance to the transfiguration and 'fusion' of contrary states that Golston sees the poem achieving, that '[transformation]' of the body 'into a vessel for the divine blood of the race' (184). His reading would fit with Lévi-Strauss's teleological definition of mythology – that mythical thought always progresses from an awareness of oppositions toward their resolution.[28] But this is not quite how the finer mesh of poetry works, even when it broods on myth. The poetic energy of 'Leda' inheres in dwelling on the threshold; in the tussle, and the denial of synthesis between the affective and the mythic. Though 'The Mother of God' is at first glance more typically unbroken in form, I hear neither the 'conversation' nor the 'conversion' that Golston finds in that poem, reading the narrative as a movement 'from a *haunt* to a *vision*' (189), the integration of the female body to a 'deep masculine resonance' leading to a 'Unity of Being' (190–2). The 'broken woof'[29] of iambs, trochees and spondees itself belies such quietism, as does the short final line of unconsoled interrogation, following upon a battery of questions. The point of turning identified by Golston is the spondaic double beat of 'blóód stóp', on the ground that 'it is heard precisely at the origin of all rhythm: in the systolic beating of the heart', so that 'wing-beat becomes heart-beat… [F]eeding her child milk, Mary looks into the face of God' as 'vision and rhythm compel each other, as the perfect human body is sensed through the flesh of speech' (190). This gives one pause; for the point of this line is that this love – which was there even in l. 1 – has not transfigured its terror but absorbed it, and it has made Mary's 'heárt's bloód stóp'. She has been called upon to recognise and accept 'the gift of death'.[30] The reason why the iambic pentameter is inaudible here is not that 'human speech and transhuman rhythm' have been fused (190), but that, as Leighton unforgettably puts it, '[m]etre never misses a beat, but rhythm can let you hear the heart stop'.[31]

The sense of a tense, vital and precariously porous border between the symbolic and the visceral, the typological and the human, is suggested not only in the poetic treatment, but seems to have been part of the process of composition of 'Leda and the Swan'. Yeats's original title for this poem about a Pagan myth was, significantly, 'Annunciation', the title under which it was sent in 1923 to the *Irish Statesman* who sent it back in outrage at its flagrant disrespect of Catholic sentiments. It appeared elsewhere in 1925 under the new title, familiar to us. The classical myth was meant merely to provide a political metaphor to Yeats, who was casting about for a vehicle to express the need of what he considered to be a country drained of energy and life-force after the Civil War, a soil exhausted and unable to bear any crop. But it was not enough – he was instinctively reaching out for a piece of Christian myth to make the pagan story resonate with full significance. 'Nothing is now possible but some movement from above preceded by some violent annunciation', he wrote in a note on 'Leda', dated 1924;[32] the swan-God was meant to be, as it were, a Lenin-figure, as Yeats explicitly invoked (to Lady Gregory) the example of Russia where democracy had to be subdued by a violent government from above.[33] Arguably, the metaphor of rape was harnessed to the male political imagination in the production of poetry – a dubious enterprise at the best of times, and particularly so as the application of the myth was itself flaunted as a radical challenge to what he perceived as a stagnant Ireland. Yet something happened half-way through the process once Yeats began his poem: 'as I wrote, bird and lady took such possession of the scene that all politics went out of it'.[34] The allegory of the felicitous destruction of an older civilisation faded out as the vividness of the figures took over: 'all things are from antithesis, and when in my ignorance I try to imagine what older civilisation she refuted ['civilisation that annunciation rejected'], I can but see bird and woman blotting out some corner of the Babylonian mathematical starlight'.[35]

'Antithesis' is, of course, what Tintoretto was depicting, but with the deep typological significance which Ruskin commented on in *Modern Painters*

(Part III) – an order of meaning that ultimately gestures towards a synthesis. Ruskin is impressed, first, by the terror, the desolation and the violence of the scene as the virgin looks up, 'startled by the rush' of 'horizontal and rattling wings':

> …houseless, under the shelter of a palace vestibule ruined and abandoned, with the noise of the axe and the hammer in her ears, and the tumult of a city round about her desolation. The spectator turns away at first, revolted, from the central object of the picture forced painfully and coarsely forward, a mass of shattered brickwork, with the plaster mildewed away from it, and the mortar mouldering from its seams…

But then he looks again, 'for there is more meant than this', and studies – and in turn makes his reader study – the 'composition of the picture' where s/he (the reader, the viewer)

> will find the whole symmetry of it depending on a narrow line of light, the edge of a carpenter's square, which connects these unused tools with an object at the top of the brickwork, a white stone, four square, the corner-stone of the old edifice, the base of its supporting column. This, I think, sufficiently explains the typical [typological] character of the whole. The ruined house is the Jewish dispensation; that obscurely arising in the dawning of the sky is the Christian; but the corner-stone of the old building remains, though the builders' tools lie idle beside it, and the stone which the builders refused is become the Headstone of the Corner.[36]

William Holman Hunt, who was greatly inspired by Ruskin's interpretation of the painting (calling him the 'decipherer'),[37] was nevertheless struck, when he went to see it, by the scale of devastation and how much vaster it was than he had imagined. Ruskin's deciphering does indeed reveal a structuring allegory, a fundamental religious vision for which the whole picture is a metaphor. Both Ruskin's response and Hunt's can, in some senses, be mapped on to the traditional fifteenth century conception of the stages (and components) of Mary's reaction to the moment of crisis. As Fra Roberto explains, in analysing the account of the event in Luke, the 'mystery' of the Angelic Colloquy can be broken down into five constituent states of mind in the Madonna: *conturbatio* or disquiet; *cogitatio* or reflection; *interrogatio* or inquiry; *humilitatio* or submission; and *meritatio* or merit.[38] When the Angel arrived and greeted Mary, writes Luke, 'she was troubled'; the second stage was cogitation, trying to figure out what was happening, and Gabriel asking her to 'fear not' as she has 'found favour with God'; the third phase is that of questioning and incomprehension, and it is not till the fourth condition arises that we see 'submission'. Yeats's Mary progresses in the first stanza from disquiet to recognition; but the poem ends as an interrogation; the vessel becomes the questioning subject, and we never settle, with her, into anything like submission or merit. And questioning the guest is antipathic to unconditional hospitality. 'Leda' also ends, syntactically, with a question; but here it is the narrator's voice, as Leda's subjectivity can only be imagined, but the narrator has travelled in the opposite direction from the scriptural one – from a sense of the symbolic magnitude of the event, to a sense of doubt and, finally, into a human, indeed female, perspective, even as Yeats was surprised by bird and woman blotting out the high symbolic vision of his 'violent Annunciation'. Ruskin and Hunt both proceeded from immediate impression to religious, typological thinking. But how do paintings affect us? Should we ignore the violent assault on the senses in favour of a 'deeper' meaning that emerges when we think, or when we have a Ruskin, or such another decipherer, at hand? Or should we let the corporeal response play against the symbolic? Ruskin cannot have been untouched by the Romantics' inheritance of the complex idea of pure perception or 'design' that evolved from Kant and got filtered through Schiller's notion of art form.[39] By the time the aesthetic concept of 'form' reached the nineteenth century, it was a complex mess of oppositions, between 'form and matter, disinterested beauty and "adventitious" representation', the intrinsic and the ornamental, as Leighton explains.[40] By the same token, it pivoted on a separation between abstract idea or concept and aesthetic representation. Victorian aestheticism was a vexed mixture of the pure and the impure, the ideal and the material, the spiritual and the secular. It is almost as if some of those contrary elements are jostling together in Ruskin's response to Tintoretto's painting, and Hunt's, after him, but settling into a hierarchy. The cognitive chronology of their readings mirrors both the stages through which Virgin comes to a full response to the angelic announcement and the sequence in which the visceral and symbolic might strike the viewer in the Scuola. But Tintoretto's raw, resolutely exposed, 'assertively loose' brushwork, the radical '*non-finito*' and uncontrolled '*fantasia*' criticised by Vasari as 'so rough that the brush-strokes may be seen',[41] may have a thematic relevance in this painting. The compositional incompleteness of the art-work corresponds to the stage of the Virgin's response which it records, incomplete in spiritual terms – her 'uncomposed' face expressing the unfinished inner self. St. Luke writes that when the Virgin heard Gabriel's salutation, telling her that 'God is with [her]', 'she was troubled'; 'the angel said to her, "Don't be afraid, Mary, for you have found favor with God."' Commentators such as Nicholas of Lyra explain that this disturbance had to do with wonder and amazement, not incredulity. Such interpretation is part of the reception history of the moment, as well as the 'Mystery' of the Colloquy as a finished theological artefact. Tintoretto's painting seems to capture the drama of the moment unmediated by such readings, offering access to a more instinctual reading of that Biblical moment. Perhaps, then, the Bible that has dropped from Mary's hands as she starts is an inscription of the possibility of a disturbance in the reading process itself, not just of her own understanding of her situation; a stripping back of the layers of familiar interpretation to open a window on to an unknown, or rather, unspoken, response caught before it is polished into known narrative and smooth art. This small detail becomes, here, a punctum that renders the physical threshold into its temporal dimension – the little rent that arrests the narrative at this instance. Significantly, Tintoretto pares away the usual symbolic details that accompany depictions of this moment: there is no caduceus, no stem of lilies, no scroll, no fountain or kettle or wash-basin, no candlestick. Some essential features aside, there are quotidian details such as the tattered wicker chair. The formal *difficolta*, in this context, works to interrogate and distance the iconographic character of the painting and accentuate the dynamic of encounter.

Leonardo warned other painters against making the mistake that Boticelli made, coming precariously close to the violent mode in his depiction of the Annunciation, with the angel almost scaring the Virgin away.[42] But Fra Angelico, who drew the delicate, beatific painting we started by looking at, was the typical embodiment of the formal quality in painting that was called *vezzoso*: a delicate, effete, bland, blithe charm.[43] In eschewing this, and giving us the extreme mode, Tintoretto is not only hurling us into the rough route to understanding, he is also letting us see the *process* by which 'the brute blood of the air' is spiritualised, the violence incipient in allegory itself. Through an unflinching use of the affective, the painting reveals the construction of the discursive. Poetry, like painting, has a direct access to the senses, and can bypass discourse and dislodge it from its 'position of mastery',[44] knowingly or intuitively. Few poets felt this more vividly than Yeats. Not only is his poetic rhythm generated at, and across, the threshold between mind and body; he speaks of, and to, an identical crossing in the reception of art and the moment of communication. As he writes in 'The Thinking of the Body', discussing two pictures of Venice by Canaletto and Franz Francken,

> [n]either painting could move us at all, if our thought did not rush out to the edges of our flesh, and it is so with all good art... Art bids us touch and taste and hear and see the world, and shrinks from what Blake calls mathematical form, from every abstract thing, from all that is of the brain only, from all that is not a fountain jetting from entire hopes, memories, and sensations of the body.[45]

So, like Yeats, we are left with girl and beast; it is the 'great wings' that '[beat] still' in our ears, beyond political or religious metaphor. Neither the fate of poetry, nor that of visual art, can be separated from 'the fate of the senses'.[46] And we remain caught, and 'caught up', in the moment where Tintoretto arrests his image – the moment of utmost perturbation, *conturbatio*, inscribed in Mary's face, in the crumbling mortar and tumbling roof; and the deluge of muscles and wings.[47] The antithesis – and interface – on which we linger is not the typological one between older and newer dispensation, but between pain and its bodily vehicle, significance and its vessel, divine and human, word and flesh, meaning and sense; and indeed between guest and host:

> They incorporate one another at the moment of excluding one another … they show they are both more and less hospitable, hospitable and inhospitable, hospitable *inasmuch as* inhospitable. (*Of Hospitality*, 81)

Annunciations, like limitless hospitality, are defined at more than one threshold; they take on the very structure of threshold experience as they remain tense with the contrary possibilities of merger and barrier, of intimacy and alienation.

Notes

1 Charles Tomlinson, 'Annunciation', in *Annunciations* (Oxford: Oxford University Press, 1989), 1–2 (1).

2 I am grateful to Yota Batsaki, Beci Dobbin and Angela Leighton for reading and commenting on a draft of this essay with generosity and acuteness.

3 Part of Lino Mannocci, 'Clouds and Myths', exhibition at the Fitzwilliam Museum, Cambridge, 9 Feb to 9 May, 2010.

4 On the integral relation between the unhomely and the homely (*das unheimlich* and what was once *heimlich*) in the 'uncanny', an idea now associated with Freud's seminal essay, see Sigmund Freud, 'The Uncanny', in *The Standard Edition of the Complete Psychological Works of Sigmund Freud*, ed. and trans. James Strachey, 24 vols (London: Hogarth, 1953–74), 17 (1955): 219–252, especially 241.

5 Lino Mannocci, 'The Angel and the Virgin: A Brief History of the Annunciation', exhibition at the Fitzwilliam Museum, Cambridge, 9 Feb to 9 May, 2009.

6 Pier Paolo Pasolini's controversial film from 1968 (based on his novel from the same year), about a seemingly divine stranger visiting, inhabiting and then just as mysteriously abandoning a bourgeois Milanese household, having transformed each member of the family and their lives forever. The magnetic stranger's unconditional giving of himself takes the form, among other things, of the act of sex with all of them – almost a metaphor for transfiguration. Unsurprisingly, the reception of the film was mixed, and interpretations vary from the visionary to the profane, and from spiritual to political allegory. See Pier Paolo Pasolini, dir., *Teorema* (Theorem) (1968; Koch Lorber Films, 2005).

7 Luke 1:26–38: 'Now in the sixth month, the angel Gabriel was sent from God to a city of Galilee, named Nazareth, to a virgin pledged to be married to a man whose name was Joseph, of the house of David. The virgin's name was Mary. Having come in, the angel said to her, "Rejoice, you highly favored one! The Lord is with you. Blessed are you among women!" But when she saw him, she was greatly troubled at the saying, and considered what kind of salutation this might be. The angel said to her, "Don't be afraid, Mary, for you have found favor with God. Behold, you will conceive in your womb, and bring forth a son, and will call his name 'Jesus'. He will be great, and will be called the Son of the Most High. The Lord God will give him the throne of his father, David, and he will reign over the house of Jacob forever. There will be no end to his Kingdom." Mary said to the angel, "How can this be, seeing I am a virgin?" The angel answered her, "The Holy Spirit will come on you, and the power of the Most High will overshadow you. Therefore also the holy one who is born from you will be called the Son of God. Behold, Elizabeth, your relative, also has conceived a son in her old age; and this is the sixth month with her who was called barren. For everything spoken by God is possible." Mary said, "Behold, the handmaid of the Lord; be it to me according to your word." The angel departed from her.'

8 On the 'punctum' as a point, a prick, a wound, that triggers the insistent gaze, the personal detail that attracts or distresses, the incision that creates a relationship with the subject inside an image (in the specific context, a photo), see Roland Barthes, *Camera Lucida*, trans. Richard Howard (London: Vintage, 2000), passim.

9 Freud, 'The Uncanny', especially 224–5 and 241.

10 Jacques Derrida, *Of Hospitality: Anne Dufourmantelle invites Jacques Derrida to respond* (Palo Alto: Stanford University Press, 2000), 77–81 (77).

11 Jacques Derrida, *Aporias*, trans. T. Dutoit (Palo Alto: Stanford University Press, 1993), 61–2.

12 Heather Dubrow, '"They took from me the use of mine own house": Land Law in Shakespeare's *Lear* and Shakespeare's Culture', in Dennis Kezar, ed., *Solon and Thespis: Law and Theater in the Renaissance* (Notre Dame: University of Notre Dame Press, 2007), 81–98 (93–4).

13 A fascinating recent example is the way in which the Palestinian refugee camps in Southern Lebanon became their host's hosts, offering refuge to displaced Lebanese citizens during the war between Israel and Hizbullah in 2006. For a suggestive reading of the paradoxical co-existence of inevitable instrumentality and the ethics of hospitality in such a situation, a sort of hosting that falls short of Derridian unconditionality but nevertheless preserves obligations of humanity and solidarity, see Adam Ramadan, 'The Guest's Guests: Palestinian Refugees, Lebanese Civilians, and the War of 2006', *Antipode* 40, no. 4 (2008): 658–77.

14 See Introduction, (xix) for Van Gennep's role in theorising the threshold in anthropological terms as the boundary marking the preliminal, liminal and post-liminal rites of passage in individual and social life.

15 But as a milder counter-example than Tintoretto's, see Simone Martini's 'Annunciation' at the Galleria Uffizi, Florence, where Gabriel's greeting *becomes* the shaft of light piercing Mary's ear while she turns her head away – she seems not to want to know.

16 'Jesus Comforts his Mother', in R. T. Davies, ed., *Medieval English Lyrics* (London: Faber and Faber, 1963), 197–8 (no. 102). Cp. 'Mary complains to other mothers', no. 112, 210–11. The double negative of 'never told me nothing' could even suggest to the modern reader a form of knowing that Freud would call uncanny – a terrifying

knowledge that both is and is not there at the moment of Annunciation, or of penetration.

17 See Leighton's essay on listening in this volume.

18 Claude Lévi-Strauss, *Myth and Meaning* (London: Routledge and Kegan Paul, 1978), passim.

19 In an alternative and less current version of the myth, Leda and the Swan's union produced Helen and Polydeucis and Leda and her husband Tyndareus produced Clytemnestra and Castor. Even if one considers this version, Clytemnestra is Leda's half-sister, and she kills Agamemnon for various reasons linked to the war of Troy caused by Helen: for sacrificing their daughter Iphigenia so that the Gods would allow the winds to let the ships sail to Troy; for leaving her for ten years to fight in the Trojan war which gave her the chance to fall in love with Aegisthus; and for bringing Cassandra back from the wars, whom Clytemnestra could not stand.

20 Cp. Yeats, 'Supernatural Songs', VIII, lines 11–12: 'What sacred drama through her body heaved/When world-transforming Charlemagne was conceived?' in Russell K. Alspach, ed., *The Variorum Edition of the Poems of W. B. Yeats* (London/New York: Macmillan, 1966), 560.

21 Geoffrey Hill, 'Annunciations' ('The Word has been abroad, is back, with a tanned look…'), in *Collected Poems* (London: Penguin, 1959, repr. 1985), 62.

22 'Jesus Comforts his Mother'.

23 W. B. Yeats, 'A General Introduction for my Work', in *Essays and Introductions* (London: Macmillan, 1961), 509–526 (524).

24 See pp. 38–40 for her analysis of the rhythmic groups in 'Leda'.

25 See Michael Golston, *Rhythm and Race in Modernist Poetry and Science: Pound, Yeats, Williams, and Modern Sciences of Rhythm* (New York: Columbia University Press, 2008), 184–8. But I do not see Dougherty arguing that passionate prose rhythms make the pentameter '*practically* inaudible', as Golston says (186).

26 Again, Yeats's own description is the most suggestive – see 'The Symbolism of Poetry', in *Essays*, 153–64 (163), for his famous comments on the kind of serious poetry, like his own, which 'would cast out…those energetic rhythms, as of a man running…and… seek out those wavering, meditative, organic rhythms which are the embodiment of the imagination…'

27 From W. B. Yeats, 'Anima Hominis', in *Mythologies* (London: Macmillan, 1959), 325–342 (331).

28 Claude Lévi-Strauss, *Structural Anthropology*, trans. Claire Jacobson (New York: Basic Books, 1963), esp. 224.

29 William Shakespeare, *Troilus and Cressida*, in *The Riverside Shakespeare*, ed. G. Blakemore Evans (Boston: Houghton Mifflin, 1974), V.ii.152.

30 The gift Mary receives during the annunciation is not unlike Derrida's notion of the gift of death, which he explores in relation to a certain attitude to divine command, through a discussion of Abraham's sacrifice of Isaac in 'The Gift of Death'. An absolute leap towards a future that cannot be anticipated is defined by Derrida as the hyper-ethical responsibility towards the wholly other, which must be premised on an estrangement from the communal needs of 'other others'. It is the burden of that radical singularity which Mary must bear, a singularity that makes her, in the medieval tradition, 'makeles' – both matchless and alone: see, e.g., the lyric 'I sing of a maiden/That is makeles', in Davies, ed., *Medieval English Lyrics*, 155 (no. 66).

31 Angela Leighton, 'Yeats's Feet', in *On Form: Poetry, Aestheticism, and the Legacy of a Word* (Oxford: Oxford University Press, 2007), 144–69 (153).

32 W. B. Yeats, *The Cat and the Moon and Certain Poems* (Dublin: Cuala, 1924), 37.

33 Daniel J. Murphy, ed., *Lady Gregory's Journals*, 2 vols (Smythe: Gerrards Cross, 1978–1987), 1 (1978): 477.

34 Ibid.

35 W. B. Yeats, *A Vision* (London: Macmillan, 1937), 268.

36 *Works of John Ruskin*, 39 vols, ed. E. T. Cook and Alexander Wedderburn (London: George Allen, 1903–1912), 4 (1903): 264–65.

37 Ibid., 34 (1908): 661–3 (661).

38 For a lucid translation of Fra Roberto's discussion, see Michael Baxandall, *Painting and Experience in Fifteenth-Century Italy* (Oxford: Oxford University Press, 1988), 50–56.

39 For a wonderfully succinct summary and, indeed, interpretation, of this process, see Angela Leighton, 'Form's Matter', in *On Form*, 1–29, esp. 3–7.

40 Ibid., 5.

41 See Tom Nichols, *Tintoretto: Tradition and Identity* (London: Reaktion, 1999), 19 and 14. This deliberately unfinished style raised eyebrows at the time, and has been read by art critics mainly in two different ways. One school has taken this to be a sign of Tintoretto's non-conformity to the pictorial taste of the time, especially the standards set by the Venetian maestro Titian. While this derives from the perception of disapproving Venetian contemporaries like Aretino, Sansovino or Dolce, or indeed Vasari, some commentators, including Sartre, have glamorised this as a socially rebellious gesture. But as Tom Nichols's judicious analysis clarifies, Tintoretto's adoption of a radically unfinished style is better seen as a strategic adoption of an artisanal professional persona, but only as part of the self-fashioning of a complex artistic identity. The very quality of inventive freedom is read by Ruskin to be a sign of 'Imagination Penetrative', committed to inward spiritual values as opposed to sensuality. But some later critics, such as David Rosand and Philip Sohm, have emphasised the naturalism and accessibility of Tintoretto's style as both an anticipation of later Venetian art which appealed to a popular level of Christian imagination, and a continuation of the earlier brushwork styles of Giorgione. The truth lies in between: Tintoretto, while he drew on and transformed known styles, was also clearly attempting something new, performative and self-consciously challenging, making both an aesthetic and a spiritual point (at once a departure from Titian intended to carve out a distinct space for Tintoretto in the fabric of both Venetian and pan-Italian patronage, and an idealisation of material poverty). See Nichols, *Tintoretto*, 13–27 and 149–52.

42 See Baxandall, *Painting and Experience*, 55–6.

43 See ibid., 147–8.

44 Phrase used by Luce Irigaray in 'The Power of Discourse and the Subordination of the Feminine'. See Margaret Whitford, ed., *The Irigaray Reader* (Oxford: Blackwell, 1991, repr. 1995), 108–32 (123).

45 W. B. Yeats, 'The Thinking of the Body', in *Discoveries: A Volume of Essays* (Dundrum: Dunn Emer Press, 1907), 37–8 (38).

46 See Susan Stewart, *Poetry and the Fate of the Senses* (Chicago: University of Chicago Press, 2002), title and passim.

47 The only image that represents *conturbatio* at the Annunciations exhibition at the Fitzwilliam is Cornelius Cort's engraving, after Titian (c. 1566): here, though the winged angel is huge and overpowering, Mary's face is relatively composed, and her book rests in her hand – not unlike Lucas Cranach's woodcut (c. 1511–13) of the angel gigantic wings met by the Virgin with the Bible nestling calmly on her lap.

Even among the rare scattering of depictions of Mary's startled disquiet, it is hard to find anything quite as startling as Tintoretto's rendering. But see Lorenzo Lotto's marvellously playful depiction of perturbation in his 'Annunciation' (Museo Civico, Recanati), where, as Tomlinson puts it, 'The cat took fright/at the flashing wing of sunlight/as the thing/entered the kitchen, angel of appearances/and lingered there' ('Annunciation'). Cats abound in Annunciation images, like those other animals who stare out of the foreground of many Renaissance paintings of momentous events – all those horses with innocent behinds, distracted dogs and greedy kittens. But typically, they are unfazed, like the soundly sleeping cat in Frederico Barocci's etching, 'The Annunciation' (c. 1584), as Mary greets the angel, or Jacob Matham's (c. 1601–5), where the cat is peacefully curled up in sleep. Lotto's cat, the centre-point of his painting, marks the dividing line between 'the thing' of light, and a surprised Virgin almost dancing her body away from the visitor, and registers the fear. But the fear is still qualified by play and rhythm and a sense of domestic miracle; the colour of God the father's robe, out there in the skies, and the direction of his arm, form a line of continuum with Mary's body. See, however, Mannocci's own 'Conturbatio' (1988), a painting eerily reminiscent of Leda and the wings, and part of 'The Annunciation', an exhibition of Mannocci's paintings at Curwen Galley, London, 11 June-11 July 1992: *The Annunciation: Lino Mannocci* (London: Curwen Gallery, 1992), plate 7. Unfortunately, I was not aware of this painting, or indeed the exhibition, in time to address either in this essay. I am grateful to the artist for showing me the catalogue.

Part Two

LIVES AND NARRATIVES, TERRITORIES AND WORLDS

Chapter Five

UNSETTLING THRESHOLDS: MIGNON AND HER AFTERLIVES

Terence Cave

The opening of the third book of Goethe's *Wilhelm Meisters Lehrjahre* (*Wilhelm Meister's Apprenticeship Years*) is one of the most arresting moments in the history of the novel. Without explanation, without context, the reader encounters a lyric poem in three stanzas, and readers of the first edition in 1795 found opposite it, on a fold-out page, a musical score that provides a setting for the poem. After the text of the song comes the context. Wilhelm is in his room when he hears someone playing a musical instrument outside his door, on the threshold. At first he thinks it is the Harpist, who had been playing and singing outside his door the previous evening. But when he hears the singer's voice, he realises it is Mignon. He opens the door, she crosses the threshold and sings the song that becomes her signature tune and one of Goethe's best-known poems: 'Kennst du das Land?' ('Do you know the land?').[1]

The positioning of Mignon and her song on the threshold both of the printed text (the third book begins the second separate volume in the first edition) and of the fictional scene is hardly an accident. Mignon will remain on the margins of Wilhelm's life and and of his angle of perception throughout the novel.[2] In one of its most fraught episodes, when Wilhelm and the company of actors he has assembled around him have been celebrating their successful performance of *Hamlet*, Mignon plans to enter his bedroom, but from the stairs, outside his door, she sees Philine go in and close the door behind her.[3] Even in the fatal scene where Mignon sees Wilhelm kissing Therese and making a public declaration of their engagement, she has just entered the room with Felix: both Mignon and Therese, in fact, come into the room at the same time, but it is Therese who is welcomed and embraced by Wilhelm, leaving Mignon definitively outside; she has a violent seizure and dies (VIII.5; p. 560). The point seems to have been taken by an early illustrator, who shows her again, this time with Felix, literally in front of an open door, looking through it towards an unseen person who is presumably listening to her song.[4]

Mignon's position on a threshold that she never manages successfully to cross is the narrative equivalent of the many forms of her symbolic in-betweenness. She is a child who is just reaching puberty and the sexual awareness that goes with it. She is a girl who prefers to dress as a boy and who only puts on female clothing when she is near to death.[5] She is a foreigner who only communicates with difficulty and has also taken a mysterious oath of silence.[6] Song, the threshold between words and music, is the medium in which she prefers to express her identity and her longings. She is already, before she dies, an angel living on the brink of the afterlife.[7] And she is also poised on generic borders, between narrative and lyric (or song), romance and the novel.

One may assume that these in-between states are central to the fascination that Mignon exerted from the outset on readers of all kinds, on the writers who retold her story, and on the poets and composers who rewrote her songs. She is a character of questions and enigmas, always open to reinterpretation, and the narrative answers that Goethe provides to many of these questions towards the end of the novel, after her death, have palpably been insufficient to settle her, since readers (including those who have invented Mignons of their own) have persistently ignored or displaced them and constructed their own answers. They take her across the threshold into sexuality, spirituality, psychopathology, high lyric, the sentimental novel and opera. They turn her into a gypsy, a fairy, a wild girl from the woods, a selfless teenager who helps a traumatised younger child back towards speech and society, a self-possessed young bourgeoise, an abused adolescent, a Freudian case-study, a Lulu or a Lolita. One might argue that these new readings and characters have little or nothing to do with the one Goethe imagined, that they are simply manifestations of a constantly shifting reception history. Yet all of them, in one way or the other, claim descent from *Wilhelm Meister*, and in so doing, they unpack features that in the novel itself are still embryonic, mere potentialities. Collectively, they designate the possible futures of Goethe's invention, and thus its specifically historical (diachronic) configuration.[8]

I want first to use one of the threshold scenes I have already mentioned as an initial focus for questions that will reappear in Mignon's afterlives. My object here is not to write a detailed account of these complex issues, but to show the ways in which a fictional work can accommodate such questions – questions of the threshold – and create a kind of chain reaction as others rethink the categories concerned. The party after the opening performance of *Hamlet* (*WML*, V.12) and the ensuing episodes constitute a watershed in the story of Mignon's relations with Wilhelm. Occupied by the festive mood, the 'adults' do not notice at first that the 'children' (Mignon and Felix) are not present. Finally, the Harpist leads them in, wearing fancy dress and playing instruments. They sing a number of songs, and Mignon does an elaborate tambourine dance. Then they sit at the table; the childrens' heads look like puppets, and they perform an impromptu Punch and Judy scenario. Liberally supplied with drink, Mignon becomes excited and aggressive, performing a wild dance in which she resembles a maenad. Eventually the party comes to an end and the participants go their separate ways, not without some suggestion of erotic afterplay. On the stairs, Wilhelm suddenly feels a sharp pain in his arm: Mignon has bitten him. All this precedes the episode of which we only get a full account later (VIII.3): Wilhelm goes to bed, but is joined there, in the dark, by a woman of whose identity he is unsure. The next morning, Mignon treats him differently: she seems to have grown physically and become more mature overnight (V.13).

Mignon's threshold position is apparent in the party scene in a number of ways. In the first place, she is classified as a child, but it becomes clear that her wildness (which might have appeared simply as childish over-excitement) also has an emotional and erotic content, culminating in the maenad-like dance and the bite. The sexual threshold coincides in this episode with a blurring of the border between the human and the animal, the rational mind and the irrational body. It has often been noted that Mignon is repeatedly referred to in Goethe's novel as a creature, as something strange and not quite human. Such references are often associated with her extreme physical agility, which resembles that of a young animal rather than a child; her difficulties with language – she speaks imperfect German, is not especially articulate except when singing, and has sworn a vow of silence about her origins – also suggest that she inhabits a domain that lies on the threshold of the human.

The number of different strands that Goethe packs into the quite limited fragments of narrative featuring Mignon is demonstrated by the wave of German Romantic and post-Romantic fictions that seize on the materials provided by *Wilhelm Meisters Lehrjahre* and work out their implications, or propose counter-fictions. In virtually all of these works, there is more than one figure who shares characteristics with Mignon.[9] Clemens Brentano's *Godwi* (1801) has at least three such figures: the sickly boy Eusebio, in exile from his Italian home and parents; a young woman variously known as Kordelia and Annonciata, whose passionately contemplative nature is coupled with a tendency to aphasia, who falls disastrously in love, is raped and abandoned, and who dies at an early age; and Violetta, whose sexually adventurous mother has exposed her to premature erotic awareness, and who is later corrupted by the invading Napoleonic armies and abandoned for Godwi belatedly to 'save', although she dies soon after he has proposed marriage to her. One striking element of the *Wilhelm Meister* parallel is that Godwi first meets her by touch, half undressed and apparently compliant, in a pitch-dark room, after which her mother displaces her and spends the night with him.[10] Splittings of this kind also occur in late Romantic novels such as Eduard Mörike's *Maler Nolten* (*Nolten the Painter*) (1832), and there can be little doubt that Bulwer Lytton's use of the same device in his experiments with the *Bildungsroman* belongs to the same genealogy, given his enthusiasm for German literature.[11] For our purposes, the crucial point is that, in each case, female adolescence is represented as a problematic threshold state.

Elsewhere, strands from Mignon's narrative are elaborated in terms that give them a precise genealogy. The clearest instance is Stifter's two stories of feral girls, *Katzensilber* (1853)[12] and *Der Waldbrunnen* ('The Forest Spring', 1866). These explore in divergent directions the consequences of an attempt on the part of well-meaning bourgeois characters to educate them and integrate them into the social world; in a scene in *Der Waldbrunnen*, Juliana is discovered on a hillside singing Mignon's 'Heiß mich nicht reden', a song about her unwillingness to speak. There can be no doubt that Stifter's interest in the feral child was at least partly nourished by the story of Kaspar Hauser, which crystallised a long-standing fascination with the question of how far the human child is a blank sheet on which the acquisitions of culture (speech, behavioural patterns, and so on) are subsequently written: an interest, in other words, in the borderlands of the category 'human'. A late addition to the Mignon canon, Gerhart Hauptmann's story *Mignon* (completed in 1944, first published in 1947), endorses this reading: the narrator, with the apparent assent of an anthropologist at a lunch-party, associates her wildness and aphasia with the condition of *homo sapiens ferus*, mentioning Kaspar Hauser as a prime example.

Pathological exacerbation of the features Goethe assigned to Mignon is another widespread feature of her afterlives. It is especially evident in German literature,[13] and it is audible, too, in Hugo Wolf's settings of the Mignon songs, which, with their recurrent syncopated ostinato like an irregular heartbeat in the piano accompaniment, are as anguish-laden as any Wolf ever composed: Wolf was a master of the miniature, but there is nothing 'mignon' about these full-scale settings. That the Lulu of Wedekind's plays is also known as Mignon[14] represents an extreme point in the projection of Mignon's characteristics into a disturbed mental world where the erotic is inseparable from the criminally violent, and it will not be long before interpreters of her story begin to avail themselves of the resources of Freudian psychology. The world of *Lolita* is by now only a step away.

What these later fictions collectively demonstrate is first of all that the Mignon narrative carries a series of concerns connecting female adolescent development with, on the one hand, the borders of the human and, on the other, the borders of rationality or mental equilibrium. In all the instances I have mentioned, the threshold is still there, but it has clearer contours, often because it is actually crossed as 'Mignon' acquires sexual knowledge or moves between her 'natural' origins and social integration. In general, too, these examples limit themselves to a single focus: mental disturbance, the characteristics of the feral child, the alienating movements of the automaton. It is when one spools these various strands backward, reversing the order of literary history, that one finds them as it were impacted on one another in Goethe's text. Something happened there, an attempt to grasp simultaneously a set of different but apparently related problems, that gave later writers an exemplary test case, a dossier they would revisit compulsively, teasing out its implications and discovering new interpretative frames.

It goes without saying that whatever it was that happened was conditioned, at least in part, by the intellectual context Goethe inhabited, and must in any case be regarded as an instance of what it was possible to imagine in the closing decades of the eighteenth century. Goethe's interest in medical explanations is clearly enough signalled in Book VIII of the *Lehrjahre* by the role of the doctor, who undertakes to treat the Harpist (with some initial success) and who also observes and examines Mignon, although his medical practice is not itself represented in the novel but conveyed by his retrospective report to Wilhelm. Essentially, his diagnosis is psychosomatic: he takes for granted the interdependence of Mignon's physical symptoms on the one hand and her anxieties, fears and largely unspoken desires on the other. The fictional doctor's discourse is the only evidence we have for what Goethe had in mind in presenting Mignon's illness and its symptoms to the reader; he did not, for example, include medicine among the topics to which he devoted scientific essays.[15] He did, however, write extensively on biological metamorphosis in plants as a model of 'development' which might also be applicable to humans. In any metamorphosis or development from one state to another, the critical question is what happens at the threshold stage, where the organism is, at it were, neither one thing nor the other, and it seems likely that this was one of the contexts for Goethe's invention of a character who not only inhabits a threshold stage of development but also participates in some sense in both genders.[16]

These medical and biological reflections belong to a broader demystifying, secularising intention which is apparent in *Wilhelm Meisters Lehrjahre* at a number of levels. Central to this intention is the replacement of the plot of destiny with a story whose chance occurrences are only retrospectively perceived as end-directed.[17] An example more relevant to our present purpose, however, is Mignon's funeral. In this extended scene, the trappings of religion are absent and the children are invited first to see Mignon's dead body as beautiful, while recognising that her wings are only imaginary, and then to return to the active enjoyment of life. By means of a fictional narrative embedded in the discursive frame provided by figures such as the doctor and the enlightened Abbé, Goethe uses Mignon to explore responses to the crossing of this ultimate threshold.

Even posthumously, the enigma of Mignon affords an opportunity to raise questions of the natural as opposed to the transcendental when the explanatory narrative of Mignon's origins touches on the validity of the moral infamy attributed to incest. The incestuous relation between Augustin and Sperata, Mignon's parents, takes place in the absence of knowledge on both sides; it is made possible, in fact, by the false shame of their father, who was reluctant to acknowledge publicly that at a relatively advanced age he had engaged in the (entirely legitimate) sexual relations that resulted in the birth of Sperata. Augustin himself maintains that nature gave no sign of any interdict on their love, nor did it immediately destroy the child that then resulted.[18]

These passages rebut the standard fictional (and ethical) notion of the 'call of the blood', the mysterious awareness that is supposed to accompany potential acts of incest, or other forms of recognition of near kin where genealogical identity has been obscured. Goethe is here reexamining another borderline that is said to be constitutive of 'the human', namely a horror of incest that is not observable in other animals, and proposing, via Augustin, a 'natural' account which strongly suggests that the aversion is produced by the religious shame and guilt that cause all the trouble both before and after Mignon's birth. In other words, the incest is constituted by a moral deformation within culture itself, not by the transgression of some fearful supernatural taboo.

In such ways, Mignon challenges established categories, revealing their borderlines to be much more porous than had commonly been imagined. The co-existence of childlike behaviour and sexual desire, the demystification of the soul, the continuity of human behaviour with the mechanical, the animal or indeed the vegetable, all these features of Mignon as she appears in *Wilhelm Meister* will recur in her afterlives, although never again in such a dense cluster. But the fusion of different physiological or biological questions is still not the whole story, since it does not include one of the most prominent and enduring of Mignon's characteristics. For Novalis, writing in the immediate aftermath of the publication of the *Lehrjahre*, Mignon and the Harpist represented poetry and music in opposition to the secular bourgeois life into which Wilhelm is finally received at their expense, and a quasi-allegorical reading of that kind (although without its polemical edge) remains a powerful tool for the understanding of Goethe's *Bildungsroman*. How are we then to perceive Mignon's musical gifts in relation to her other characteristics?

In the history of ideas up to the Enlightenment, poetry and music were in general assigned to the higher realms of experience, whether as the harmony of the spheres, the utterance of angelic choirs, or the outcome of a potentially supernatural inspiration. The Muses are always indisputably goddesses of one kind or another. Even a text as late and as secular as Gerhart Hauptmann's *Mignon* insists on the immateriality of music as the pure domain of the soul,[19] and Novalis uses what is essentially a Platonising approach as the foundation for his Romantic allegory in *Heinrich von Ofterdingen*. Goethe, on the other hand, was writing at the culmination of eighteenth-century reflections (one thinks here in particular of the work of Baumgarten) that connect aesthetics, via the original Greek sense of the word, with sensibility. This is also the historical moment when determined efforts were being made, in particular in France, to understand what the consequences of a purely materialist model of the organic (including the human) world might be for the relationship between mind and body. Such questions were raised in fictional and quasi-fictional form by Denis Diderot in *Le Neveu de Rameau* (*Rameau's Nephew*) which Goethe was later to translate, in *Le Rêve de d'Alembert* (*D'Alembert's Dream*) and in other works. For our purposes, what is critical here is the intersection between (rational) thought, affect and sensation. Diderot characteristically uses musical analogies – the vibration of strings as a model for what happens in the mind, for example – and he also imagines sexual scenarios, such as the erotic dreams of d'Alembert and their consequences as observed by a female observer, in order to think about the body as a site of mental and affective phenomena. In *La Religieuse* (*The Nun*), these two lines of thought come together in a remarkable scene where the young novice Suzanne, who has earlier been forced into the convent and abused there, plays the harpsichord while her new, much more indulgent, Mother Superior leans against her, caresses her, and finally has what the reader recognises as an orgasm, although Suzanne is too naïve and inexperienced to understand this.[20] Diderot's interest in this novel in a pubescent female body exposed to painful and unfamiliar experiences turns precisely on a question of the threshold: the girl has reached an age where the body begins to know about sexuality before she is capable of formulating that experience rationally and discursively.

We have no evidence that Goethe had read these works before he began the first draft of his novel, probably in the early 1770s. But we know that they were disseminated in German intellectual circles via the manuscript journal *Correspondance littéraire*, and it is likely that Goethe had access to them at some stage. At least they indicate the horizon of innovative thought on such questions in the later eighteenth century, and it is also instructive to see such thought motivating new kinds of narrative and new fictional techniques: the naïve or unconscious protagonist is very much a product of this era. Goethe does things very differently, but he too uses music – or more specifically song – as a metaphorical extension of the affect of his characters, associating it on several occasions with semi-pathological states: thus the scene in *Wilhelm Meister* where Mignon has a seizure in Wilhelm's arms, a scene which has clear erotic associations, is immediately followed in the narrative sequence by Mignon's performance of her song 'Kennst du das Land', a performance described in some detail. This grouping may be juxtaposed with the scene where Wilhelm, still suffering from the wounds inflicted on him by robbers, hears the Harpist and Mignon sing 'Nur wer die Sehnsucht kennt'. Although an expression of their melancholic yearnings, the song resonates also with Wilhelm's yearning (*Sehnsucht*) for the mysterious woman who came to his aid, and, not least, with his physically vulnerable state.[21]

I would argue that Mignon and the Harpist, as embodiments of the aesthetic domain, offer a secularised, naturalistic way of understanding the relation of music and poetry to human experience. One could derive from this the conclusion (essentially, Novalis's) that the close yet in the end failed relation between Wilhelm and his musical protégés is determined by the assumption that excessive preoccupation with the aesthetic domain is an error, a confusion of categories, which may thwart or at least retard entry into the social and moral life. But that simply returns us to the common conception of the novel as a story about the maturation of an exemplary male figure. What interests me more particularly is the splicing of this further strand – a remarkably prominent one – into the amalgam of features we have already considered. Wilhelm's muse is not a heavenly being but an awkward adolescent whose sensibility has been wrought amid traumatic circumstances, a gifted but disturbed child who is backward with language but precocious in music. She usurps the place assigned to allegories in earlier narratives, much as Dorothea stands in for Santa Teresa, or Daniel Deronda, Mirah and Mordecai for legendary and indeed anagogic figures, in George Eliot's secularising fiction. Angela Carter provides a powerful postmodern variant: in *Nights at the Circus*, Mignon is resurrected as a sexually abused and abjected adolescent whose singing has redemptive powers on an Orphic scale.[22] Everything depends here, once again, on where the threshold is placed and how permeable it is.

Neither the templates that I have drafted in here from the history of ideas nor any other can wholly account for Goethe's invention of this complex character and her story. In particular, they are liable to elide the affect which is such a powerful catalyst for the release and transmission of their seminal possibilities, and which arises from the anxieties attached to fundamental changes in ways of thinking about how the human organism works, how the mind is related to the body, or how thought and aesthetic experience operate if there is no immaterial soul. It seems rather that we are speaking in such cases of an amalgam of interdependent elements, a single bomb that can only explode when all the components are present. And that amalgam again derives its explosive force from its placing at a particular moment in history: inconceivable at an earlier moment, at a later point it would have come 'too late': it would no longer have had the effects, triggered the ever-proliferating number of responses, that Goethe's text in fact did.

Wilhelm Meisters Lehrjahre is indeed in an exemplary sense positioned at a diachronic threshold, between Enlightenment and Romanticism, between a moribund feudal order and a new bourgeois society founded on trade and industry, between eighteenth-century genres such as the picaresque novel and the nineteenth-century novel of the adventitious and the everyday, between romance and realism (these conventional oppositions may be defined in a variety of different ways without much altering the point made here). That Goethe's contemporaries were conscious of this portentous positioning is shown by Friedrich Schlegel's often-quoted aphorism, 'The French Revolution, Fichte's philosophy of knowledge and Goethe's "Meister" are the most significant trends of our age.'

Complex literary works, especially those that make a considerable impact on later times, often appear to be placed on or across such thresholds, at moments when ideological and intellectual frames of reference are shifting, or at points of intersection between different cultural perceptions. The work they do, both in their own time and for future generations, is cognitive: they provide heuristic models with which to redraw the boundaries of received conceptions. Their asymmetries, their loose threads, their occasional awkwardness, are symptoms of their positioning in relation to a threshold that may not previously have been perceived in such ways, and of the necessarily unresolved states of reflection they embody. Non-resolution is a precondition of their capacity for engendering further reflective transformations.

Pursuing this nexus on to a still more general plane, one may ask what 'Mignon' is in studies of her afterlives, and hence what such studies may hope to achieve other than the collection of a set of more or less comparable literary materials. The answer one might give in the context I have evoked might be first that Mignon, in Goethe's fiction, is already structured like a category; and secondly, if this hypothesis is accepted, that Mignon and her afterlives collectively develop, extend and explore that category in ways that are historically bound.

My aim in transferring the word 'category' to a fictional character is to bring about a modification of both terms. This becomes clear if one adopts for a moment, instead, the standard procedure of identifying the character with a *concept* or a single conceptual area – 'Mignon' as a type of the vulnerable adolescent female, of pubescent sexual desire, of the abused child, or an ideal identification of music and poetry. The project of studying Mignon's afterlives would then be the project of studying one of these, or perhaps more than one if a plurality of types turned out to be compatible with thematic unity. One could then write a conceptual history, or a cultural history with a conceptual focus, of which Mignon would be the emblem, the 'figure'.[23] To call her a category, on the other hand, allows plurality without reduction. I take the word here in the sense in which Wittgenstein uses it to qualify sets of phenomena that have a family resemblance but no single unifying definition. He offers the category 'games' as a prime example: we use this word holistically, and think we know what we mean by it, but there is no single definition that captures the essence of a game.[24]

George Lakoff and others have developed this strategy further in ways that are relevant to my discussion. In particular, they point out that one corollary of focusing on categories (instead of definitions and concepts) in this way is that one will be led to consider their boundaries, the point where a given example may no longer be regarded as belonging to the category. Typically, categories have fuzzy edges, and the fuzziness here is not a conceptual muddle that one then strives to clear up: it is an inherent aspect of how categories work. When one asks what a given category is, one may therefore look at an exemplary case, a 'prototype', which seems to have many if not all of the features shared by the other members of the category, or one may look at the borders, the threshold beyond which the category comes into effect (or, conversely, is no longer operative); ideally, in the end, one should define one of these procedures in terms of the other.[25]

When applied to cultural materials of the kind we have been looking at (including cultural history itself), the notion of the category brings into view the powerful forces that meet and dispute the terrain at critical thresholds. In that light, we may pursue the interest and value of 'Mignon' as an imaginative (cognitive) resource without either reducing her to the personification of an abstraction or, on the other hand, to the status of a colourful, moving, but in the end purely aesthetic phenomenon. She becomes a figure to think with, both for the authors who imagined and reimagined her and for their readers. More particularly, she challenges established categories by embodying (in a quasi-literal sense) a set of features that is both unique and disturbingly mixed. By the very way she is framed in and by the narrative, as we have seen, she works from the margins and across thresholds, and even a cursory analysis of what is at stake here shows that she inhabits a whole cluster of fuzzy borderlines between categories that are in general supposed to be distinct or even mutually exclusive.

The number of different strands connected by the impulse to rethink the human and its limits through the figure of Mignon is startlingly rich and differentiated. Gender (tested at puberty, where the supposedly sexless child becomes powerfully gendered), the incest taboo, the relation to the feral and the automatic, the pathological effects of severance and abuse are some of the most prominent of these, but there are others that seem less connected. The relation of the aesthetic and the social, or the borderline between language and music as embodied in song, invite one to make a thematic division, assigning such questions to an enquiry of their own. Yet the primary assumption I am making here is that this would be a fatal error. Mignon is a strange, complex, conflicted creature, but the impact she has had on readers and later writers (not to mention composers and singers and their audiences) depends, initially at least, on the coexistence of all the strands in the bundle. As I have indicated, they subsequently become separated, but there would be nothing to separate if the strands had not been tangled in the first place. Thus, for example, when the reverberations of Mignon's zither, of her untrained voice and her defective speech are juxtaposed with her seizures, where emotional and sexual response are hard to distinguish from epilectic spasms and cardiac malfunction, it becomes impossible to think of song (or the high lyric poetry represented by 'Kennst du das Land') merely as an aesthetically pleasing and moving supplement to the serious business of living.

When Mignon travels, then, whether fictionally across the Alps into unknown territory or in literary history across genres, modes of expression, or horizons of reception, she carries with her a potentially explosive package of materials. She also, wherever she goes, remains on the borders, unresolved, a figure of painful but productive tension; you can hear it in her songs, you can read it in the narratives through which she passes. The threshold she occupies between categories and habits of thought is always unsettling, and by the same token a threshold that she repeatedly unsettles.

Notes

1 Johann Wolfgang Goethe, *Wilhelm Meisters Lehrjahre*, ed. Erich Schmidt (Frankfurt am Main: Insel Taschenbuch, 1980), 150–1 (III.1). I have chosen this edition (referred to subsequently in the notes as *WML*) for the purposes of this paper both because it is readily accessible and because it reproduces the illustrations and the musical settings I refer to (composed by Johann Friedrich Reichardt). Readers using other editions and translations will easily locate examples by chapter-numbers, which are supplied for all examples (III.1 = Book III, Chapter 1); chapter-numbers only are given where the reference is to an episode as a whole. All translations are my own.

2 A brief conspectus of the plot as far as it concerns Mignon will be helpful here. The youthful Wilhelm, stage-struck from childhood, leaves home and falls in with a wandering band of actors. While on the road, he sees a girl (dressed as a boy), barely adolescent, being mistreated by the leader of a troupe of acrobats who have apparently abducted her; he rescues her, she becomes his devoted servant. She falls in love with him, but he seems largely unaware of her affection. Nicknamed 'Mignon', she is Italian

and speaks only broken German. However, she sings spontaneously and beautifully; four of her songs are included in the novel. She is represented throughout as enigmatic, fascinating and highly vulnerable; she suffers from alarming seizures when emotionally disturbed. One of these seizures eventually kills her when she sees Wilhelm kissing a woman (Therese) he is said to be engaged to. After her death she is found to be the daughter of an Italian nobleman and his sister; this nobleman also plays an important role in the novel as the mysterious wandering Harpist, who befriends Mignon and sometimes sings with her.

3 This episode is presented in two perspectives, the first in V.12–13, the second in VIII.3; for further details, see below.

4 The illustrations, by Franz Ludwig Catel, were published separately in 1799 (for the image referred to here, see *WML*, 338).

5 Other female characters in the novel wear masculine attire, but only temporarily and without creating a comparable degree of gender ambiguity.

6 The oath is explained in *WML*, VIII.5 (538–9); it is anticipated both by Mignon's general reluctance to answers questions and, more specifically, by her song 'Heiß mich nicht reden' ('Don't ask me to speak'), which is placed, without contextual explanation, at the end of Book V – another threshold, since it marks a major break in the narrative, the point where Wilhelm abandons his theatrical career and shifts to a different milieu and a wholly different phase of his life.

7 See *WML*, VIII.2, where Mignon appears dressed as an angel at a birthday party organised by Natalie for the young girls under her care; it is in this context that Mignon sings her last song, 'So laßt mich scheinen, bis ich werde' ('Let me appear thus, until I become [an angel]').

8 The fullest account of Mignon's reception history to date is provided by Carolyn Steedman in *Strange Dislocations: Childhood and the Idea of Human Interiority, 1780–1930* (London: Virago Books, 1995). My own book, *Mignon's Afterlives: Crossing Cultures from Goethe to the Twenty-First Century*, which offers a comprehensive study of the Mignon corpus in German, French and English culture and includes a chapter on her musical manifestations, will be published by Oxford University Press in 2011. The themes sketched in this essay are explored there in a much wider context.

9 It is true that *WML* also features a series of woman figures, but the splitting of characteristics exclusively assigned by Goethe to Mignon is demonstrable in all these later cases.

10 Clemens Brentano, *Godwi*, in *Werke*, 4 vols (Munich: Carl Hanser Verlag, 1963–68), 2 (1963): Part II, Chs 32–3.

11 In the double novel *Ernest Maltravers* and *Alice, or the Mysteries*, for example, Alice and her adoptive daughter Evelyne are twinned by virtue of Maltravers' attachment to both at different points in the narrative: Alice allows herself to be seduced, while Evelyne, with whom Maltravers has had a first tactile encounter while she is still a child, remains virtuous. For an example from George Eliot, see my article 'Mignon's afterlife in the fiction of George Eliot', *Rivista di letterature moderne e comparate* 56 (2003): 165–82.

12 'Katzensilber' is a mineral, a variety of mica.

13 In Mörike's *Maler Nolten*, for example, mental disturbance becomes generalised. Here, the innocent Agnes is pursued to madness and death by the demented half-gypsy Elisabeth, who herself shares features with Mignon and who appears in a series of quasi-supernatural scenarios.

14 See Frank Wedekind, *Erdgeist*, in *Werke*, vol. 3, ed. Hartmut Vinçon (Darmstadt: Häusser, 1996), Act I Scene ii, Act II Scene iv, Act IV Scene viii.

15 Acquisition of medical knowledge forms an important strand in the sequel to the *Lehrjahre*, *Wilhelm Meisters Wanderjahre*; doctors with their resolutely secular attitudes also feature regularly in nineteenth-century fictions such as Immermann's *Die Epigonen*.

16 See Goethe's essays on the formation of sexual organs in plants, discussed in a wider historical context by Steedman, *Strange Dislocations*, Ch. 3 (see especially 46–7 and notes).

17 See my article 'Written on the scroll: Diderot, Goethe and Blixen', *Oxford German Studies* 33 (2004): 51–69.

18 *WML*, VIII.9 (598–600).

19 One might contrast this perspective with the way music is presented in Thomas Mann's *Doktor Faustus*, published not long after Hauptmann's *Mignon*.

20 Denis Diderot, *La Religieuse*, in *Œuvres romanesques*, ed. H. Bénac (Paris: Garnier, 1962), 235–393 (340–1). The passage ends: 'Truly that crazy woman was endowed with an extraordinary sensitivity, and her enjoyment of music was particularly intense; I have never known anyone on whom it produced such singular effects.' In other episodes, Suzanne sings suggestive songs to the Mother Superior and other nuns while accompanying herself on the keyboard. *La Religieuse* was first published posthumously in 1796, the year in which the publication of the *Lehrjahre* was completed.

21 Further examples of 'sympathetic resonance' between singers and their accompanists occur in Goethe's later novel *Die Wahlverwandtschaften*, where they are linked to the theory of 'elective affinities' that gives the novel its title.

22 See my article 'Singing with tigers: recognition in *Wilhelm Meister*, *Daniel Deronda* and *Nights at the Circus*', in Philip F. Kennedy and Marilyn Lawrence, eds, *Recognition: The Poetics of Narrative: Interdisciplinary Studies on Anagnorisis* (New York: Peter Lang, 2009), 115–34; reprinted in slightly modified form in Terence Cave, *Retrospectives: Essays in Literature, Poetics and Cultural History*, ed. Neil Kenny and Wes Williams (Oxford: Legenda, 2009), 168–85.

23 This is in fact the strategy adopted by Carolyn Steedman in *Strange Dislocations*.

24 I refer here to *Philosophische Untersuchungen (Philosophical Investigations)*, with translation by G. E. M. Anscombe (Oxford: Blackwell, 1953), §65–7. See also my article 'Lapin ou canard? Essai sur les binômes littéraires', in Delphine Denis, Mireillel Huchon, Anna Jaubert, Michael Rinn and Olivier Soutet, eds, *Au corps du texte: hommage à Georges Molinié* (Paris: Champion, 2010), 257–66.

25 See George Lakoff, *Women, Fire, and Dangerous Things: What Categories Reveal about the Mind* (Chicago and London: Chicago University Press, 1987), Book I, Part I.

Chapter Six

DANGEROUS LIAISONS: DESIRE AND LIMIT IN *THE HOME AND THE WORLD*

Supriya Chaudhuri

A threshold is physically crossed in one of the most striking visual sequences in Satyajit Ray's 1984 film, *Ghare Baire* (The Home and the World). It is a cinematic moment filled with expectation, prefaced by the narratorial voice of the film's protagonist, Bimala. On this day, we learn, the 12th of Agrahayan, B.S. 1314 (26 November 1907), the young mistress of the *zamindari* of Sukhsayar, for the first time in the family's history, stepped out of the inner, women's quarters (the *andarmahal*) of the house to entertain a guest in its outer apartments.

The diegetic framing of the sequence appears to cite the film's own framing by a literary text, Rabindranath Tagore's novel of the same name (serialised 1915–16). But this is an illusion. The moment itself belongs entirely to the film's field of vision; it is missing in the novel, which contains no textual counterpart to Bimala's voiced commentary. With the exception of that voice, the sequence is silent. The pale green doors of the *andarmahal* swing open, and two graceful, formally-dressed figures – Bimala and her husband Nikhilesh – emerge into a light-filled gallery. The camera's eye focuses for a moment on the pair's feet, shod in decorative slippers, then moves up to track their transit through the corridor, panelled in stained glass that casts an unearthly radiance on the scene. As they reach the open doors at its end and emerge into the long, pillared verandah, with its slender European statues on raised pediments, the pace diminishes to lyrical slow motion. In a series of overlapping shots, the director focuses on their deliberate, self-absorbed, thoughtful steps, making them appear to float rather than walk, like characters in a dream. Two sets of doors remain open behind them, but they do not look back. In the last shot of this wordless sequence, they stand framed by the curtains until Bimala crosses a final threshold into the sitting-room (*baithak-khana*) of her marital home.

The sequence occupies just over one minute of screen time, though it may seem longer because of the leisurely, poetic movement of the camera as it records the pair's progress through the verandah. Those seventy seconds may indeed correspond to the actual time taken to traverse such a distance, and in that respect Ray might appear to be quoting the first seven-and-a-half minutes of his own earlier, greater film, *Charulata* ('The Lonely Wife', 1964). There too, as Charulata crosses the long verandah from the inner apartments to her husband's study and sitting-room, screen time and real time coincide. But while the 'realistic' tracking camera here follows Charu's own rhythms – busy, preoccupied, curious, idle – the camera-work in *The Home and the World* is completely different: time is elongated, non-naturalistic, made to fill the recessive, over-lapping shots and dreamlike motion. In both films, though, Ray offers a highly self-conscious use of the lens's gaze to assert 'the symbolic functions of the frame and the scene as spatial orders', at the same time as he establishes the spatial economy within which relationships and characters must be understood.[1] *The Home and the World*, with its contrast of *ghar* (home) and *bahir* (outside), is firmly articulated in terms of this spatial economy.

The house in colonial India constituted a space roughly divided into outer and inner precincts, the outer areas reserved for the men of the house, for male visitors, and for business, and the inner or women's quarters, referred to in Northern India as the *antahpur*, *andarmahal* or *zenana*. The separation was reflected in the architecture of the traditional dwelling, though the distinction could only be strictly maintained in households above a certain economic level (if the dwelling was substantial enough to be divided), and was open to modification in the heterotopic sites constituted by religion or pleasure – for instance, in the transgressive space of the brothel, or through the socially sanctioned practice of pilgrimage. For women, this demarcation of household space allowed for a degree of freedom as well as privation, both characteristically internalised to become a norm of virtuous conduct. Domestic confinement was constituted not only by external restrictions but also by proscriptive fear or 'shame' (*lajja*). The East Bengal housewife, Rassundari Debi (1810–99), writing the first Bengali prose autobiography in the second half of the nineteenth century, realises that even her children would not be able to understand the prohibitory shrinkings that formed their mother's consciousness. In a remarkable passage, she describes herself as retreating to an inner room to avoid being seen by her husband's horse when it came into the courtyard to be fed.[2]

This distinction between outer and inner regions, so vital to the self-understanding of the colonial bourgeoisie, was preserved in the new town houses built in the European style. But in a seminal study, Swati Chattopadhyay notes changes in the treatment of interior space from the eighteenth to the nineteenth centuries:

> Pre-colonial architecture emphasised the experience of the interior spaces and the many thresholds that connected the rooms with the interior open space, be it a courtyard or a garden. The eighteenth-century buildings of Calcutta designed for affluent Indians shared this tradition. They ignored a prominent street entrance, and lavished attention on the four interior faces of the courtyard… In other words the envelope was de-emphasised to celebrate the interiority of domestic space. This focus on interiority would change in the nineteenth century for two reasons. One was the popularisation of the European notion of a façade, and the second was the desire to *connect* with the increasingly busy street life, rather than withdrawing from it… This interest in generating a "front" was symptomatic of the new urge to outwardly *display* residences as symbols of wealth and status.[3]

Tagore's grandfather Prince Dwarakanath built a house in the new style in 1823, a *baithak-khana bari* consisting of reception rooms and offices erected next to the eighteenth-century family mansion in Calcutta's Jorasanko district. After his death, as the artist Abanindranath Tagore recalls in his memoirs, the second floor of the house was reconfigured to accommodate the *andarmahal*, with screens, curtains, and shutters, as well as extensions, verandahs and passageways on multiple levels. Complex rules governed the shutting of doors and window-blinds, scrupulously maintaining the separation between the *andarmahal*, inhabited by the women, the children and their servants, and the offices and salon on the first two floors, ruled over by the men of the house.[4] For the poet as for his nephews Abanindranath and Gaganendranath, who repeatedly return to it in their paintings, the Jorasanko house, with its intricate gradations of interior space, its internal boundaries, the multiple frames of windows, doors and shutters, the possibilities both of *looking out* and *looking in*, became a mysterious and haunted place. It is this interior space, the space of early childhood, that is for them the site of creative imagination.

Yet during the same period, as Tagore movingly chronicles in *The Home and the World*, the bourgeois house also becomes the physical site of a project of social modernisation which might, in some enlightened families, require the bringing of women out of the *andarmahal* to the public apartments. This passage from inner to outer, a transition attended by extreme risk and difficulty, seeks to re-configure the values of domestic space by recasting women's lives. Typically, it is a *male* project, like the many social reform movements of the nineteenth century which focus on the condition of women. At the same time, the careful spatial articulation of *The Home and the World* reminds us that physical space can never be treated *merely* as a function of ideology: there is always something in it that exceeds the use to which it is put. Bodily experiences of place, distance, and proximity accompany the ceaseless transformation of space into the mental categories that organise our relationships with others; objects are touched only to be converted into signifying forms.

Tagore's novel is composed as a sequence of alternating personal narratives ('autobiographies') by Bimala, her husband Nikhilesh, and Nikhilesh's friend Sandip. Each looks back at the history of desire and self-delusion that breaks open their triangular relationship, a sequence of events commencing with Bimala's 'emergence' from the *andarmahal.* For the liberal, educated Nikhilesh, this projected emancipation is a necessary constituent of the companionate marriage he desires. Given the historical period in which the novel is set, just after the first Partition of Bengal in 1906, this would not have been a novel proposition. From the second half of the nineteenth century, reformist interest in women's education (*strishiksha*) had enabled the articulation of a new ideal of partnership in marriage, towards which some liberal husbands sought to educate their wives. Tagore's own sister-in-law Jnanadanandini, wife of his elder brother Satyendranath (the first Indian member of the imperial Civil Service) had been taken out of the *andarmahal* by her husband in the 1860s. Her emergence from their Jorasanko home to ride in a carriage and to attend a party in the Governor's House attracted considerable public attention. A relation by marriage belonging to the Pathuriaghata family, Prasanna Kumar Tagore, met her at the Governor's party and was so overcome by mortification that he left abruptly. Through a long process of experimentation with styles of wearing the sari, especially the Parsi mode of western India, Jnanadanandini also initiated new forms of dress appropriate for women who were to be seen in public. In *The Home and the World*, it is Nikhilesh who lovingly provides his wife with these items of dress – chemises, blouses, jackets, slippers – which had already become part of the wardrobe of the urban elite. In a remarkable early scene in the novel, Bimala is subjected to the ironic, critical gaze of her widowed sister-in-law as she dresses for her first meeting with Sandip.

Yet despite the advances made by a westernised bourgeoisie, rural society remained more conservative. This was above all the case with traditional Hindu aristocratic families living on their country estates, especially if they had large numbers of Muslim tenants (as in the *zamindari* of Sukhsayar). While Nikhilesh wishes to introduce his wife in Calcutta society, she is reluctant to accompany him there, and the novel is wholly set in the country. Within this physical context, Nikhilesh's insistence is presented as an act of love, filled with the egoism of that emotion:

> One day I said to Bimal: you must come out. Bimal was within my house – she was a household Bimal, made by the trivial, set rules of a small place. Was the love that I regularly got from her gathered from a deep source within her heart, or was it like the daily ration of tap water provided by the municipality's pump?... I did not realise then that if one truly wishes to see a human being in wholeness and freedom, then one must abandon the hope of retaining a definite claim upon her.[5]

As this passage indicates, Nikhilesh's project is also a test: a love-test, exposing both parties to unprecedented risk. The 'world' (referred to in the novel as *baire*, i.e. *bahir*, literally 'outside') in which he seeks to place Bimala, the world which, so he says, *needs* Bimala in order to achieve its proper plenitude, is for him a space of freely articulated desire where *her* love can be measured. It is important to note the exclusively affective bias of this projected emancipation, its de-linking (unusual in the period) from social, educational, even political goals. In execution, Nikhilesh's liberating idea draws uncomfortably close to the classic love-test exposing a wife to the proximity – and attractions – of her husband's best friend. Yet it is conceived under the influence of a wholly modern emotion, a love painfully inflected by anxiety, seeking reassurance from the world for an inward, almost inaccessible state of feeling, compounded of sentiment, idealism, desire and hope. The tenor of Nikhilesh's love alienates him radically from its object, his wife Bimala, since it is an emotion she cannot reciprocate without surrendering her own sense of self.[6]

As Rilke said, lovers are always on the brink, always arriving at each others' boundaries.[7] In its treatment of love, *The Home and the World* contributes as much to a history of the emotions as to the political history with which it is more usually associated. In both aspects, it has been much misunderstood. Early reviewers in the West were shocked on the one hand by its travesty of the home (E. M. Forster described it as 'a boarding house flirtation') and on the other by its devaluation of the world (Georg Lukaćs called Sandip 'a contemptible caricature of Gandhi', and thought that Tagore had played into the hands of the colonial police).[8] Mistaken identifications apart, the novel undoubtedly places a scandal at the heart of both politics and domestic life.

The Home and the World is set against the background of the first Partition of Bengal, accomplished on 16 October 1906 and revoked only in 1911. This was a comprehensive territorial readjustment which made Bengali Hindus a minority in both the newly formed states of Bengal (a Hindu majority state comprising the capital Calcutta and eleven districts of West Bengal, Darjeeling and the whole of Bihar and Orissa) and Eastern Bengal and Assam (a Muslim majority state with its capital at Dacca). The division sparked off intense political protest all over Bengal. The *swadeshi* movement, commencing around 1905, advocated not only a constructive recourse to indigenous manufacture and services, but economic and social boycott (of foreign goods and those who used them), and gave rise to organised extremist violence. Tagore, who had been at the forefront of the *swadeshi* movement and anti-Partition campaign at its inception, and led a demonstration in the streets of Calcutta to tie *rakhis* on the wrists of Muslims in 1906, found himself in active retreat from its narrowly chauvinistic premises within a year or so. In a number of articles written at the time, Tagore set out the terms of his disillusionment with the politics of boycott – especially because of its deep alienation of the Muslim population – and of terrorism.[9] But his retreat from political activism was unpopular, and the historian Ranajit Guha, analysing the fractures in civil society following Partition, speaks of the head wound suffered by Nikhilesh in his attempt to save the lives of Muslim villagers as a 'metaphor for the author's own battered reputation of 1908'.[10]

Tagore's own convictions are seen as reflected in Nikhilesh's liberal universalism. Sandip, by contrast, with his complete lack of sexual and moral scruple, his unashamed egoism, and his unchecked appetite, offers a bitter parody of *swadeshi* politics and of the nationalist leader as self-serving charlatan. Bimala's infatuation with Sandip's rhetoric and his flattering identification of her with the newly-born nation are vitiated from the start by the erotic charge of their relationship and its game of power, its deliberate confusion of politics with sex. Yet it would be a mistake to see her only as under the spell of that relationship. She is the novel's centre, drawing to herself not only private desire but public hope, inhabiting the boundary between inside and outside, constituting herself as a project for modernity itself. It is her narrative voice that mediates the moral and ideological disjunctions between Nikhilesh and Sandip, and records a trajectory of desire that in the ultimate analysis has nothing to do with either, but is almost wholly directed at finding a location for a self that can never be at home in the world. The nostalgia she expresses at the start of the novel for a lost way of life, the urgency with which she embraces a future that is always out of reach, marks her with the signs of a radical discontent, the discontent that Freud makes a condition of modernity, or of civilisation as we know it.

The immediate catalyst for Bimala's emergence from the *andarmahal* is Sandip's arrival at Sukhsayar with a band of fiery, ochre-clad young nationalists, an extraordinary scene which Bimala watches, with the other women of the house, from behind a screen. His impassioned address to his followers in the courtyard of the house draws her to push the screen briefly aside, and for an instant she sees his glance fall on her, caught, in that act of transgressive eagerness, on the threshold of inner and outer. As Tagore describes it, this passage of glances – absent in Ray's film – is at once revelatory and profoundly deluded. Bimala sees in Sandip the face of the newly awakened nation, looking at her, as 'the sole representative of all the women of Bengal', to respond to its call to arms. Yet something more is at stake in this liminal encounter. For the first time in her adult life, Bimala is conscious of having been seen by another man; of having exposed herself to the world – or, in the novel's terms, the *bahir* or 'outside' – as connoted by the gaze of the other. If she seeks to identify herself with the resurgent nation, she also desires the full reciprocity of that gaze. It is this that takes her from *andarmahal* to *baithak-khana,* a journey critically captured in Ray's film, but never physically described in the novel, which has, as it were, already enacted its liminal moment.

Viewers of Ray's film are likely to be disturbed by its deliberate scopophilia, its fascination with what Ray himself, in an interview with Shyam Benegal, called 'the visual aspect of opulence', and the extent to which it insists on arresting or prolonging the gaze, composing its sequences in highly elaborate, almost static frames. The film's visual pleasures, its warm, rich golden tones, the slow eye of the camera as it dwells on objects, furniture, clothes, persons, might seem to confirm a new fetishisation of the gaze, wholly distinct from the lyrical, ironic, many-angled camera-work of *Charulata.* In some ways, certainly, both films bear out Laura Mulvey's analysis of the pleasures of the gaze in narrative cinema, allowing the spectator unimpeded visual access to the fetishised object of desire in patriarchal culture.[11] But by contrast with the earlier film's capacity for an under-emphasised but critical examination of the gaze itself, *The Home and the World* appears to have allowed that gaze to harden and settle. Rarely, if ever, are we drawn into the frame. We are outside, looking in: at Bimala as she views the scene in the courtyard, at Sandip framed by pillared arches as in a Renaissance painting, as he addresses the assembly. What holds the eye, moreover, is the rich detail of surfaces, textures, lines and colours: holds it *at the level of surface,* so that even in an interior, there is no interiority. While this may seem at odds with the novel's construction as a series of interior monologues, both retrospective and introspective in content, I would like to argue that Ray's choice of treatment is not only deliberate but necessary.

The film's visual excess is a stylisation (with the element of distortion that such stylisation involves) of Bimala's own obsession with her self-image as the novel records it. When, at the start of her narrative, she recalls an idealised image of her mother as a traditional Hindu wife, wearing a red-bordered sari, with vermilion in her hair, the image serves as an iconic marker of the values of the *andarmahal*, uniting chastity with power. Yet it is an image she cannot approximate in her own life, however much she may romanticise the acts of worship that express the chaste wife's devotion, drawing to her through her own self-abnegation the power of patriarchy as a whole. This self-ideal, placed on the one hand against the widows and neglected wives in Nikhilesh's family, and on the other against Bimala's own marriage to a man who wants not devotion but a wholly modern love, is both inaccessible and threatening. At the same time, Bimala cannot reciprocate Nikhilesh's 'freeing' love (also a form of egoism) because, in her profound, unthinking narcissism, she will not risk the self-surrender of the ego in such a relationship. Sandip's seduction of her, as Tagore makes clear, is founded on the blandishments of the image: the resurgent nation with which Bimala is identified, and the deliberate sexualisation of that figure so as to coincide with Bimala's physical body, clad in the rich deep colours of blood and earth.[12] Repeatedly, Bimala's narrative returns to the images into which she seeks to project herself: the iconic figure of her mother as chaste wife, the country she sees in a night-time vision 'a woman like myself, standing expectant', the female body which Nikhilesh wants to clothe in the latest foreign fashions, the sexually-awakened woman Sandip identifies, transgressively, with the nation not as motherland but as beloved. Perhaps it was inevitable, then, that instead of adopting Tagore's open ending, where the extent of Nikhilesh's injury is still unknown, Ray should have fixed Bimala's fate in and *through* the image: in a final dissolve, she is invested with the cropped hair and white sari of a Hindu widow. But in the novel, none of these projections is fully realised: the desiring subject, locked into the narcissism of her ego-ideal, is never able to make her self coincide with her self-image, which is, we realise, in each case a projection on to her of *male* desire. What is reflected back at her from 'the threshold of the visible world' – as Lacan describes the mirror stage – is what the world wants her to be.[13]

Lacan's memorable pronouncement, 'the mirror-stage would seem to be the threshold of the visible world', places the entry into the field of vision at a point where narcissism and alienation coincide, to the extent that the image is both the *same* and the *other*:

> The *mirror stage* is a drama whose internal thrust is precipitated from insufficiency to anticipation – and which manufactures for the subject, caught up in the lure of spatial identification, the succession of phantasies that extends from a fragmented body-image to a form of its totality that I shall call orthopaedic – and, lastly, to the assumption of the armour of an alienating identity, which will mark with its rigid structure the subject's entire mental development.[14]

The formation of the bodily ego, involving both idealisation and identification, is also, Lacan suggests, a form of *méconnaissance.* In a fine study, Kaja Silverman reflects on the mirror image as a limit: 'that which cannot be crossed', at the same time that it is a threshold, so that all our visual transactions (gaze, look, screen) are inflected by the narcissism through which we enter the scopic domain.[15] This notion of the threshold as an invisible but persistent limit is useful, I would suggest, in understanding the way in which the subject is always confined by its bodily image, which both confirms identity and produces a deep sense of alienation.

Thus it is not simply in the domestic restriction of women's spaces, though these are most visible and 'enacted' in Tagore's novel and Ray's film, that we are to look for the idea of a threshold. For women, the long and apparently interminable process of socialisation involves the repeated referral to an image-ideal that is both insistently viewed and entirely secluded: that is, never viewed at all except in imagination. That paradox, also very much part of the text of *The Home and the World,* makes it impossible to read the novel in terms of the simple transition of a woman from the inner quarters of her *home* to the public space of the *world.* That the transition should also involve a dangerous liaison, sexually charged if not involving the physical act of adultery, compromises the status of the world, by inflecting it with 'private' passion, just as it imperils the home. Desire can only be understood through this ceaseless activity of constituting and transgressing limits, wherever they are placed, within the space of the 'inner' as much as in the realm of the 'outer'. Ultimately, and no doubt expectedly, the opposition of inner and outer, home and world, breaks down: but we cannot do without the idea of a threshold, as Lacan understood when he placed it at the inaugural moment of the ego.

The spatial trajectory through which Bimala passes, then, does not represent release, and the opposition of *ghar* and *bahir*, home and world, is always purely notional. If the *ghar*, or home, can be spatially configured in both novel and film, the *bahir*, or outside, is a floating signifier with no fixed location. Ray, discussing this film with Andrew Robinson, recalled a story related by Tagore's sister-in-law Jnanadanandini. Her husband Satyendranath, wishing to introduce her to his friend Manomohan Ghose prior to her emergence from the *andarmahal*, could find no way of doing this other than to bring his friend secretly into his bedroom at night, so that he might converse with his wife on their marital bed, within the enclosed space of the mosquito net. No conversation ensued, and after a period of tongue-tied silence Satyendranath escorted his friend from the room, satisfied at having made a symbolic point.[16] This extraordinary incident (and Ray's recalling of it) demonstrates the perceived fluidity of the category of the 'outer', which is constituted as much by the male gaze as by a social or physical location. If Ray's film produces, through Bimala's journey from the *andarmahal* to the *baithak-khana*, a visual emblem of the passage from inner to outer, it also produces, with a deeper sense of shock, an image of the entry of outer into inner: Sandip waiting in the sitting-room to 'receive' the married couple. That room itself, permitting entry to Sandip from without, and free of prohibition to Bimala from within, is an intermediate space, 'of ambiguous species mingling inside and outside' as Sandip remarks in the novel. Bimala is never released into the wider sphere of the 'world', since she never leaves the house: she attends no assemblies, visits no tenants, meets no British officials. The purpose of her daily visits to the sitting-room is to meet Sandip; but the room itself is not wholly beyond the regulatory control of the *andarmahal*, since one day Sandip's entry is barred by an officious servant posted by Bimala's sister-in-law. It is in this dangerous, liminal space *between* home and world that the two conduct their relationship.

If Bimala's transition from innocence to experience is governed by a desire that always returns to the self, the two male protagonists, too, make her a project of the ego. Nikhilesh's love, a novel emotion that appears to inaugurate a new phase of cultural sensibility, seeks to remake Bimala both as Galatean model (the analogy is used in the novel) and as universal exemplar. Sandip's amoral passion openly enlists her in the cause of self-love; as sexually desired object, she reflects back to him, like the reborn nation, his dream of power. In the specular dynamics of this circuit of projection and return, the distinction of inner and outer may appear to collapse. Yet in both novel and film, the represented experiences of space, distance and boundary are crucial. It is in and through space, in the imagined distance between the desiring self and the desired other, in the crossing of a limit that can never be left behind, that the individual subject realises its profound, insurmountable loneliness. Nikhilesh carries this loneliness into the bedroom he had shared with Bimala, inexpressibly moved by the physical signs of her body in its absence: her comb, her hairpins, her slippers. And at the end of the novel, looking out through the window at a desolate landscape in which she had once seen the nation as 'a woman like myself, standing expectant', Bimala realises the impossibility of escape into that 'outside'. It is through the careful tracing of these spatial trajectories, through the material witness of location and movement, that the human individual is realised in terms of the unavoidable and painful self-separation of bodies.

In its confusion of the realms of the private and the public, the domestic and the political, *The Home and the World* may seem to point to yet another kind of boundary-crossing. Partha Chatterjee placed the distinction of inner and outer at the heart of early nationalist discourse, dividing the world of the colonised into two realms, the material and the spiritual. 'The material is the domain of the "outside", of the economy and of statecraft, of science and technology…the spiritual, on the other hand, is an "inner" domain bearing the "essential" marks of cultural identity.' Over time, Chatterjee argues, this inner world of 'language or religion or the elements of personal and family life' is increasingly made the vehicle of colonial difference, its familial, personal and spiritual aspects actively guarded against the touch of the coloniser. In the outer domain of the state, however, nationalism sought to erase the marks of cultural difference in order to share, and ultimately to take over, the 'modern regime of power'.[17]

I have argued elsewhere that Bimala's relationship with Sandip, driven by his own corrupt version of a nationalist ideology, confuses inner with outer, and that by drawing the spiritual model of Hindu womanhood out of the inner realm of cultural practice into the outer world of political struggle, she risks its corruption and distortion.[18] I am no longer sure that this is true, nor that Chatterjee's distinction holds. Rather, it seems to me that in the project of colonial modernity, especially the social reform movements of the nineteenth century (including the taking of women out of seclusion), 'language or religion or the elements of personal and family life' were distinctively inscribed by the marks of 'external' change. Conversely, political action never hesitated to mobilise images and ideas from the realm of religious or cultural practice; the ideology of the nation always drew upon the vocabulary of the sacred. The dangerous liaisons of *The Home and the World* indicate Tagore's own discomfort with the ease of these transitions. The novel is not a conservative work, but it is certainly a deeply unhappy one. Bimala's sentimental education leads her from a traditional ideal of womanhood to a state of radical incompleteness where the models she seeks have disintegrated, leaving her in the confusion and uncertainty that Tagore saw as characteristic of modernity.

Ray's decision to film this work may be seen a culturally belated venture, and indeed the film's slow pace, its rich formal compositions of scene and frame, its glowing, sombre colours and visual excess, may seem to confirm a quality of memorialisation, rather than representation *per se*. As viewers, I have suggested, we are drawn particularly to surfaces and textures: Nikhilesh and Bimala, sitting on richly upholstered chairs to converse with Sandip as though it were a strange marital duty, are not so much individuals as figures in a tapestry. It is as though Ray in 1984, more than twenty years after his penetration of aristocratic and bourgeois interiors in films like *Jalsaghar* (The Music Room, 1958), *Monihara* (in *Teen Kanya* (Three Daughters, 1961)) and *Charulata* (The Lonely Wife, 1964), was now content to recall the experience of viewing, allowing the cinematic screen to acquire the aura of a museum piece. It is in this context that we may remind ourselves of another threshold experience. In a lecture given in 1967, Michel Foucault recalled Gaston Bachelard's phenomenological celebration of spaces, both interior and exterior, to propose his own category of 'other spaces', or heterotopias. The heterotopia is a site of contradiction, a place that runs counter to the places where we normally live and work, and is therefore socially construed as other, like the cemetery or the prison. One such heterotopia, Foucault says, is the cinema theatre, precisely because it is constructed out of a set of superimpositions, and also because it is in some sense a heterochronia, admitting us into another time just as it is sited as another place:

> The heterotopia is capable of juxtaposing in a single real place several spaces, several sites that are in themselves incompatible. Thus it is that the theater brings onto the rectangle of the stage, one after the other, a whole series of places that are foreign to one another; thus it is that the cinema is a very odd rectangular room, at the end of which, on a two-dimensional screen, one sees the projection of a three-dimensional space.[19]

The Home and the World, like its predecessors, is a film made to be viewed in the cinema theatre where, in darkness, silence and anonymity, we can allow ourselves to be drawn into the recessive depths of the screen and its glowing surface, as to a limit that is also a window. From within the prison of interiority, we are seduced by the power of the gaze into a liminal transaction with the figures of our fantasies. Nothing could be further from the postmodern experience of viewing these films on DVD through a television screen or computer monitor, assailed throughout by interruption, conversation, noise. *The Home and the World*, in its curiously static, formal, and auratic use of the language of cinema, seems to wish to preserve against the odds those older conditions of viewing; indeed, to impose them as conditions rather than accidents. In so doing, it appears to quote or cite the experience of cinema as the prime agent of our cultural modernity, and to make us conscious of the light-filled surface of the screen – like the light-filled corridor into which Bimala emerges – as the threshold of a newly visible world.

Notes

1 Ravi Vasudevan, 'Nationhood, Authenticity and Realism in Indian Cinema: The Double-Take of Modernism in Ray', in Moinak Biswas, ed., *Apu and After: Revisiting Ray's Cinema* (London: Seagull Books, 2006), 80–115 (101).

2 Rassundari Debi, *Amar jiban* (My Life), in N. Jana et al., eds, *Atmakatha* (Autobiographies), 5 vols (Kolkata: Ananya Prakashan, 1981–86), 1 (1981): 1–81 (33). On Rassundari, see also Tanika Sarkar, *Words to Win: The Making of 'Amar Jiban': A Modern Autobiography* (New Delhi: Kali for Women, 1999).

3 Swati Chattopadhyay, *Representing Calcutta: Modernity, Nationalism and the Colonial Uncanny* (London: Routledge, 2005), 157.

4 Abanindranath Tagore, *Apan Katha* (My Story) (Kolkata: Ananda Publishers, 2005), 25–6.

5 Rabindranath Tagore, *Ghare Baire* (Kolkata: Vishva Bharati, 1994), 34. My translation.

6 For a fuller discussion, see Supriya Chaudhuri, 'A Sentimental Education: Love and Marriage in *The Home and the World*', in P. K. Datta, ed., *Rabindranath Tagore's 'The Home and the World': A Critical Companion* (Delhi: Permanent Black, 2003), 45–65.

7 Rainer Maria Rilke, 'The Fourth Elegy', in *Duino Elegies*, ed. and trans. J. B. Leishman and Stephen Spender (London: Hogarth Press, 1963), 48–53 (48): 'Treten Liebende/ nicht immerfort an Ränder, eins im andern'.

8 See E. M. Forster, *Abinger Harvest* (London: Andre Deutsch, 1996), 367, and Georg Lukács, 'Tagore's Gandhi Novel', in *Reviews and Articles for Die Rote Fahne*, trans. Peter Palmer (London: Merlin Press, 1983), 8–11 (9–11).

9 Notably the presidential address delivered to the Pabna Pradeshik Sammilani in February 1907, published in *Prabasi*, Phalgun 1314; 'Byadhi o Pratikar', *Prabasi*, Shravan 1314; 'Path o Patheya', *Bangadarshan*, Jyaishtha 1315; 'Samasya', *Prabasi*, Asharh 1315; 'Sadupay', *Prabasi*, Shravan 1315; and 'Deshahit', *Bangadarshan*, Ashvin 1315 (i.e. between February 1907 and September–October 1908).

10 Ranajit Guha, *Dominance without Hegemony: History and Power in Colonial India* (Cambridge, Mass: Harvard University Press, 1997), 109.

11 See Laura Mulvey, 'Visual Pleasure and Narrative Cinema', *Screen* 16, no. 3 (1975): 6–18.

12 See Rabindranath Tagore, *Ghare Baire*, 73. Tanika Sarkar, in 'Many Faces of Love: Country, Woman and God in *The Home and the World*', in Datta, ed., *A Critical Companion*, 27–44, observes that 'the transgressive eroticising of the nationalistic impulse was perhaps the most disturbing aspect of the novel for contemporary Bengalis' (35).

13 Jacques Lacan, 'The Mirror Stage as Formative of the Function of the *I*', in *Écrits: A Selection*, trans. Alan Sheridan (London: Routledge, 1989), 1–8 (3).

14 Ibid., 5.

15 Kaja Silverman, *The Threshold of the Visible World* (New York: Routledge, 1996), 3–11 and passim.

16 See Indira Debi Chaudhurani, ed., *Puratani* (Kolkata: Indian Associated Publishing Company, 1957) and Andrew Robinson, *Satyajit Ray: The Inner Eye* (Delhi: Oxford University Press 2004), 268.

17 Partha Chatterjee, *The Nation and Its Fragments: Colonial and Postcolonial Histories* (Delhi: Oxford University Press, 1994), 6 and 26.

18 See my article in Datta, ed., *A Critical Companion*, 63–4.

19 Michel Foucault, 'Of Other Spaces', trans. Jay Miskowiec, *Diacritics* 16, no. 1 (1986): 22–7 (25); originally published in French as 'Des espaces autres: Une conférence inédite de Michel Foucault', *Architecture-Mouvement-Continuité* (October 1984): 46–49. Online: http://foucault.info/documents/heteroTopia/foucault.heteroTopia.en.html (accessed 26 June 2010).

Chapter Seven

WRITING THROUGH OSMOTIC BORDERS: BOUNDARIES, LIMINALITY AND LANGUAGE IN MEHMET YASHIN'S POETICS

Rosita D'Amora

In the poem *Savaş Zamanı* (Wartime) the Turkish Cypriot author Mehmet Yashin's (Yaşın) writing self confesses: 'I was often unsure in which language to shed my tears, / the life I lived wasn't foreign, but one of translation – / my mother-tongue one thing, my motherland another, / and I, again, altogether different…'[1] Some of the most important threads of Yashin's poetics intersect here in these lines. Mehmet Yashin was born in Nicosia in 1958, when Cyprus was still a politically undivided territory under British colonial rule, but already torn by fierce intercommunal conflicts between the two major ethnic groups populating the island, the Greeks and the Turks. His family is of Turkish origins and Turkish is his mother tongue – the language he learned before any other in what, in another poem entitled *Bir Hayalet* (A Ghost), he describes as the 'polyglot house, now silenced'[2] that he was raised in. And this language still remains the main means of his literary writing. Yet, throughout Yashin's oeuvre, both in his literary works and in his essays,[3] it is possible to trace a constant hesitation about the language he finds more appropriate to resort to in order to express himself, even when his poetical urge leads him to disclose his most intimate sorrows. Furthermore, at times, the author blatantly admits that his mother tongue does not suffice, and, in doing so, he openly reveals the precarious ability of a mother tongue to encompass and convey multiple identities and different cultural belongings, and, conversely, the impossibility of any mother tongue to coincide with, or be kept within, the bounds of the often arbitrary national borders of its 'motherland'. Hence his compelling need to trespass fictitious linguistic frontiers questioning the idea as well as the definition itself of mother tongue.

The following comment by Yashin suggests a deeper complexity to what is usually perceived as a natural, familiar correlation between languages and national identities (mother tongue/motherland), adding to it a degree of estrangement, a 'step-ness' (step-mothertongue):

> Mothertongue is relative, multiple, and shifting, and what I would like to propose is that there is a 'step' quality latent in it… Language is a step-mother by its very nature. Individuals are born into languages they have not themselves created and which cannot express human beings totally. Particularly writing-language as the basic element of literature, does not come to life from a natural mother, but is precisely geared to create the sense of a 'mother' in the context of fictionalised national histories. The '*step*-tongues', which have enforced themselves as so-called '*mother*tongues', partly through literary works, on particular communities, are the primary forces that attach individuals to a modern sense of national belonging, re-creating an imaginary notion of 'us'.[4]

Here, Yashin takes a firm stand especially against Cyprus's most recent history where linguistic identities have increasingly become ethnically identified and politically charged. In the same poem, 'Wartime', with a few verses of pregnant clarity, the poet reminds us how in a conflict-zone such as Cyprus, divided between two imported and contrasting nationalisms, crossed by contested political boundaries, demarcated by tangible divides, any linguistic choice inevitably involves unambiguous political consequences. Thinking of his childhood he remembers: 'Turkish was dangerous, must not be spoken, / and Greek was absolutely forbidden… […] / English remained right in the middle, / a slender paper-knife for cutting schoolbooks, / a tongue to be spoken at certain times / especially with the Greeks!'[5] The resolute indeterminacy of the poet in choosing his language of expression can be seen, therefore, as an extreme act of revolt. If such uncertainty aims to reveal how linguistic boundaries do not necessarily overlap with political ones, such as the *Green Line* that separates north and south Cyprus – the Turkish and the Greek sides – it also allows Yashin to create a parallel interstitial space, an osmotic threshold with multiple, porous entrances and exits that represents the vanishing point of the dividing lines between conflicting national and linguistic identities.

If one understands a threshold in its figurative meaning of 'border', 'limit' but also as 'the line that one crosses in entering' (OED) a place – or in exiting from it – it can be perceived as a crucially functional space even within the fixity of political and cultural divisions imposed by opposing nationalisms. From this perspective, a threshold delimits two other contiguous spaces, on each one of its sides, and implicitly defines them in terms of opposition to each other (outside/inside, inclusion/exclusion, mother tongue/foreign language). At the same time, it is itself a space that enables passage between these two: hence the need to exert a strict control on such passages or to try to obstruct them completely with checkpoints, border control stations, barbed wire, walls. Yet, each passage in either direction inevitably leaves behind traces of often involuntary interactions, also giving thresholds the more engaging dimension of unguarded and utterly contaminated spaces.

There is then no other possible choice left to the poet but to be in constant transit through these liminal spaces, shunning any fixed identification, and to write his verses in-between the two sides of a threshold: 'Then in my poems, the three languages got into a wild tangle.'[6]

The 'Poet of No Country', His Step-mothertongue and the Divided Island

The quest for a more complex and multifaceted linguistic identity influences Yashin's entire writing process pervasively, spurring his language towards a constant search for hybrid zones. This can be traced in the author's biography, but also in Cyprus's long history where language use is situated against a very intricate background and, as we shall see, has represented, in the last decades, a fairly turbulent political issue.

As for Yashin's personal past, interesting reflections upon the problematic yet enriching linguistic legacy bequeathed to him are scattered in many of his poems but can also be found in an autobiographical essay entitled *Üveyanadilim* (My Step-Mothertongue). In this essay, in particular, while examining the different layers of his 'step-mothertongue', the impossibility of disentangling his use of English and Greek from his Turkish and, at the same time, his condition of not being able to express himself properly, either 'as a Greek from Athens', 'an Englishman from London' or 'a Turk from Istanbul', the author confronts, and confronts us with, these questions:

> 'If that's the case, like whom do I speak and write? As a Cypriot Turk from Nicosia? Or as a cosmopolitan Turk who lives in Istanbul, Athens, London? Or rather as a European Turk essentially connected to Istanbul? The answer to all these questions is both yes and no…'[7]

In the attempt to reconstruct his linguistic identity, he harks back to a natural sense of coexistence and merging of multiple linguistic spaces in his own family. Turkish itself was spoken in slightly different ways by the various members of his family. Yashin, for instance, recalls from his childhood memories how his father, known as the 'Cypriot poet', was actually brought up in Istanbul, and how the people of the literary circle he was part of, as well as his language, 'his style, his way of speech, his slang, his vocabulary', were also mostly from Istanbul.[8] The Turkish of his mother, instead, was a pure, modern Turkish (*öz Türkçe*) – the distilled product of Mustafa Kemal Atatürk's language reform also imported from mainland Turkey – as was at that time regarded appropriate for a well-educated woman with an urban upbringing. Her language was consciously selective and she would never confuse her Turkish with the English she learned at school, which was perceived by her generation as the language of the colonisers, or the Greek Cypriot dialect (*Kypriaka*) which, in the opinion of the Cypriot Turkish urban elite, had an intrinsic provincial nature. On the contrary, his beloved great aunt Süreyya who brought him up had no such intellectual anxieties. In a poem entitled *Teyzedil* (translated into English as 'Aunt-ology', but literally meaning 'Aunt-tongue') written in her memory, he describes her versatility as follows: 'In the English era, the widow lady teacher / was Süreyya at home and Judith to all others, / Flax-haired Lâmia to her friends [...] / And then, the Turks came. / She was now Judith at home and Süreyya outside'.[9] With the same ease with which she constantly adapted to the many names given to her, she would also use a permeable Turkish open to all sorts of influences. Yashin remembers the fluidity of her language accepting Ottoman Turkish 'openly', Greek and English 'indirectly' and Arabic and Latin 'secretly',[10] as well as her natural tendency to resort to each one of these languages according to the different circumstances. And with the same amazement he must have felt as a child, he recalls in verses her ability 'to read the Koran in Arabic for the dead; / to make olive-magic in Latin, / correct my Turkish in red'.[11]

All these elements came together in Yashin's 'step-mothertongue': the 'pure Turkish' of his mother, the Turkish his father used in order to write his nationalistic poems, the Istanbul variety he spoke, and alongside them the knowledge that a language could be assumed as a distinctive mark of identity and used on this basis to legitimise national and political boundaries. On the other hand, it is his 'Aunt-tongue', the almost unaware and unceasing shifting from one language to another of the poet's 'dear old aunt' Süreyya, that seems to have encouraged him to position his language use on the porous thresholds of contiguous linguistic spaces and retrace such spaces in the history of his island – the entire island, regardless of its current political divisions.

Indeed, for centuries, language contact has been 'the rule rather than an exception' in Cyprus.[12] Being strategically located at the crossroads of Europe, Asia, and Africa, succession or coexistence of different communities and cultures has been long inscribed in the island's history. Since ancient times, Cyprus has been annexed by every ruling empire in the region. It was conquered by the Greeks, Phoenicians, Egyptians, Persians, Romans, Byzantines, Lusignans and Venetians, until 1571 when the Ottomans gained control. It was during the three centuries (1571–1878) of Ottoman rule that the island acquired its current ethnic character. After the Ottoman conquest, the local population, at the time predominantly composed of Orthodox Greeks, was enriched by the settlement of a community of Muslim Turks who came to represent approximately 20% of the inhabitants of the island. Within the framework of the Ottoman *millet* system, which under the overall control of the Ottoman state granted non-Muslim religious groups considerable autonomy to regulate their internal affairs, the two communities lived side by side peacefully, maintaining their religious, cultural and linguistic differences, but also sharing a variety of spaces and experiences.[13] It was only from the first half of the nineteenth century, with the increasing spread on the island of a Greek national consciousness imported directly from mainland Greece – Greece obtained its independence from the Ottoman Empire in 1832 – that their coexistence began to show the first signs of what would later became an unbridgeable rift. The period of British rule on the island (1878–1960)[14] led to a further reinforcement of Greek Cypriot national claims that progressively grew into an anti-colonial struggle and prompted, at the same time, analogous feelings among the Turkish Cypriot community. On the one hand, Greek Cypriots were advocating union (*enosis*) with 'mother Greece', while on the other hand, Turkish Cypriots were closely following the nation-building process in Turkey. Fearing for their survival as a minority in Cyprus if it unified with Greece, the Turkish Cypriots eventually countered the politics of *enosis* with a request for *taksim*, or partition of the island between the two groups. In the imagery of Turkish Cypriot nationalism, 'Turkey became the idealised romantic motherland that would protect 'the lonely children', who perceived themselves as 'the helpless remains' of the collapsed Ottoman Empire'.[15]

The stage had been set for the kindling of an intercommunal conflict of great intensity that in the end resulted in the military occupation of the Northern part of the island by the Turkish army in 1974 and the subsequent unilateral proclamation, in 1983, of the Turkish Republic of Northern Cyprus, which has been, so far, internationally recognised only by Turkey.

Borders Between Countries, Thresholds Between Languages

As the Greek Cypriots and the Turkish Cypriots began to perceive themselves as two distinct groups whose respective national identities drew their roots from outside the island, from the motherlands' soil, the demarcation between their languages was also given a new sharp emphasis and used as a strong reassertion of boundaries.[16] In particular, in locating their sense of national belonging in their respective nation-states, they chose to enshrine their linguistic differences in the acceptance of their motherlands' newborn national languages, which were increasingly superimposed on the local varieties of Greek (*Kypriaka*) and Turkish (*Kıbrıs Türkçesi*) traditionally used on the island.[17] Paradoxically enough, the imported national idioms were the recent and artificial products of large scale linguistic engineering campaigns which, despite using different strategies, intended in both Turkey and Greece to engender a national consciousness based on the recognition and institutional promotion of one 'pure' language that could further secure the borders of the two new states. The 'Language revolution' (*Dil devrimi*) launched by Atatürk in Turkey in the early 1930s, for instance, aimed to uproot from Ottoman the numerous Arabic and Persian borrowings and grammatical features, regardless of the fact that they had long been part of this language, and replace them with often unknown or consciously manufactured 'pure' Turkish words. In the context of the new republican, secular state these 'foreign' words had became symbols of a decadent Ottoman past and antiquated Islamic traditions that had to be completely erased. Conversely, in Greece, where the 'language question' (*glossikó zìtima*) had been debated since the middle of the eighteenth century and was mainly concerned with the controversy about which of the varieties of Greek should be used as a written language, the advocates of the most 'purifying' tendencies persistently opposed the use of the numerous Ottoman Turkish loanwords that were perceived, in this case, to be mere lexical traces of the Dark Ages of the long Ottoman rule.[18]

These new languages, despite their undeniable initial 'precariousness',[19] immediately assumed strong ideological connotations in the context of the two incipient nationalisms in Cyprus as well. In this way, the two major linguistic spaces of the island, which, for centuries, though maintaining their distinctiveness, had been in constant contact, began gradually to be perceived and used as separate and irreconcilable. The Turkish Cypriot elite, for example, had been attracted by the language reform in Turkey since its very beginning and actively encouraged its adoption on the island. Even though this adoption did not seem to have a large impact on the majority of Turkish Cypriots in the years to follow, by the 1950s, as Turkish Cypriot nationalism increasingly became a separatist ideology fostering a sense of complete identification with the motherland, a systematic programme of linguistic homogenisation was enforced. One of the most significant examples of this attitude was the *Citizen, speak Turkish!* campaign organised in 1958 by the Turkish Cypriot nationalist leadership that, besides promoting educational programmes aiming to teach standard Turkish, imposed fines on anyone speaking Greek or even using Greek words.[20] Despite similar attempts to deny the historical development of Turkish and Greek as contiguous languages by abruptly interrupting the dialectical interactions between them, doors of access to non-national linguistic contact zones could not easily be bolted and interactions still continued. Such interactions, moreover, besides being embedded in both spoken languages, could additionally draw on a semi-official but long-established literary tradition.

In his essay 'Introducing Step-Mothertongue', Yashin presents as an 'anomaly' the fact that in the latter half of the twentieth century 'there has been limited contact between Turkish and Greek languages and literatures'.[21] In this way he offers two remarkable examples of literary productions that cannot be ascribed to only one community. Although not directly related to the most recent linguistic developments in Cyprus, a significant episode of osmotic contact between Turkish and Greek is historically represented by the hybrid language usually referred to as *Karamanlıca* in Turkish and *Karamanlidika* in Greek. This was a form of spoken Turkish written in the Greek alphabet and used for many centuries as an unofficial language by Turkish speaking Orthodox Greeks living in central Anatolia, which eventually fell into disuse by the early 1930s, when most of the members of this community were re-settled in Greece as a result of the exchange of population that took place between Greece and Turkey in 1923.[22] Alongside this complete merging of the spoken form of one language into the 'alphabetical contours' of the other, another important example of contamination is to be found in Cyprus and is represented by a group of Turkish Cypriot folk poets (*poetarides*) who use as their literary language the Greek dialect of the island, constantly interweaving it with Turkish words and expressions or loanwords of French, Italian, and Arabic origin.[23]

Significantly enough, in both cases, the contiguity and mingling of Turkish and Greek linguistic and cultural elements can be traced in literary traditions lying outside the margins of the clear sense of belonging and identification that each community has elaborated in more recent times, as well as outside their respective official and canonised literary discourses. Yet, these seem to be the traditions that inspire Yashin's works more, and it is along these same margins that it is possible to locate the language he recreates with his writing. This is a language whose supporting structure is represented by standard Turkish but that by turns switches with ease from Cypriot Turkish to modern Greek and English, recovering the semantic riches of Ottoman Turkish and at times also proposing, as in his second novel *Sınırdışı Saatler* (Deportation Hours),[24] a revived contemporary version of *Karamanlıca* with the aim of rejoining all these languages to a pre-modern and pre-national permeability. Through the use of this language, Yashin aims to blur univocal representations of his island, disclosing its rich history and re-opening obstructed passages of mutual exchange. Even though, since his early youth, he has spent prolonged periods of time abroad, mostly living between Turkey and England, Cyprus remains the epicentre of his poetic universe as well as his main source of inspiration. His search for a complex language therefore couples with the main trajectories of his poetry that run parallel to the island's troubled history. Cyprus becomes both a concrete and an abstract space, a place the author is constantly going back to, both in person and through his writing, in order to explore his memories, visit his house, return to his home.

Hovering on the Threshold

'They wrote ΕΛΛΑΔΑ[25] on our door while we slept / and when we opened our eyes / we found ourselves in Greece!'[26] These initial lines of the poem *Bir Sabah Yunanistan'da* (One Morning in Greece) condense a multiple violation, unknown hands writing in a foreign alphabet the name of the nation of the Other on the threshold – the public, yet private, surface of the door to the family house. The family is asleep, eyes are closed, and when they reopen the house is in another country and the idea of home is irretrievably dislocated elsewhere. The house has suddenly lost its lights and sounds, as well as the possibility of access to the outside world, now potentially hostile: 'Afraid to turn on the lights / and even to talk, / we now live like guests in our own house. / And we can't even go out in our garden / without asking the landlord's permission!'[27] But the outside world can still enter the house, finding his way in through a window that filters the sad glancing of some trees. Alongside the displacement of the home, identity itself is questioned: 'Through the window they stare at me, / the troubled trees: / Either we are not who we are / or our house is not ours.'[28]

This poem contains one of the most recurrent themes that pervade Yashin's poetry, where the conflicts lacerating Cyprus are mostly recounted with intense autobiographical accents often revolving around the representation of the poet's house. This house, that in this poem seems almost empty, is elsewhere described in great detail with an utterly uncomplicated yet eloquent language as the house 'taken captive in every war, shot at, set alight, looted of dowries in Ottoman chests', filled by a multitude of dusty, inert objects and lifeless family pictures in frames.[29] At the same time, this house cannot be exactly located outside the poet's memories and the poet himself seems unable to enter into it: 'Only as a ghost can I now return to my home / emerging from blurred mirror…'[30] Access is granted by poetry alone: 'Nothing but poetry can bring me back'.[31] In 'One Morning in Greece', instead, the impactful use of another language, through the mere insertion of an initial capitalised word, adds a dramatic tangible dimension to the representation of the personal as well as collective sense of loss and dislocation and efficaciously complicates the relation between the poet and the reader.

The lines from the poem 'Wartime' quoted at the beginning of this essay convey the image of a hesitant poet, a poet unable to identify himself with the national symbols around him and trying to negotiate the precarious edges of concurrent linguistic spaces. In 'One Morning in Greece', however, the poet clearly shows us how even the use of a single word, ΕΛΛΑΔΑ, standing as an epigraph at the beginning of the poem but far from being an indictment against those who are on the other side, reveals the immense evocative force that contamination can engender. The juxtaposition allows the poet to articulate his multiple identities outside the singularity of one language, and forces the reader to a halt too, a little hesitant pause, as when crossing the threshold to enter a place never before visited.

Notes

1 The poem, which was composed in 1991, was originally published in the poetry collection *Sözverici Koltuğu* (The ChairMan, 1993). For the English translation see Mehmet Yashin, *Don't go back to Kyrenia*, trans. Taner Baybars (London: Middlesex University Press, 2001), 25, lines 12–15. For Yashin's collected poems see Mehmet Yashin, *Toplu Şiirler (1977–2002)* (Istanbul: Everest Yayınları, 2007).

2 This poem, written in 1997, is included in the poetry collection *Hayal Tamiri* (To Repair a Daydream, 1998). For the English translation see Yashin, *Don't go back*, 3, line 7.

3 Although he is manly known as a poet – since the publication in 1984 of his first acclaimed poetry collection *Sevgilim Ölü Asker* (My Love the Dead Soldier), he has published another seven poetry collections – Mehmet Yashin has also published two novels, *Soydaşınız Balık Burcu* (Your Kinsman Pisces, 1994) and *Sınırdışı Saatler* (Deportation Hours, 2003), as well as several essays, most of which have been recently collected in the volume *Toplu Yazılar (1978–2005)* (Istanbul: Everest Yayınları, 2007).

4 Mehmet Yashin, 'Introducing Step-Mothertongue', in Mehmet Yashin, ed., *Step-mothertongue: From Nationalism to Multiculturalism: Literatures of Cyprus, Greece and Turkey* (London: Middlesex University Press, 2000), 1–21 (1–2).

5 Yashin, *Don't go back*, 25, lines 3–4, 8–11.

6 Ibid., line 20.

7 Yashin, *Üveyanadilim* (My Step-Mothertongue), in *Toplu Yazılar*, 74–79 (75). The translation is mine.

8 Ibid. Mehmet Yashin's father is the poet Özker Yaşın (1932-), considered among the major representatives of a literature that emerged in Cyprus in the 1950s and thematically engaged almost exclusively with the Greek-Turkish conflicts on the island and the related nationalistic issues.

9 This poem, written in 1995, is part of the poetry collection *Işık-Merdiven* (Ladder of Light, 1986). For the English translation see Yashin, *Don't go back*, 67, lines 5–7, 14–15.

10 Yashin, *Üveyanadilim* (My Step-Mothertongue), 76.

11 Yashin, *Don't go back*, 69, lines 11–13.

12 Dionysis Goutsos and Marilena Karyolemou, 'Introduction' to *International Journal of the Sociology of Language* 168 (2004): 1–17 (2).

13 Niyazi Kizilyürek and Sylvaine Gautier-Kizilyürek, 'The Politics of Identity in the Turkish Cypriot Community and the Language Question', *International Journal of the Sociology of Language* 168 (2004): 37–54 (39–40).

14 In 1878 the Ottoman empire ceded the administration of Cyprus to the British Empire, which in 1914 would annex the island in consequence of the outbreak of World War I and the entry of the Ottomans on the side of the Central Powers. With the Treaty of Lausanne (1923) the newborn Republic of Turkey relinquished its rights on Cyprus and in 1925 the island formally became a British Crown colony, which it remained until independence was granted in 1960.

15 Kizilyürek and Gautier-Kizilyürek, 'The Politics of Identity', 41.

16 For the centrality of languages in the making of nationalism, besides the seminal work of Benedict Anderson, *Imagined Communities: Reflections on the Origin and Spread of Nationalism* (London: Verso, 1983), see also Paul Gubbins and Mike Holt, eds, *Beyond Boundaries: Language and Identity in Contemporary Europe* (Clevedon, England: Multilingual Matters, 2002) and Stephen Barbour and Cathie Carmichael, eds, *Language and Nationalism in Europe* (Oxford: Oxford University Press, 2000). In this last volume, see especially Peter Trudgill, 'Greece and European Turkey: From Religious to Linguistic Identity', 240–63.

17 On the complex and ever-changing relations between standard and local varieties of Turkish and Greek, as well as the perception of them as higher- or lower-register languages and their consequent use in specific domains, see Goutsos and Karyolemou, 'Introduction', Kizilyürek and Gautier-Kizilyürek, 'The Politics of Identity', and Dimitra Karoulla-Vrikki, 'Language and Ethnicity in Cyprus under the British: A Linkage of Heightened Salience', *International Journal of the Sociology of Language* 168 (2004): 19–36.

18 Both linguistic questions have received much scholarly attention. On the Turkish Language Reform see in particular the comprehensive study by Geoffrey Lewis, *The Turkish Language Reform: A Catastrophic Success* (Oxford: Oxford University Press, 1999); for a recent analysis of the Greek language question within the context of nation-building and identity formation see Peter Mackridge, *Language and National Identity in Greece 1766–1976* (Oxford: Oxford University Press, 2009).

19 The 'precarious' familiarity with the new Turkish language, for example, is effectively described in the following anecdote. In autumn 1934, at a banquet in honour of the Swedish Crown Prince and Princess, Mustafa Kemal Atatürk gave a speech, originally written in Ottoman but 'translated' for the occasion in *öz Türkçe* (pure Turkish), which was so crammed with outlandish neologisms that Atatürk, famous for his rhetorical skills, delivered it 'with the awkwardness of schoolchildren who have just begun to read'. See Lewis, *The Turkish Language Reform*, 56.

20 Kizilyürek and Gautier-Kizilyürek, 'The Politics of Identity', 41. A similar campaign with the same name was carried out in Turkey in the first decades of the Turkish Republic and aimed to put pressure on non-Turkish speakers to speak Turkish in public, in order to create a more homogeneous nation-state. See Marcus A. Templar, 'Tasting the Bitter *Pekmez*: Causes of Turkey's Instability', *Journal of Global Change and Governance* 1, no. 2 (2008): 2, 12. Online: http://dga.rutgers.edu/JGCG/vol_I_2.html (accessed 26 June 2010).

21 Yashin, 'Introducing Step-Mothertongue', 1.

22 Ibid., 2, n. 2. For the history and a bibliographical survey of works in Turkish language written using Greek letters see the work by Sévérien Salaville and Eugéne Dalеggio, *Karamanlidika: bibliographie analytique d'ouvrages en langue turque imprimés en caractères grecs*, 3 vols (Athens: Institut français d'Athènes, 1958–1974), and the subsequent additions by Evangelia Balta, *Karamanlidika Additions: bibliographie analytique (1584–1900)* (Athens: Centre d'Études d'Asie Mineure, 1987), *Karamanlidika XXe siècle: bibliographie analytique* (Athens: Centre d'Études d'Asie Mineure, 1987), *Karamanlidika Nouvelles additions et compléments: bibliographie analytique* (Athens: Centre d'Études d'Asie Mineure, 1997).

23 Yashin, 'Introducing Step-Mothertongue', 5–7.

24 The novel tells, through a series of 'tales', the surreal journey of a man, Misail Oskarus, in a wandering search for his own identity, his homeland, his language, and his writer,

Mehmet Yashin. This search takes place in a blurred buffer zone, a limbo populated by the liminal beings who have been deported here and are kept in a timeless wait, having been prevented from expressing themselves in the undefined 'upper world'. Many phrases and entire sections of this novel, even though in modern Turkish, are written with Greek letters that the author himself has adapted to the phonetic peculiarities of Turkish.

25 ELLADA (Greece).

26 This poem was originally published in the poetry collection *Pathos* (1990). For the English translation see Yashin, *Don't go back*, 11, lines 1–3.

27 Ibid., lines 5–8.

28 Ibid., lines 11–14.

29 These lines are from the poem *Ölü Ev* (Dead House, 1988), originally published in the poetry collection *Sözverici Koltuğu* (The ChairMan, 1993). For the English translation see Yashin, *Don't go back*, 123.

30 From the abovementioned poem 'A Ghost', see Yashin, *Don't go back*, 3, lines 1–2.

31 Ibid., 124.

Chapter Eight

DANCING AND ROMANCING: THE OBSTACLE OF THE BEACH AND THE THRESHOLD OF THE PAST

Jonathan Lamb

> *I ask myself what past historians of the castaway state have done – whether in despair they have not begun to make up lies.*[1]

Keith Thomas's latest book, *The Ends of Life*, ends with a couplet taken from Dryden's Horace:

> Not Heav'n itself upon the past has pow'r,
> But what has been has been, and I have had my hour.[2]

In her review of his book Hilary Mantel, winner of this year's Man Booker Prize for a splendid historical novel based on the life of Thomas Cromwell, had this to say about his quotation:

> As a comment on a career, this is graceful; as comment on the discipline to which Thomas has devoted himself, it is not quite true. Historians can do what heaven cannot: for all practical purposes they can change the past behind them… We understand the past in the light of evidence we select… It is not only the voiceless workers of England who have been subject to what E. P. Thompson famously called 'the enormous condescension of posterity;' it is our ancestors as a class, made fodder for theories.[3]

When someone fresh from inventing a fiction based on history makes this sort of remark it is interesting to probe it. Does Mantel silently admit there was a time before theories when historical evidence was proof against selection and ancestors immune to the condescension of their posterity; an era when history was as self-evident and inevitable as Thomas suggests? Is changing the past now inescapable in the face of the myriad facts lodged in the archive – a subterfuge practised by those who edit their way to a flattering picture of the present, or an act of piety enjoined on those who would prefer not to patronise the dead? Or does she mean that the fairest way to alter a past which is going to be altered anyway is not to manipulate the facts but to imagine them? Is fictionalised history better than selected evidence because it is less dishonest, or because it is more vivid, shapely and probable; and maybe more true? In her conversation with Henry Tilney about history and historical novels in *Northanger Abbey*, Catherine Morland certainly thought so. I want to test some of these queries first of all in a time and space where theoretical history met its first great challenge, and what it hoped would be its vindication, namely the South Seas. And then I mean to bring the discussion home, or almost home, again by examining Samuel Johnson's sole attempt at ethnographical history, his *Journey to the Western Isles of Scotland.* I want to identify how individual stories about crossing the beach, that strange limit identified by Greg Dening not simply as the dividing line between the sea and the land – the place where the visitor and the indigene meet – but also as the observance of naval customs, the structure of Tahitian temples, the litter of no-man's land and, I would suggest, a Highland track. The beach is what costs those who traverse it a change or metamorphosis not easily recorded as factual testimony.

In the mid-eighteenth century European navigators found islands not known by them to have existed, places where modes of production and reproduction were so novel that even a man as literal-minded as James Cook thought he might have stumbled across the terrestrial paradise. In places such as Tahiti and Hawai'i men and women, he observed, went naked without shame, had sex in the open, and found their bread not in the sweat of their brows but in the branches of trees. Bougainville's report of Tahiti gave Diderot the idea for one the subtlest Enlightenment speculations on sexuality and its relation to social structures. Diderot suggested that the Pacific was an 'ocean of fantasy', a place where all experiences appeared to have been imagined, either because they were so incomparably exotic, out of time, and were entered like a dream, or because the civilised mind stands in need of alibis for its most daring imaginings. Rousseau and the Abbé Coyer had exploited earlier voyages, chiefly Anson's, for reports of uninhabited islands whose lavish supplies of fruit, herbs and fish afforded their discoverers exquisite sensations of pleasure – equal (according to Coyer) to the delights of the most refined palate. Enthusiasts and skeptics alike were fond of comparing these extravagances to the passages of romance. Peter Heylyn had already imagined that *The Faerie Queene* had been situated in the terra incognita, that mysterious cartographical entity one of whose actual fragments, Aotearoa/New Zealand, was illustrated and explained by Sir George Grey with quotations from Spenser's romance. There were giants too, such as the Patagonians who towered over their European visitors, and cannibals almost everywhere, not to mention naked damsels who made lascivious offers of their bodies to Odyssean seamen, all of which earned the genial incredulity of Diderot, Walpole and Voltaire when they invented their fictions of the strange customs of the Southern Hemisphere.

One of the strangest of these was the anonymous *Adventures of Hildebrand Bowman* (1778). The story begins with an actual cannibal event which befell the crew of the *Adventure*'s cutter on Cook's second voyage, when eleven men were killed and partly eaten at Grass Cove, in New Zealand's Queen Charlotte Sound. The fictional twelfth, Bowman, makes his escape and commences a journey through time that corresponds to the aesthetic development of the human senses, culminating in the modern age of Luxo-Volupto whose inhabitants experience 'Touch or Feeling in as exquisite a degree as human nature is capable of supporting without turning pleasure into pain'.[4] *Hildebrand Bowman* is interesting not simply because it emphasises the importance of pleasure in European encounters with strange places and peoples, but more significantly because it unites an idea of history, specifically stadial history's four eras of hunting, herding, farming and commerce, with a narrative of encounters between the hero and societies at different stages of advancement. Despite the violent outset of the story and its deliberate adjustment of aesthetics to levels of production, it is plain the author sees no definite calibration between civility and technology since Luxo Volupto is represented as both sophisticated and corrupt. For him and for others cannibalism is not necessarily a zero degree of savagery, nor do (or did) the events on the beach at Grass Cove accuse the Maori of unequivocal aggression, where it seems the clumsy seizure of Maori property by one of the crew precipitated the violence that ended in a scene which James Burney could never mention except in a whisper. Cook himself refused to punish the perpetrator, a chief called Kahura, because he was not convinced that the blame lay entirely on his side – a decision which cost him (according to Anne Salmond) the respect of his crew, isolating him and leading to the bizarre acts that preceded his death in Hawai'i.

So this blunder on the beach propels two singular narratives, the perpetually imperfect historical account of Cook's demise (explosively rehearsed in the exchanges between Marshall Sahlins and Gananath Obeyesekere in the 1990s), bringing full circle a tale of fatal violence committed on the shore, and the fictional travels of Bowman, which begin and end with questions of taste. That Bowman's fictional history should correspond to stadial or conjectural history is intriguing on two counts: first that it is obviously fictional embroidery of an actual historical event, and second that it offers itself in proper experimental form as eyewitness testimony. With regard to stadial historians Mary Poovey has pointed out, 'What they wanted to describe – the origins of modern society, and especially how "rude" societies became "civilized" – had not been recorded by witnesses.' So they had to fill up the empty spaces in the account with abstractions that were treated by them as real entities, but which were in effect no different from fictions.[5] In order to buttress these abstractions stadialists such as John Millar, as well as anti-stadialists such as Adam Ferguson, were raiding the voyage literature of the mid-century for eyewitness evidence of the truth or fiction of conjecture – in Millar's case, facts that would show human society evolving in a predictable four-part sequence. In his *Observations Concerning the Distinction of Ranks in Society* (1771) he had traced human progress from hunting and gathering to pastoral nomadism, thence to agriculture and finally to *doux commerce*, ending at exactly the same terminus as Bowman but with a very different inflection. While no single witness had access to the whole process, as Bowman claimed to have, merely to momentary encounters such as that which went so badly wrong at Grass Cove, it was possible now to frame a stadial history based on evidence, not conjecture. There was a risk of course that empirical knowledge would disturb the symmetry of what had been conceived, shattering its narrative and convicting it of fiction.

Stadial history was built on the rivalry between two theories concerning the origins of humans. There were those who believed in polygenesis, namely, that inhabitants of different regions were originally quite distinct, growing from a unique stock, and always bearing the same distinguishing features of their race or nation. Thus Lord Kames, a powerful advocate of this position, argued that chance has nothing to do with differences in what he called national character, and that national history was inscribed in this character, not in the development of techniques of production:

> Where the greatest part of a nation is of one character, education and example may extend it over the whole; but the character of that greater part can have no foundation but nature. What resource then have we for explaining the opposite manners of the islanders [of the South Seas], but that they are of different races?[6]

The stadial position was founded on monogenesis, where a single human species acquired wide variations as the factors of soil, climate and geology operated on it; but with the advance of time such transformations were affected by many other supplemental causes, such as material culture, technology, travel, systems of law, education, government, property, relations between the sexes and exchange.

One of the most eminent advocates of monogenesis was the cantankerous Johann Reinhold Forster, the official natural historian on Cook's second voyage to the South Seas (1772–5), who used the laboratory of the Pacific to make the first serious attempts at comparative ethnology. Correctly assuming that the Polynesian islands, stretching from Aotearoa/New Zealand in the west to Rapanui (Easter Island) in the east, had been colonised in a general migration eastwards from Malaysia by a people of the same original culture and language, he had on the *Resolution* an unrivalled view of how variations in environment resulted in changes not only in politics and wealth, but also physique, complexion and temperament: 'Nay, they often produce a material difference in the color, habits, and forms of the human species.'[7] In terms of the Polynesian diaspora, the inhabitants of the Society Islands (Tahiti and its neighboring islands) came out on top, in Forster's opinion, with a climate so pleasant, vegetation so lush and seas so bountiful that there emerged not only an opulent chiefly system of government which defended property rights for everyone, but also distinctive coloring, muscle tone and stature. Near to the bottom came the inhabitants of Dusky Bay, in the south of New Zealand's South Island, who were poor, violent and ill-conditioned; but not so utterly wretched as the non-Polynesians of Tierra del Fuego, a benighted people who represented the bottom of Forster's scale.

Forster's study of Polynesian cultures was very different from Pierre Lafitau's of the Iroquois or Peter Kolb's of the Hottentots, where the focus on a single national object precluded comparative judgements.[8] When Burke said that navigators such as Cook had unrolled the great map of mankind, he was using a cartographical metaphor to make sense of the kind of anthropological history Forster was writing. Here spread out was a history of the human world, proceeding from its most primitive beginnings to its flourishing amidst property, trade and civility, and yet quite detached from European influence. For the first time the early sequences of conjectural history were available for comparative experimental study.[9] The different eras of social development were accessible by ship, and the curious observer could travel back and forth between them, discriminating as minutely as he pleased. However, it soon became clear to Forster that it was not quite so simple. The map of humanity in the Pacific did not reveal an advancing set of coordinates between lines of latitude and stages of development, which is what he first hypothesised. Clearly some nations had done well, and others poorly; and even within one nation, such as the Tahitians, a privileged class (the *arioi*) had thrived while those beneath (whom Forster suspected to be the remains of a vanquished population) were visibly less wealthy and physically smaller and darker. The regular four-part pattern was contradicted not only by examples of primitivism that were clearly derived, not original, but also by degeneration occurring in places of great natural amenity, often alongside manifest proof of its opposite. What is more, Forster was often indebted to brief meetings amidst inauspicious circumstances, hampered sometimes by his own irascible temper, for observations which he had to generalise if they were to make any sense. For example, his visit to Dusky Bay in New Zealand's South Island was made after a hideously uncomfortable voyage in which he was manifesting the first signs of scurvy; and his view of the four people he met there, one of whom had a large wen on her cheek, seemed to coincide with his opinion of the chaotic state of the vegetation which had lowered, he said, his opinion of the country.[10] From our point of view it is one of Forster's strengths that whatever was problematic in his witnessing, as Nick Thomas has pointed out, `tended to be paraded rather than disavowed'.[11]

However, this tendency did not do much for authentication of history, and kept bringing Forster back to the perplexities of the encounter itself, and the scantiness of what it could be made to yield in terms of amity and information. Many personal histories of the South Seas are like this and often follow the pattern of one of the most successful fictions ever invented: a man is driven ashore under inauspicious circumstances, contrives to preserve a miserable existence, grows happy, witnesses horrid feasts on human flesh, is terrified, forms a close association with a native, and not knowing when he is well off, decides to leave his island and return to Europe. Give or take a few details, this is the story of Herman Melville in the Marquesas, William Mariner and George Vason in Tonga, William Lockerby in Fiji and John Young in Hawai'i.[12] Ian Campbell has identified four broad categories of beach crossing, and may be summarised as the reluctant, the hybrid, the acculturated and the transculturised.[13] Horace Holden's life on Tobi Island was pure hell; he was forced to survive on leaves and insects until he was so skeletal his bones broke through his skin. He was in no condition to adapt in any degree to his life of a slave, and all he wanted was to get back home. William Pascoe Crook was not quite so miserable on the Marquesas, but he didn't understand or like what was happening to him there, and was extremely keen to get away. On the other hand, Melville's sojourn in the Marquesas was much more pleasant, though seasoned with fear, and for a while he lived like one of the Taipi; but when an opportunity of joining a ship presented itself, he was in no doubt about taking it. This equivocal engagement with native life was perhaps the typical pattern of beach-crossing, where limited but inevitable concessions were made to cultural difference, while basic affiliations remained intact. William Mariner is one of the most interesting examples of this kind of hybridity, a European who was fully adopted by his Tongan tribe but himself not entirely absorbed by their culture. Then there were men such as Edward Robarts in the Marquesas and David Whippy in Fiji who acquired a detailed knowledge of local culture and a perfect command of the local language in order to make a living by crossing back and forth over the beach, trading information and goods. As entrepreneurs they facilitated traffic between islanders and visiting ships, sometimes giving crucial aid to missionaries; and in effect they were settlers. One of the best narratives of early New Zealand is written by this kind of acculturated settler, Frederick Maning's *Old New Zealand*.[14] But men such as George Vason, Jean Cabri, John Young and Isaac Davis were transformed by life on the beach's other side, and those who were forced to leave it (Vason and Cabri) mourned what they had lost. The transformation was expressed socially – Vason, Davis and Young became landowners and chiefs, janissaries of the South Seas – and physically: Cabri's body was covered with intricate Marquesan tattoos. One of the best of this kind was John Jackson, 'Cannibal Jack', who concludes his memoir by trying to explain what his purpose was in writing it: 'Well, the answer is, I did not know any more than I do now, excepting perhaps, that I might have been running around the world for sport, or, better still, that I was trying to run away from myself, or chasing shadows… If I enjoyed myself as I went along, I don't know whose business it is, excepting my own.'[15]

The same fantastic incoherence haunts all these tales, either because the transit of the beach is never made, and experience remains inchoate, or because the crossing is achieved, and the result is incommunicable to those who have no inkling of it. Maning's digressions are Shandean extravagances, all made at the expense of historical time and the European reader, and he calls the narrative effect *dancing*:

> But I must confess I don't know any more about the right way to tell a story, than a native minister knows how to 'come' a war dance. I declare the mention of the war dance calls up a host of reminiscences…in such a way that no one but a few, a very few, pakeha Maori can understand. Thunder! – but no; let me get ashore; how can I dance on the water, or before I ever knew how?[16]

Maning's dancing seems to belong in many instances to the first moment of encounter, such as this, his first landing in New Zealand. James O'Connell danced for his life on the island of Ponape in front of a terrifying audience of armed men: 'I struck into Garry Owen,' he recalled, 'and figured away in that famous jig to the best of my ability and agility, and my new acquaintance were amazingly delighted thereat'. And when O'Connell got home, he made a living re-performing a once-familiar dance made exotic.[17] Trevor Howard, as Captain Bligh in the Brando version of *Mutiny on the Bounty*, dances very uncomfortably to the Tahitians; and in Kate Grenville's *A Secret River*, her settler hero Thornhill tries to identify himself to his Aboriginal neighbours, who cheerfully echo what he says, '*Yes*, he shouted, *only it ain't you, mate, it's me that's Thornhill!* He was almost dancing, poking himself in the chest.'[18] There is evidently a difference between petitionary dancing and impatient dancing. Inga Clendinnen makes a case for something in between, a sort of sympathetic dancing, when she tells the story of a British officer, William Bradley, whose men were danced at by Aborigines at Sydney Cove and who, being destitute of other means of communication, danced back at them, with everyone finally mingling in an extempore ball.[19] She represents this dancing as a demonstration of speechless goodwill, a provisional state of affairs dominated by hope for the best: not yet an achievement or a fact, more of an expectation.

This sort of dancing fits well into the category of beach exchange Greg Dening calls performance, which he distinguishes as a kind of instant ritual which works because it is suffused with sufficient energy to impart a kind of necessity and precision, or what J. L. Austin would call happiness and Marshall Sahlins *mana*, to the spectacle. In his study of the failure of Bligh's command of the *Bounty*, Dening showed how unhappily Bligh performed the rituals of a captain, never using the right words or the right gestures, until his clumsiness had reduced the vessel to a state of anarchy.[20] From the start, performance ruled the beach, whether it was the crude exhibition of power evident in the firing of the four pounder, or bringing down sea-birds, or even the local population, with a musket; or whether it was the arrival of an *arioi* performing troupe ready to give a pantomime, their drums beating and their flags streaming from canoes sitting just beyond the surf, performance seems to have prevailed all over the beach.[21] Anne Salmond has told us that Polynesians were brilliant improvisers, and at a moment's notice could reenact some notable event, such as the clever theft of British equipment, to huge applause. On Tahiti these displays included mimicries of hornpipes and English country dances, danced back as it were to the first dancers of them.[22] There was a daring performance by a Fijian of a British sailor: He wore pegs in his mouth to represent rotten teeth, slashed at the grass idly with his cutlass, addressed his chief as 'old bloke' and offered him a puff of his pipe.[23]

But how this back and forth of drama and dancing contributed to knowledge, apart from the instinctive knowledge of how to survive in unpredictable circumstances, it is hard to say. Dening finds an analogue for the beach in the no-man's land of the First World War, as described by Edmund Blunden: 'In this vicinity a peculiar difficulty would exist for the artist to select the sight, faces, words, incidents, which characterised the time. The art is rather to collect them, in their original form of incoherence.'[24] This advice resembles the conclusion of Herbert Guthrie-Smith's autobiography when, to summarise the history of the changes, both rapid and long-term, which overtook the land on which he was farming sheep in the Hawke's Bay region of New Zealand, he says: 'If the following pages have any value it is because of the insistence on the cumulative effect of trivialities...only to a small number of observers opportunity is offered of marking and tracing them; only a trifling minority continue in long enough occupation of any one area, fully to be cognisant of their marshaled immensity.' And how does he marshal that immensity? Why, as miracles such as those wrought by the earthquake of 1931 which neatly severed every cigar in a closed box in his study without harming the box or breaking any of the windows in the house, and which then caused the whole chimney stack to fall in a curve off the roof, to come in at the verandah, then out again on to the path, without breaking the roof or the railings of the verandah. With these momentous enigmas he can fix the attention of his reader and give the immensity of his particulars a chance.[25] They are agreeable to one of the first imagined sightings of things on a beach, facts without a context, so incoherent they might be taken equally for history or fiction: 'Three hats, one cap, and two shoes that were not fellows'.

A fascinating but mordant debate was started in Australia after the publication of Kate Grenville's *The Secret River* (2005). In this historical tale of the settlement of the Hawkesbury River in New South Wales, Grenville was concerned with a settler family called Thornhill, and she made no attempt to include the Aboriginal side of the events, other than descriptively. The closest she got to dancing was the scene where Thornhill proclaims his identity to the Aborigines, and hops in exasperation as they fail to comprehend what he is telling them. She confessed, 'I don't pretend to understand or be able to empathise particularly with a tribal Aboriginal person from 200 years ago.' But evidently she could manage this feat with a white convict, actually her ancestor, and one to whom she was determined not to condescend. Inga Clendinnen thought the result of this re-enactment was a dubiously partial and 'untutored' empathy with white settlers. To the question Grenville posed herself in writing the story, 'What would I have done in that situation, and what sort of a person would that make me?' Clendinnen answered shortly, 'Grenville would not have been Grenville in that situation. We cannot post ourselves back in time.'[26] Two grievous errors are made here by Grenville, Clendinnen persuasively argues. The first is to cheapen the passion that ought to inspire history – the horror, the moral rage, the compassion – in favour of the illusion that we can share the feelings of people in the past who seem to be the same as we are now, Europeans on our side of the beach. The second is to set aside not only the cultural difference of Aborigines but also the difference of history. Two hundred years presents the same obstacle to the historian as tribal culture does to the settler; but both need to be tackled if justice is to be done. The question is, how? By dancing? She suggests dancing of Bradley's kind is a way of marshalling the immensity of what is witnessed but not known, a representation of things in their incoherence: a method of according facts a kind of miraculous singularity without being overwhelmed by them. What one might then go on to ask is whether this has anything in common with history at all, and whether it is not a private romance, the work of a single performer retailing wonders in no apparent sequence, facts not necessarily connected and therefore not really facts at all – just like Hildebrand Bowman's.

Of the information brought home from the South Seas Samuel Johnson was generally contemptuous. He thought the younger Forster's *Voyage round the World* (1777) was tedious[27] and Hawkesworth's redaction of Cook's not much better: 'Hawkesworth can tell only what the voyagers have told him; and they have found very little, only one new animal, I think.'[28] That new nations with unique sexual customs had been discovered in places hitherto not known to exist appears not to have impressed him at all. A summary of his views of the anthropological importance of the South Seas is to be found in an exchange with Boswell, who was filled with a romantic desire to live on the beach in Tahiti or New Zealand long enough fully to understand the customs and beliefs of people living in a state of nature. Johnson demanded of him,

> What could you learn, Sir? What can savages tell, but what they themselves have seen? Of the past, or the invisible, they can tell nothing. The inhabitants of Otaheite and New-Zealand are not in a state of pure nature; for it is plain they broke off from some other people. Had they grown out of the ground, you might have judged of a state of pure nature. Fanciful people may talk of a mythology being amongst them; but it must be invention. They have once had religion, which has been gradually debased. And what account of their religion can you suppose to be learnt from savages? Only consider, Sir, our own state: our religion is in a book; we have an order of men whose duty it is to teach it…yet ask the first ten gross men you meet, and hear what they can tell of their religion.[29]

As well as providing a summary of the non-knowledge to be garnered on this side of the beach, Johnson establishes a perfect equality between the ignorance of the enquirer and that of the native informant. A savage life is only the sum of what can be collected from an imperfect memory; mythology is a fiction either invented by the savages themselves or by those who wish to render them interesting; and whatever the visitor is told it has scant connection with the actual state of affairs, which is emphatically not a state of nature. There is no truly primitive state of savagery to be observed, and what scoundrels such as Rousseau dignify with the name of a state of nature, or British conjectural historians for that matter, is really always corrupt, for nobody grows out of the ground – and even if they did, their lack of pity, curiosity and letters would mean that what we mistook for innocence would really be imbecility. At the same time Johnson's repudiation of fieldwork reveals a canny but largely submerged estimate of what is at stake in the discussions generated by the elder Forster and Kames. For example, everyone agreed that savagery is always a relative estimate of progress or degeneration; for when Forster discovered what he took to be the degree zero of prehistoric life in the inhabitants of Tierra del Fuego, he was at length inclined to believe that humans so poor, so dull and so unlovely somehow must have been reduced to this condition. Clearly Johnson had read enough of the voyages to know that no one believed in an autochthonous origin of any Polynesian nation in the South Seas, that these were migratory cultures that had risen or fallen according to the amenity of the landfall or, in the case of the Rapanuians, their own profuseness, or for some other reason altogether. What Johnson wishes to impress upon the naïve and ardent Boswell is that the history of that rising and falling is purely conjectural, and that conjecture is worth nothing. Lord Monboddo's conjectures concerning the ape-like origins of humans he found not offensive but stupid: 'What strange narrowness of mind now is that, to think things we have not known, are better than the things which we have known.'[30]

Johnson set off with Boswell for the Highlands in 1773, the year Hawkesworth published his *Account of the Voyages* and a year after Cook set sail on his second voyage through the Pacific, accompanied by the two Forsters. This was the closest Johnson came to doing fieldwork on his own account, and what he meant to collect was information of facts, things which were known. If he might be said to be testing any kind of theory, it was one that he embodied: his own version of stadial development where civil society reaches its apex in the rich material and intellectual culture of metropolitan London (Bowman's Luxo-Volupto as it happens), a triumph of physical and mental exertion that was unequalled in the contemporary world. It caused Johnson great pleasure to catch sight of the silhouettes of Lord Mulgrave and Omai as they stood talking by a window, and to find he was not to be able to tell one from the other.[31] In his *Journey to the Western Islands of Scotland* (1775) he aimed to measure the distance separating the primitive stage of development of the region (hovering somewhere between pastoralism and subsistence farming) from the standards of politeness which he himself and his companion represented. Here are his alpha and omega: old traditions and antiquated manners on the one side, and a modern, civil nation on the other. Of his host at Anoch he reported that his life was 'merely pastoral', his wealth consisting entirely of 'one hundred sheep, as many goats, twelve milk-cows, and twenty-eight beeves ready for the drover'.[32] He explains how such a mountainous fastness defends 'the original, at least the oldest race of inhabitants' (43); and so it is with a sort of comical vainglory he takes his first step towards Loch Ness and into the past: 'We were now to bid farewell to the luxury of travelling, and to enter a country upon which no wheel has ever rolled.' (29) Nevertheless he detects many signs of progress in the circulation of money and the reach of the law, concluding with apparent approval, 'There was perhaps never any change of national manners so quick, so great, and so general, as that which has operated in the Highlands, by the last conquest, and the subsequent laws.' (57) There is only one way for the Highlands to go, and that is rapidly into the present.

Such certainty about the movement of history is undercut however by melancholy reflections: 'We came thither too late to see what we expected, a people of peculiar appearance, and a system of antiquated life.' (57) If Forster was troubled by evidence of time going forwards and backwards in the same place, no less is Johnson. When he beholds antiquated manners he is for the most part impatient with them, especially if they require him to go to bed on straw, to travel without wheels and to listen to a pack of lies from people who will tell the curious traveler anything they think he wants to know. It is then that he catches a strong flavour of clan life and its 'muddy mixture of pride and ignorance' (89). At the same time he reports the general discontent among Highlanders of all classes owing to the rise of rents, the plague of emigration, and the laws against wearing the plaid and the carrying of arms. He recurs to the same theme that Cook was to rehearse when on his return he saw Tahiti blasted by venereal disease, and accurately predicted in the South Seas the same miseries of disease and depopulation for the indigenous people that had been endured for so many centuries in the Americas. In a solemn moment Johnson assesses the damage to what was once a cultural focus with a lot of heat in it: 'The clans retain little now of their original character, their ferocity of temper is softened, their military ardor is extinguished, their dignity of independence is depressed, their contempt of government subdued, and their reverence for their chiefs abated.' (57) What is he describing but the degeneration incident to modernisation, the retrogradation that accompanies progress? If he came too late to witness antiquated life, he came also too early to see the progress he wished to welcome. Like Forster he finds himself witness to a conundrum he cannot solve.

There are a number of symptoms of Johnson's failure to find the right time for his history. His pleasure and impatience are alike expressed as litotes, as if he has trouble positively affirming that things are either pleasant or inconvenient, caught as they are on the threshold between an equivocal antiquity and an awkward modernity. A house of entertainment is 'not ill-stocked with provisions', a young woman is 'not inelegant either in mien or dress', and he consumes barleycakes 'without unwillingness' (33–7). Alternatively, when he is shown a tree of insignificant size, but informed that there is a much larger one a few miles away, he recalls, 'I was still less delighted to hear that another tree was not to be seen nearer.' (10) What objectively he identifies as the intellectual poverty of a nation that has no historians (50), or the intellectual starvation of the Highland traveler who 'knows less as he hears more' (51), is finally thoroughly internalised as his own inability to process facts that seem to belong to different eras, confounding his ability to distinguish between true knowledge and fiction.

Opulence, for example, is alive and well in the Highlands and all the more surprising for its sudden appearance amidst scenes of natural barrenness. The house of McLeod at Raasay was 'such a seat of hospitality, amidst the winds and waters, [as filled] the imagination with a delightful contrariety of images…without is the rough ocean and the rocky land, the beating billows and the howling storm: within is plenty and elegance, beauty and gaiety, the song and the dance' (66). A rocky shore that divides a howling storm from a charming dance, it is an interesting pairing. The same coalition of positive and negative impulses that drives Johnson's prose into litotes here stimulates fantasy of Keatsian extravagance, 'The same that oft-times hath / Charm'd magic casements, opening on the foam / Of perilous seas, in faery lands forlorn.'[33] This was the minstrelsy to which Johnson was prepared as it were to spread his kirtle. He compared the effect on the mind to the fictions of Gothic romance: 'Whatever is imaged in the wildest tale, if giants, dragons, and enchantments be expected, would be felt by him, who, wandering in the mountains without a guide, or upon the sea without a pilot, should be carried amidst his terror and uncertainty, to the hospitality and elegance of Raasay or Dunvegan.' (77) Despite his perpetual reminders to the reader of the ignorance of bards and genealogists in the Highlands, it is in these Gothic havens, watching the dancing to the accompaniment of the billows, that Johnson learned the tales of the McLeods and the traditions of the Macleans and had no difficulty in believing them as family history. Although he warns us not to fill the vacuum of information with the pseudo-primitivism of *Ossian*, he spends pages discussing evidence of second sight. Of this faculty, which might have been suspected of being the most romantic of all, Johnson says, 'The local frequency of a power, which is nowhere totally unknown… where we are unable to decide by antecedent reason, we must be content to yield to the force of testimony.' (107) No conjectural historian could be more ready to admit that things we have not known are more interesting than those we have; no ethnographer could more willingly accept the testimony of native informants; no witness could be more partial in admitting evidence whose grounds of authenticity (partly known almost everywhere) is asserted solely as a denial of its opposite, 'nowhere totally unknown'. Like many another inhabitant of the beach faced with the obstacles of culture and history, Johnson has started to dance and romance.

Notes

1 J. M. Coetzee, *Foe* (London: Penguin, 1988), 88.
2 Keith Thomas, *The Ends of Life: Roads to Fulfillment in Early Modern England* (Oxford: Oxford University Press, 2009), 267.
3 Hilary Mantel, 'Dreams & Duels of England', *New York Review of Books*, 22 October 2009, 8–12.
4 Anonymous, *The Travels of Hildebrand Bowman* (London: W. Strahan and T. Cadell, 1778), 267.
5 Mary Poovey, *A History of the Modern Fact* (Chicago: Chicago University Press, 1998), 215, 228.
6 H. Home, Lord Kames, *Sketches of the History of Man*, 4 vols (London: W. Strahan and T. Cadell, 1778), 1:39–40.
7 Johann Reinhold Forster, *Observations Made during a Voyage Round the World*, ed. Nicholas Thomas, Harriet Guest, and Michael Dettelbach (Honolulu: University of Hawai'i Press, 1996), 152.
8 Nicholas Thomas, '"On the Origin of the Human Species": Forster's Comparative Ethnology', in Forster, *Observations Made during a Voyage Round the World*, xxiii–xl (xvi).
9 Poovey, *A History of the Modern Fact*, 215–28.
10 Georg Forster, *A Voyage Round the World*, 2 vols (London: White, 1777), 1:127.
11 Nicholas Thomas, *In Oceania: Visions, Artifacts, Histories* (Durham: Duke University Press, 1997), 80.
12 See H. E. Maude, *Of Islands and Men: Studies in Pacific History* (Oxford: Oxford University Press, 1968), 170–7.
13 I. C. Campbell, *'Going Native' in Polynesia: Captivity Narratives and Experiences from the South Pacific* (Westport, Conn.: Greenwood Press, 1998), 79.
14 See John Nicholson, *White Chief: The Colourful Life and Times of Judge F. E. Maning of the Hokianga* (Auckland: Penguin Group, 2006); and F. E. Maning, *Old New Zealand and Other Writings*, ed. Alex Calder (Leicester: Leicester University Press, 2001).
15 Quoted in Campbell, *'Going Native'*, 74.
16 F. E. Maning, *Old New Zealand* (London: Smith Elder, 1863), 7–8.
17 Susan Milcairns, *Native Strangers* (Auckland: Penguin, 2007), 121.
18 Kate Grenville, *The Secret River* (Melbourne: The Text Publishing Company, 2005), 213.
19 Inga Clendinnen, *Dancing with Strangers* (Cambridge: Cambridge University Press, 2005), 8.
20 Greg Dening, *Mr Bligh's Bad Language* (Cambridge: Cambridge University Press, 1992).
21 William Ellis, *Polynesian Researches*, 2 vols (London: Fisher and Jackson, 1830), 1:318–19.
22 Anne Salmond, *The Trial of the Cannibal Dog* (London: Allen Lane, 2003), 201; Ellis, *Polynesian Researches*, 2:319.
23 Campbell, *'Going Native'*, 79.
24 Dening, *Performances*, 203.
25 Herbert Guthrie-Smith, *Tutira: The Story of a New Zealand Sheep Station* (Edinburgh and London: William Blackwood, 1969), 195.
26 Inga Clendinnen, 'Who Owns the Past?' *Quarterly Essay* 23 (2006): 20.
27 James Boswell, *The Life of Samuel Johnson, LL.D.*, ed. R. W. Chapman (Oxford: Oxford University Press, 1980), 860.

28 Ibid., 537.

29 Ibid., 751.

30 Ibid., 460, 723.

31 Roxann Wheeler, *The Complexion of Race* (Philadelphia: University of Pennsylvania Press, 2000), 192–7.

32 Samuel Johnson, *A Journey to the Western Islands of Scotland*, ed. Mary Lascelles (New Haven: Yale University Press, 1971), 37. Further references to this edition are given as page numbers in my text.

33 John Keats, 'Ode to a Nightingale', lines 68–70, in *The Poetical Works of John Keats*, ed. H. W. Garrod (Oxford: Clarendon Press, 1958), 257–260.

Part Three

MATTER, MIND, PSYCHE

Chapter Nine

'REMEMBER ME'

Michael Witmore

Captain: [To crew] Pull the power back. That's right. Pull the left one [throttle] back.
Copilot: Pull the left one back.
Approach: At the end of the runway it's just wide-open field.
Cockpit Unidentified Voice: Left throttle, left, left, left, left…
Cockpit Unidentified Voice: God!
Cabin: [Sound of impact]

— Cockpit Voice Recording, United Flight 232, 19 July 1989[1]

Modern aviation has given us the purgatorial technology of the CVR or cockpit voice recording, the so called 'black box' that captures instrument information and audio from the cockpit in the last moments of a disaster. In the case of United Flight 232, whose final moments in flight are recorded above, the pilots managed to land their plane in Sioux City Iowa after three hydraulic systems failed simultaneously at 33,000 feet. Just after the first impact is heard – the left wing of the DC-10 clipped the landing strip before the tail end of the aircraft tore away from the cabin – flight 232 flipped upside down and crashed in a corn field near the airstrip. All three pilots survived, but in the end, 110 people were killed in the incident.

The mere existence of such recordings is unnerving. On some of them, pilots call out people's names before the audio cuts off, knowing their voices will be played to loved ones after they are dead. The men and women whose voices are captured on these tapes are mindful of the fact that, even as calamity unspools, whatever they say will survive them. The technological intervention here is perverse: through a kind of grim foresight on the part of designers and safety officials, the interval between life and death has been made to speak. 'God!' It's happening. But who or what listens?

When Hamlet hears the voice of his father in the opening scene of Shakespeare's play, it is very like this disembodied voice of disaster. 'Remember me', the ghost says, setting the plot of Shakespeare's tragedy into motion.[2] Shakespeare's audience would have been fascinated by the possibility that a spirit only – a being without a body – had returned to the world in order to tell the truth about his death. There was sectarian debate about just this topic, one I will explore briefly below, but the theatrical function of the ghost is more straightforward: it must deliver a message in the absence of a living speaker. Memory must live on, even when no person alive can carry it forward. And when it is a memory like this one, 'murder will speak with most miraculous organ'. Like a modern day black box, the ghost is Shakespeare's theatrical version of that impossible voice from the past, the one that speaks about the worst after it has happened.

Something will happen to those who hear this voice. In the following pages, I would like to explore the effects of hearing this story from the ghost, suggesting that *Hamlet* provides us with a particularly rich phenomenological meditation on the ways in which we are estranged from ourselves when disturbing memories are preserved without a live person to deliver them. My aim here is not simply to suggest that *Hamlet* is, in a sense, the transcript of a disaster but to suggest as well that the play is very deliberate in setting out the consequences of entertaining the kind of impossible memories that King Hamlet delivers to his son. Whether they come from a real ghost or the devil, a 'spirit of health or a goblin damned' (I.v.19), these words from the threshold have the power to split the listener from his own proper sense of self, to send him spinning off into a world where bodies, voices, memory and even political authority cannot be located in the right places.

* * *

We suspect that there would be no play if Hamlet had nothing to go on but the promptings of his 'prophetic soul'. The ghost must speak to him, when the prince is watching with Horatio, in order for the machinery of the Senecan revenge plot to creak into motion. But as soon as we begin to talk about a machinery or plot devices, we have entered a conversation about causes and effects, pushes and pulls. Just what kind of thing is a ghost and how can it move anything, not just figuratively, but literally?

This seems to be a question that Shakespeare himself entertained, and it is connected to some of the early modern debates about ghosts and specters of the period. As Stephen Greenblatt has shown, Protestant hostility toward the doctrine of Purgatory would have caused audiences to consider the ghost's presence with some care.[3] The figure who arrives on stage to urge a killing would have presented audiences with a startling set of choices: the 'old mole' might represent a (Catholic) soul returned from the dead, for example, or a demonic apparition inviting the prince to commit a mortal sin. It might also be a brainsick, melancholic fantasy. Ghost theorists such as the French demonologist Pierre Le Loyer were curious about the mechanics of ghostly apparition and action, and debated the issue in print. Writing against what he called 'Athiests and Libertines' who did not admit 'any substances in being, but such only as [are] corporall and having bodies', Le Loyer advocates the reality of 'Specters' as an object of sensation. A specter is a 'substance without a body, presenting it self sensibly unto men', he writes, adding that because they lack 'thickness' they cannot be 'palpable' or 'subject to handling'.[4]

There was really no way around this issue of 'handling', since any version of the ghost (except a theory of fraudulent simulation) started with the idea that a ghost lacked the proper, extended body of the living. Aristotle had said, and it was frequently repeated, that 'everything that is moved is moved by something' (*Physics* 7.266b). But while this idea had acquired the status of a philosophical maxim or proverb (*omne quod movetur ab alio movetur*), it was difficult to apply to a creature that lacked thickness, could not be handled, and yet was capable of impressing itself on the senses. When Hamlet says 'Rest, rest perturbèd spirit' (I.v.190), the listener does not have to be a master of Aristotle's organon to sense that a paradox is being broached. How can a ghost trouble the senses – put their subtle parts into motion – if a ghost is not itself a thing that can push other things? Protestantism could only magnify this intuition, making the moving power of the ghost something to be worried in thought. If the age of miracles had ceased, as Protestants believed, why would God suspend the workings of the world to endow a non-body with some extraordinary liminal push? Common sense and reformed theology both suggested that the threshold separating bodies could only be breached by another body. Two things would have to *touch* for such a change to take place.

We get an even more vivid sense of this threshold problem – the problem of explaining how a body is moved by a something that is also a nothing – when we notice the recurrence of the word 'voice' in the play. Voice can mean many things in Denmark's elective monarchy: it can mean the sound associated with the speech of an individual, but it means also the collective voice of the kingdom and, more technically, the voice one gives as an elector to a candidate for the monarchy. Margareta de Grazia has explored the ways in which this elective structure, one actually in force at the time of the play's composition, creates uncertainty in succession by allowing the crown to pass by vote rather than primogeniture.[5] One can plausibly assign Hamlet's famous 'distraction' to this kink in the lineal descent of the crown, enabled (as de Grazia points out) by his mother's dynasty-shifting marriage to her husband's brother. Perhaps, de Grazia argues, the surplus anxieties and delays that the Romantics perceived in the plot of *Hamlet* were their own.

But the voice is a marvel within a marvel: like the visible presence of a ghost, the sound of the voice does not respect punctual boundaries. It is the sound of one, but it often comes from another. Given this strange mobility, which we will explore in a moment, I think that the play is doing more than explicating the consequences of filial dispossession, or at least, is using that drama to illustrate more complicated intuitions about political legitimacy and bodily self-possession. For in *Hamlet*, possession of one's body is both physical and symbolic, and this latter, symbolic dimension of proper or embodied being can be troubled, compromised or interrupted by political events.

Consider, for example, the portability of the voice in the play – its capacity to be lost, found, and repossessed. A voice can be given to someone, for example, as when the mortally wounded Hamlet, himself a speaking dead man, says:

> O, I die, Horatio…
> But I do prophecy th'election lights
> On Fortinbras. He has my dying voice.
> So tell him, with the occurrents, more and less,
> Which have solicited – the rest is silence. (V.ii.305–311)

Hamlet here is both giving his voice in election and transferring, in an odd way, his own voice to Fortinbras through the intermediary of Horatio. There can be little doubt that this voice, in the context of the play's plot, is the legitimate voice of the kingdom. Indeed, given the way in which voices and bodies merge and separate in the play, it would seem that *Hamlet* proposes a metaphysics of vocal succession that parallels some of the legal mechanics of the King's Two Bodies.[6]

For in *Hamlet*, it is clearly in the voice that the dynastic, collective and – in this historical context – metaphysical force of kingship mingles with the material, embodied fact of personhood. 'Never alone / Did the King sigh, but with a general groan' (III.iii.22–23), says Rosencrantz to Claudius. He is glossing a commonplace of early modern political theory. A king may have one body, but when a voice issues out of that body, it is the voice of a multitude.[7] A king's vocal chords are special: they constitute an 'ingenious instrument' (to borrow a phrase from *Cymbeline*), one that produces sounds which are not, strictly speaking, those of a person. But does Claudius really have this voice? Is it possible that the mystical voice of the kingdom, the one that must be passed from one monarch to the next through the mechanics of election, could have been mis-placed, misremembered? The mere presence of the ghost suggests that this is the case.

For above all, the speaking thing on the ramparts is a voice without a body. Marcellus strikes it with his partisan, but it is like the air, 'invulnerable'. It will only speak to Hamlet of course, perhaps because Hamlet has himself been put into a strange, displaced relationship to his own body. Presumably, his father had settled election on him, establishing the line of vocal succession. But Gertrude's marriage to Claudius has left Hamlet too much in the sun/son, which in this case means too much in the disenchanted receptacle that is his body. By the end of the first act, it is obvious to the audience that the prince is uncomfortable in his 'too solid flesh', wishing that it would 'thaw and resolve itself into a dew' (I.ii.129–30). Thinking perhaps as much of the crown as the human body, he declares, 'things rank and gross in nature / Possess it merely' (I.ii.136–37). Once the succession has been interrupted in this vocal realm, individuals such as Hamlet become orphans of the flesh.

Mere occupation as opposed to legitimate possession, communal or customary right as opposed to singular ambition. To the extent that a voice is invisible but sensible, it encompasses the legitimacy of the crowd as opposed to the singular desires of a usurping individual.[8] On my reading, which really only follows Hamlet's, Claudius has stolen the diadem and put it in his pocket. This one act, premised as it is on fratricide and an abused 'process' or story that makes this event seem accidental (a snake in the garden), shakes and upends everyone who has a bodily stake in the monarchy. The old King is now a voice without a body, the errant representative of a kind of spooked monarchical power. The sitting king is powerful but also hollow. As Hamlet says riddlingly to Claudius, 'the body is with the King but the King is not with the body. The King is a thing – …of nothing' (IV.ii.25–27).

What is fascinating about this structure of dependency in the play is its chiasmatic nature: a disruption in the physical realm (murder) creates metaphysical ripples in the symbolic (where royal legitimacy is conserved), only to fracture the connection between the body and its daimonic voice (Hamlet's being put far from the 'understanding' of himself). The murder of old Hamlet does something to his son, but also does something to the murderer and the one who has died: all of these effects surface in the gaps where voices or sounds come out of bodies. Like Glen Gould highlighting the inner melodic lines in his hyperarticulate playing of Bach's Goldberg Variations, Shakespeare seems to find all manner of cross-melodies to play on the theme of sound and voice. Claudius, for example, likes to have the cannons sound whenever he proposes a toast – a kind of aural prosthetic, 're-speaking earthly thunder' (I.ii.128). He has the body of the king (he is sleeping with the old King's wife), but his voice requires a ballistic second or augment. The ghost delivers the news of Claudius' murder, but cannot reveal the sufferings of the afterlife: he is exiled from both the living and the dead, 'unhouseled, dis-appointed, unaneled' (I.v.77).

Critics rarely comment on the fact that the ghost employs prefixes of negation, all of which refer to some forced withdrawal from bodily experiences with metaphysical force (Eucharist, vocal confession, anointing). Yet the command to Hamlet reverses this pattern: 'Remember me!' It means, put the body back with the voice. Underlying the command is an insight: there is something ghostly even about legitimate kings. Whatever they are hedged with, kings exhibit a certain preternatural mismatch between the voice and the body that produces it. They speak with more than one voice. It will only be when Hamlet is mortally wounded and Claudius is dead – when the prince is the conduit for the migratory voice of kingship – that Hamlet's disdain and disgust for the body and its desires will be relieved. Perhaps this is the price of being a certain kind of son, one who cannot, as Laertes reminds Ophelia, 'carve for himself'. Rather, his choices are circumscribed 'unto the voice and yielding of that body / Whereof he is the head'. He can only act on choices 'that the main voice of Denmark goes withal' (I.iii.22–24, 28).

Once the voice of succession has been spooked, Hamlet, as heir to that voice, becomes a kind of machine. 'While this machine is to him', Hamlet signs his halting love letter to Ophelia, suggesting the profound self-estrangement and bodily alienation he experiences in the wake of his father's death. Ophelia will not fare much better. Like the reeds that whisper the story of Midas' indiscretion in Ovid's *Metamorphoses*, Ophelia produces sounds that cannot be connected to who and what she is. As she sings snatches of old songs, clothes soaked in water, she is almost inanimate – 'incapable of her own distress' (IV.vii.153). They are alike in this way: neither is in a position to produce the right sounds.

* * *

Let us say, then, that the ghost is a device in Shakespeare's theater, one he inherited from Senecan tragedy and infused with sectarian and political lore. It seems perfectly reasonable to argue that in *Hamlet*, Shakespeare articulates a metaphysics of kingship that takes shape when he begins to probe the gap between voice and body – a gap that becomes particularly interesting when a ghost arrives on stage to tell a story about regicide. We can align this metaphysics with the Elizabethan doctrine of the King's Two Bodies and, indeed, even connect it to anxieties about the succession at the time the play was written. But I suspect that the pattern of bodily and vocal displacements traced in the play cannot be exhausted by discussions of monarchical politics. What the play is circling around in the interval between the ghost's charge and the performance of revenge is the issue of bodily and community integrity: the way these two things become intertwined with one another in a particular dynastic or familial scene.

Perhaps we ought to look at the play as a hypothesis about how body, voice, identity and memory are bundled together in a world full of 'accidental judgments and casual slaughters' (V.ii.335). Horatio, the penultimate speaker in *Hamlet*, is the last black box: he tells the truth of this familial and dynastic disaster, having been preserved to speak by Hamlet at the end of the play. The tale he tells will have a certain conserving effect. In agreeing to report Hamlet's cause 'aright', Horatio becomes the next curator of the ghostly voice of memory, situating it somewhere else, providing the story and details necessary to make it rest where it is put. Clearly this is the outcome that Hamlet is aiming at: it is the fulfillment of the ghost's command. When rest becomes silence, which it is, the 'rights of memory' claimed by Fortinbras in Denmark will include the right to speak in a certain sort of way. As political theory, this is the kind of mystification of monarchy that we would expect from an Elizabethan thinker. But as a phenomenology of memory, it is something more profound.

In his last work, the *Visible and the Invisible*, Maurice Merleau-Ponty writes powerfully about the ways in which the visible body and ultimately, the body as such, emerges from our traffic with the world:

> When I find again the actual world such as it is, under my hands, under my eyes, up against my body, I find much more than an object: a Being of which my vision is a part, a visibility older than my operation or my acts. But this does not mean that there was a fusion or coinciding of me with it: on the contrary, this occurs because a sort of dehiscence opens my body in two, and because between my body looked at and my body looking, my body touched and my body touching, there is overlapping or encroachment, so that we must say that the things pass into us as well as we into the things.[9]

Here Merleau-Ponty describes a kind of reflexive 'overlapping' that occurs when the sensing body is both an agent and patient at the same time, touched and touching. The name he ultimately gives to the medium of this overlap is flesh, a substance that is not simply the organic basis for our bodies, but the medium in which all forms of self-relation and worldly inter-relation are possible. The flesh touches, but also senses itself touching: it is the medium and object of touch at the same time.[10] When flesh obtains this dual, reflexive role, touch ceases to be a phenomenon of contiguity, something that occurs when a boundary or limit is crossed. Rather, it is a threshold whose generative or world-accommodating powers cannot itself be breached or touched. 'Things pass into us, and we into things.'

When Merleau-Ponty writes about a dehiscence in the body, an overlapping that is not a coincidence, he is identifying as foundational a situation that Shakespeare's play depicts as aberrant. The time is, by definition, out of joint for the 'I' who finds the world under his or her hands and eyes in Merleau-Ponty's scheme, which is also the case in *Hamlet*, but only because the metaphysical structures of sovereignty in the latter have, in effect, forced the symbolic divorce of body and voice. Strangely enough, *for this culture*, Shakespeare's culture, the underlying non-coincidence of the body and its memories – memories that are brought to bear on the body at precisely the moment when one speaks – becomes thinkable only at a point of political rupture or 'disappointment'. The ghost, Hamlet, and all those displaced by the symbolic swerve of power in this play are the early modern period's unlucky, if fictional, phenomenologists. Only from their displaced location in the world and problematic status *as speakers* can what Merleau-Ponty called the 'flesh of the world' become an object of thought.

And what is the flesh of the world? The play has its own rumblings on this question. Judith Butler, in a recent reading of Merleau-Ponty's *Phenomenology of Perception* and *The Visible and the Invisible*, has discussed the phenomenologist's use of flesh as a metaphor for the intertwining of social, linguistic and embodied being.[11] She argues that our 'inability to ground ourselves' as independent beings of only *one* sort (political agents, language users, bodies in motion) is 'based on the fact that we are animated by others into whose hands we are born and, hopefully, sustained'. It is an ongoing liability of our thought that the flesh strikes us – not just Hamlet – as sullied precisely because it is a medium of dependency, she argues. We are, after all, connected to others by flesh, by a fabric of connections that cannot be gamed or undone: 'We are thus always', Butler writes, 'done to as we are doing…undergoing as we act… touched in the act of touching' (203).

There are only certain historical situations, certain configurations of flesh, power and memory, in which this insight could be pleasurable. In *Hamlet*, it is not. Flesh is, of course, precisely the thing that haunts both Hamlet the character and *Hamlet* the play – what becomes of it, what it sustains, what needs it has, and what the world might be in its absence. The play is a ghost world. But perhaps what we can take from Hamlet the political phenomenologist is the conviction that this same intertwining of bodies, memories and voices which he finds so troubling is ultimately the threshold at which we connect with the literary past. What if memory is a ghost that constantly needs to be placated, situated – one that survives the wreck of history, as the Adrienne Rich poem suggests? What if literature, *Hamlet* for instance, is a spectral voice that speaks from the grave? Like a stranger, it arrives from an elsewhere unseen. And this is why, Hamlet-like, we give it welcome.

Notes

1 Malcolm MacPherson, ed., *The Black Box: All-New Cockpit Voice Recorder Accounts of In-Flight Accidents* (New York: Quill, 1998), 184.

2 William Shakespeare, *Hamlet*, ed. G. R. Hibbard (Oxford: Oxford University Press, 1987), I.v.91. All subsequent references to *Hamlet* are to this edition.

3 Stephen Greenblatt, *Hamlet in Purgatory* (Princeton: Princeton University Press, 2002).

4 Pierre Le Loyer, *A Treatise of Specters* (London: Val. S., 1605), 1, 4. As the quotation makes clear, Le Loyer was entering a discussion in print in 1605 (the book appeared in both English and French the same year) that was already exploring the issue of the ghost's body and non-extended substances. Much of the thinking about non-extended substances had already been done in debates about the Eucharist.

5 Margreta de Grazia, *'Hamlet' Without Hamlet* (Cambridge: Cambridge University Press, 2007).

6 Ernst H. Kantorowicz, *The King's Two Bodies* (Princeton: Princeton University Press, 2007). See also Lorna Hutson, ed., 'Forum: Fifty Years of the King's Two Bodies', special issue, *Representations* 106 (Spring 2009).

7 In a sense, the voice of a king represents a collapse of a political plurality into the immanent presence of a single individual, just the opposite of the kind of polyphony envisaged by Italian feminist philosopher and political theorist Adriana Cavarero in her *For More Than One Voice: Toward a Philosophy of Vocal Expression*, trans. Paul A. Kottman (Stanford: Stanford University Press, 2005), 193–4. Paul Kottman has argued that *Hamlet* is about the prince's struggle to inherit a broken form of sociality, a claim I would extend to include the ghost's fractured form of vocal inhabitation. See Paul A. Kottman, *Tragic Condition in Shakespeare* (Baltimore: Johns Hopkins University Press, 2009), Ch. 3. On the paradoxes of vocal origination in the Renaissance, see Gina Bloom, *Voice in Motion: Staging Gender, Shaping Sound in Early Modern England* (Philadelphia: University of Pennsylvania Press, 2007).

8 The psychoanalytic theorist Mladen Dolar suggests that all vocal performances must shade into ventriloquism – a situation where something speaks that cannot properly speak – when he argues that the lack of a visible origin for speech makes it more difficult to assign to a speaker. See Mladen Dolar, *A Voice and Nothing More* (Cambridge: MIT Press, 2006), 70.

9 Maurice Merleau-Ponty, *The Visible and the Invisible*, trans. A. Lingis (Evanston: Northwestern University Press, 1968), 123.

10 This reflexivity in function was noticed by Aristotle and developed by commentators in Late Antiquity and the Middle Ages under the heading of the *sensus communis* or common sense. On this fascinating tradition, see Daniel Heller-Roazen, *The Inner Touch: The Archaeology of a Sensation* (New York: Zone Books, 2007).

11 Judith Butler, 'Merleau-Ponty and the Touch of Malebranche', in Taylor Carman and Mark B. N. Hansen, eds, *The Cambridge Companion to Merleau-Ponty* (Cambridge: Cambridge University Press, 2005), 181–205 (203).

Chapter Ten

BETWEEN SLEEP AND WAKING: MONTAIGNE, KEATS AND PROUST

Jeremy Lane

This brief essay emerges from an ongoing study of relations between imaginative writing and liminal states or movements of consciousness, especially those on the threshold between waking and sleep, or between consciousness and its loss or inhibition. In the examples considered here, such writing is meditative and self-reflective, and brings the first person into the centre of its concern. Its literary realisation is as both product and process, involving transitions between consciousness and its absence, between waking and sleep, between everyday consciousness and an obscure consciousness of the night. It may include dreaming but also less defined, more intermediate mental activities and phenomena brought under the term 'hypnagogia', a leading towards or away from sleep proper.[1] Falling asleep and waking up, 'dropping off' and 'coming to' – movements into or out of unconsciousness, lapses, syncopes and myoclonic episodes, losses and recoveries of consciousness, consciousness expressed through musing and dreaming, partial, drifting thought or imagination, rhythmicities and fluctuations of consciousness: these are the experiences and phenomena I'm trying to probe, as they are reflected and articulated in literature. Finding versions of these movements in a range of literary kinds and forms, my concern is to explore possible relations between them and the activity of the creative imagination. Also crucial for the three very different examples discussed here, is the question of the self's or first person's status and persistence during such movements away from full consciousness, clarity, and wakefulness. In focusing briefly on these three writers, sharply differing in period, language, and genre, I hope to suggest ways in which they all raise questions about the functioning and importance of movements away from everyday consciousness towards imagination, reverie, and fantasy, as well as about the philosophical imperative of clarity set against a poetic interest in exploring and rendering kinds and movements of awareness which might transcend or evade that imperative.

At a very general level, it can be argued that, in the Western tradition at least, and particularly in its metaphysics, the honours belong to clarity, wakefulness, full consciousness, from the divine fiat of Genesis through to the withdrawal of the veil, apocalypse (from the Greek *apo-kaluptô*, an uncovering of what is concealed or buried). A biological disposition toward light, the day, the visible, and a primeval fear of darkness, night, the unseen, are symbolically extended and articulated to constitute the pervasive cultural bias. Both Greek and Judaic traditions underwrite this, neither of course in any simple or uniform way, and with profound differences between them, but both nonetheless with persistent force. With Plato, the Ideal which as a concept is at once epistemological, ethical, and aesthetic, consists, as the term itself indicates, in visibility, the root verb *eidô* meaning both to know and to see. The principle of light, *phaos*, corresponds with and enables that of reason, *logos*, as well as the capacity for perfect sight and knowledge intrinsic to the *eidos*, the Idea or Form, to be inferred from the imperfection of reality. Scripture presents a divine principle equally conceivable by the same tokens as the epitome of clarity, bringer of light into darkness, all-knowing and all-seeing, ever vigilant. Consider, for example, the Jewish *menorah*, the seven-branched lamp which represents 'the eyes of the Lord, which run to and fro through the whole earth'.[2] The predominant affirmation of light and lucidity is subject to qualifications, including such fundamental instances as the dual theophany of Exodus where Jehovah signals his presence as the fire by night and cloud by day, a chiasmic light in darkness, darkness in light.[3] There are also certain obvious resistances to this affirmation, for example in elements of religious mysticism or materialist or irrationalist philosophy, yet nonetheless what opposes or negates it is most often construed pejoratively. Darkness, obscurity, the absence or failure of full consciousness, all are 'bad objects' for the most part in the discourses of our culture, seen as the negative 'other' of its positive excellences, light, clarity, conscious mind, the enlightened soul.

In the history of philosophy parallel antitheses and valorisations apply. The Cartesian *cogito*, in particular, seems to imply in principle an unceasing wakefulness since, if sleep depends on the withdrawal of consciousness, this appears to result in the loss of self. Michel Covin rather sardonically notes that one can imagine the distress felt by Descartes at getting into bed at night – 'On imagine avec quelle angoisse il [Descartes] devait se mettre au lit'.[4] By definition the *cogito* cannot cease from thinking, and in principle the ego cannot withdraw from consciousness. Major and contrasting philosophical positions, idealism, materialism, scepticism, empiricism, all seem thus to be fundamentally based upon the assumption of the lucid and wakeful observer. The quest for enlightenment, for the secure foundation and universal application of rational principles, announces itself eventually as *Aufklärung*, as a movement out of the darkness of superstition and ignorance into light, encouraging or leading the awakening soul out of the sleep of reason. Modern philosophy's intimate association with the growth of scientific thought, from Descartes onward, provides the most extensive articulation of the overall propensity I am seeking to describe, even and especially when, as neuroscience, for example, it makes the vacillations of consciousness themselves material for its vigilant analysis.

At the same time, modern thought from its Romantic origins onward, appears in important ways to propose the converse, in various formulations, to that propensity – movements, that is to say, away from or counter to the privileging of light, clarity, vigilance. Humanist and Enlightenment confidence in those powers and goods is challenged by various forms of materialism or irrationalism or sensationalism. The phenomenality of the unconscious in sleep and dreaming in particular dramatises that challenge. Attention to the hypnagogic from Romanticism through to Surrealism, from Coleridge's 'Kubla Khan' to Aragon's *Paysan de Paris*, reflects this counter-movement, where the critique of the active waking self, will, consciousness, reason, light, is conducted in many and various ways.

The foregoing brief outline provides, I hope, a broad frame for considering the three writers discussed here. All three variously relate alternations in consciousness, its coming and going, metaphorically or experientially realised as transitions between light and darkness, most evident and dramatic in the experience of hypnagogia (not a state but a condition of lability), as itself intermediate between the overall alternation of wakefulness and sleep. An awareness of imagination as experience of and on the threshold is enabled, and is recognised as itself enabling an imaginative literature, of a kind that seeks engagement with precisely this experience through a sustained and mobile introspection; but it also works through the imaginative resource of some form of mediation, which is that of a language artfully structured. All three, Montaigne, Keats, and Proust, for all their differences, engage with and try to realise in some form the issue of the vagary and vacillation of consciousness and the attendant questioning of the status of the self.

Montaigne's exploration, Essay 6 of Book II of his *Essays*, titled 'On Practice'[5] ('De l'exercitation')[6] exfoliates around a narrative stem, his account of an accident he meets with when out riding with his retinue. A servant on horseback runs, unintentionally but violently, into him, and Montaigne is knocked out and quite severely injured. The essay begins by arguing the need for a practical training or 'exercitation' (405, 406) of the soul through experience and not merely through theoretical procedures, reasoning and education, 'le discours et l'instruction' (405). Yet practice, he says, 'is no help in the greatest task we have to perform: dying' (416) – this supreme challenge to the soul, for which it needs to be best trained, cannot for obvious reasons be rehearsed. There is, however, some sort of equivalent experience, which is falling asleep, the lapsing of one's waking self, given overtones of a deliberate, even military exercise, perhaps with ironic qualification:

> Yet it does seem that we have some means of breaking ourselves in for death and to some extent of making an assay of it. We can have experience of it, not whole and complete but at least such as not to be useless and to make us more strong and steadfast. If we cannot join battle with death we can advance towards it; we can make reconnaissances and if we cannot drive right up to its stronghold we can at least glimpse it and explore the approaches to it. It is not without good cause that we are brought to look to sleep itself for similarities with death. (417)

This finality, death as goal and resolution, cannot be directly known but may be touched upon, glimpsed, glanced at, approached, essayed indeed through Montaigne's reflection upon experience which fringes the lapse of consciousness dramatised in this violent episode but also typified in the routine experience of falling asleep. And this recognition leads into the lyrical exclamation on the passage from waking to sleep. 'How easily we pass from waking to falling asleep! And how little we lose when we become unconscious of the light and of ourselves!' (417) Montaigne shifts from the emphasis on the ethical value of sleep's resemblance to death to one on the lability of waking and sleep, which might suggest even a kind of interfusion – as echoed in the famous quasi-doublet in the 'Apology for Raymond Sebond': 'We wake asleep: we sleep awake' ('Nous veillons dormans, et veillans dormons'),[7] which in the French plays on the assonance of the second person plural and the participle, to point up the claimed indiscernibility of these conventionally antithetical states. Another shift marks a return to the ethical, with a humanistic Christian-Stoic recognition.

> It could perhaps even seem that our ability to fall asleep, which deprives us of all action and sensation, is useless and unnatural were it not that Nature by sleep teaches us that she has made us as much for dying as for living and, already in this life, shows us that everlasting state which she is keeping for us when life is over, to get us accustomed to it and to take away our terror. (417–18)

The familiar Renaissance theme of the soul's preparation for death is sounded: compare, for example, George Herbert's 'Mortification':

> When boyes go first to bed,
> They step into their voluntarie graves,
> Sleep binds them fast; onely their breath
> Makes them not dead:
> Successive nights, like rolling waves,
> Convey them quickly, who are bound for death.[8]

However, it is not falling asleep that will be Montaigne's main subject but a more traumatic loss of consciousness and self, which is even closer to death. For death itself (as opposed to dying, the approach to death) is too precipitate to be discernible, and the closest parallel to it is falling 'into a swoon after some violent accident' (418) – the riding accident which results in his sudden and total loss of consciousness, which he here describes and reflects on. He considers that 'those whom we see failing from weakness in the throes of death find themselves in that same state' (420) which he experienced and is here re-evoking, and have both 'their body and soul buried in stupor' (420) and are unable therefore, despite any evidence of reflex, unconscious movement or response, to 'sustain any inward powers of self-cognition' and without 'any thoughts to torment them and to make them feel, or be aware of, their miserable condition' (421) are consequently in no need of pity. The weakness and incoherence of response to the external world manifested by the dying are explicitly related to the hypnagogic condition:

> The same thing happens to us when we are hesitantly drifting off to sleep, before sleep has taken us over completely: we are aware of what is going on about us as in a dream, and we follow any words spoken with a cloudy uncertain sense of hearing which seems to touch only the edges of our soul; and, to the last words spoken to us which we could follow, we make replies more marked by chance than by sense. (421)

Montaigne also notes unconscious reflexes, in injury, dying, or in sleep, 'movements independent of our reasoning' (422), which he therefore considers merely external, corporeal, 'passive movements, which only touch our outsides' (422) and 'cannot be called ours' (422), since only awareness involving 'the whole man' (422) can be.

Unconscious activities appear paradoxically, however, to be able to enter the domain of consciousness, of reasoned discourse. Montaigne goes on to relate how, approaching his home following the accident and still in a state of shock, he reports that he answered questions from his distraught family and even ordered a horse to be provided for his wife, struggling along the 'difficult and steep' (422) roadway. But these responses, he claims, were unconscious and automatic: they did not come from 'a soul which is awake' (422) but were

> empty acts of apparent thinking, provoked by sensations in my eyes and ears: they did not arise from within me. I had no idea where I was coming from nor where I was going to; nor could I weigh attentively what I was asked. My reactions were trivial ones, produced by my senses themselves, doubtless from habit. Any contribution from my soul, which was only very lightly involved and as though licked by the dew of some light impression of the senses, came only in a dream. (422)

The lyrical, faintly erotic simile reflects the languid and pleasurable quality of this state of dissociation, painless, 'most agreeable and peaceful' (423) and evocative of the ease of transition from life to death which he anticipates, a happy death in which only a gentle dissolution would be registered. Put to bed, 'I felt myself oozing away so gently' (423), welcoming it seems an easeful death, in Keats's phrase, of the kind condemned by Pascal as pagan, lacking the rigour, the clarity of intention, the vigilance of Christian dying. Montaigne's delicious death is indeed the classical and pagan brother to sleep.

Evidently however, Montaigne does not die, but begins to recover, regaining consciousness, which means consciousness of pain, after-effects of which he can still feel at the time of writing. Indeed, a couple of nights later, he comes close to dying for a second time, but this is 'a livelier death' (423), a waking death, as it were. Recovery is gradual, with an amnesia regarding the accident itself as the last point of obscurity to be resolved. Reflection on the incident, trivial in itself, is valuable to Montaigne personally because of its Stoic instructiveness: intimacy with dying helps 'inure' one to death, though this is not a doctrine, of general or universal application, a lesson for others, but, Montaigne says, a study for himself alone, though its publication may help others. It is predicated on experience, precisely on the accidental and subjective, and it points to the heart of his 'thorny undertaking' (424), which is 'to follow so roaming a course as that of our mind's, to penetrate its dark depths and its inner recesses, to pick out and pin down the innumerable characteristics of its emotions' (424), whatever the risk he runs of being charged with egotism, self-obsessiveness – for the risk is intrinsic to the enterprise.

The engagement is with a self that evades the clear delineation and active manifestation of the human agent in a waking world: 'I am chiefly portraying my ways of thinking, a shapeless subject which simply does not become manifest in deeds. I have to struggle to couch it in the flimsy medium of words.' (425) The aim is not to record deeds but to reveal the self, an aspiration based not on self-love but on humility, the willingness to portray inconsistencies, incoherences, unclarities of the self, revealing ultimately 'the nullity of the human condition' (426), here in the temporary but emphatic loss of that multifarious personality, its hiatus. The essay itself embodies a kind of vacillation that can be seen as a figuration of the hypnagogic, in its shifting passage through a fairly exiguous narrative, and in particular in its oscillation between a Christian-Stoic affirmativeness and something very different, a kind of experiential nonchalance, a sense of the value and necessity of letting go, ultimately of oneself, a self that is constituted informally, almost adventitiously. Merleau-Ponty speaks of Montaigne's characteristic astonishment at himself – 'un certain étonnement devant soi'[9] – here that astonishment is literally dramatised in loss of consciousness with the accompanying unconcern at a selfhood haphazardly lost and recovered in a partial and provisional coincidence of body and soul.

The obvious contrast is with the determinedly meditated, far from merely 'essayed', ideal of self-possession which is the Cartesian task and goal, initiating the drive towards enlightenment. Merleau-Ponty distinguishes that mixing, the 'mélange'[10] of soul and body, in Montaigne from the determined dualism of Descartes, their separation for the sake of clarity. For Descartes the acknowledgement of the hypnagogic, though not lacking in its own interest as part of the drama of methodical doubt, is the preface to the attainment, in the *cogito*, of a radical certainty. The unclarity and uncertainty of the hypnagogic are at first affirmed and absolutised in the First Meditation, ironically as 'plain seeing', the lucid insight that leads into the dazedness of epistemological doubt. 'I see plainly that there are never any sure signs by means of which being awake can be distinguished from being asleep. The result is that I begin to feel dazed, and this very feeling only reinforces the notion that I may be asleep.'[11] But this movement is nonetheless a traversing of the territory of the doubtful, identified with sleep and dreaming, in the interests of eventual wakefulness and clarity. Sustained, intent meditation on the doubtful thus is the operation of vigilance, a refusal to be deceived, opposed to the 'laziness' of habitual assumption, also identified with sleep, as the First Meditation concludes:

> I shall stubbornly and firmly persist in this meditation; and even if it is not in my power to know any truth, I shall at least do what is in my power, that is, resolutely guard against assenting to any falsehoods, so that the deceiver, however powerful and cunning he may be, will be unable to impose on me in the slightest degree. But this is an arduous undertaking, and a kind of laziness brings me back to normal life. I am like a prisoner who is enjoying an imaginary freedom while asleep; as he begins to suspect that he is asleep, he dreads being woken up, and goes along with the pleasant illusion as long as he can. In the same way, I happily slide back into my old opinions and dread being shaken out of them, for fear that

> my peaceful sleep may be followed by hard labour when I wake, and that I shall have to toil not in the light, but amid the inextricable darkness of the problems I have now raised.[12]

And the resolution in favour of the *cogito* requires the denigration of imagination, also analogised with sleep and dreaming, as in the Second Meditation:

> Once this point [recognition of the *cogito* and the consequent logic of dualism] has been grasped, to say 'I will use my imagination to get to know more distinctly what I am' would seem to be as silly as saying 'I am now awake, and see some truth; but since my vision is not yet clear enough, I will deliberately fall asleep so that my dreams may provide a truer and clearer representation.'[13]

Recuperation of the imagination in the face of this project of epistemological grounding in vigilant clarification may then call for a dramatised reflection of the hypnagogic as itself a constitutive and sometimes an initiating condition of the fiction or the poem, and through this of an imaginative and experiential sense of the self. Such a recuperation is an important aspect of the Romantic revalorisation of the imagination, finding particular salience in Coleridge and Keats. Here I want very briefly to consider the importance of the threshold of sleep and waking in Keats, focusing predictably enough on the 'Ode to a Nightingale', while pointing beforehand to a few features of the consistently contradictory Keatsian obsession with the movements into and out of sleep. *Sleep and Poetry*, with its Chaucerian epigraph suggesting both restlessness and ease, with its opening apostrophe and acknowledgement near its close, evokes the motility of sleep as the hypnagogic, 'Light hoverer around our happy pillows!' (13)[14] as well as the degree of its power as an agency for the poetic imagination, the 'trains of peaceful images' (340) it brings. *Endymion* begins famously with the 'sleep / Full of sweet dreams, and health, and quiet breathing' (I.4–5)[15] as antidote to the 'unhealthy and o'er-darkened ways / Made for our searching'(I.10–11), imaginative ease and rhythmicity set against effortful investigation. Later in Book I, Endymion's restorative sleep under Peona's 'patient watch' (I.447), will invite the apostrophe to sleep that sees it, first through the Miltonic allusion to the Holy Spirit, then in an oxymoronic coupling, as calming, beneficent, restorative, but also, with exclamatory force, as imaginatively fecund and exciting, a whole grotesquerie of moonlit imagination:

> O magic sleep! O comfortable bird
> That broodest o'er the troubled sea of the mind
> Till it is hush'd and smooth! O unconfin'd

Restraint! Imprisoned liberty! Great key
To golden palaces, strangemintrelsy,
Fountains grotesque, new trees, bespangled caves,
Echoing grottos, full of tumbling waves
And moonlight; aye, to all the mazy world
Of silvery enchantment! (I.453–461)

Later, yet still in the first Book of the poem, in a further contradictory movement, Endymion will lament the loss of his dream to sleep, 'stupid sleep' (I.678), no longer seen as restorative, as freeing the imagination, but rather, with 'his pinions dark' (I.674), as overpowering and nullifying, as mere torpor or stupefaction. Finally, in Book IV, in a shift of the 'bower motif' that runs through the poem, there is the 'den / …of remotest glooms / …the proper home / Of every ill' (IV.513–22), a place of suffering, where, however, sleep seems to provide an ultimate anaesthesia – where

But few have ever felt how calm and well
Sleep may be had in that deep den of all. (IV.524–5)

The structural and narrative vagaries and inconsistencies of *Endymion* have received much critical comment which I do not propose to rehearse. I simply want to note the alternating reflections on the passage from waking to sleep and sleep to waking, lushly evoked, thick with sensuousness and sometimes spiced with adolescent sensuality (the notorious 'sweet-shop' Keats),[16] with their differing and sometimes opposing or incompatible valorisations of the loss of waking consciousness and the descent into slumber, figured through the poet's or Endymion's voice, or associated with characters in the narrative (Peona, Adonis, Cynthia/Phoebe, and most of all the eponymous poet-hero). The play of the hypnagogic can be sensed beneath the allegorical patina.

With the Odes, the ornamentation of neoclassical allegory, the surface Hellenism, is reduced, distilled, and for the poems which engage with the sleep/waking threshold, the 'Ode on Indolence', the 'Ode to Psyche', and above all the 'Ode to a Nightingale', the poetic power of the hypnagogic is intensified. I want to foreground a reading of the 'Ode to a Nightingale' which Helen Vendler, in her analysis of the poem, disparages, 'as rather a random succession of impressions, a drift of mind' reflecting 'its abandonment to reverie'.[17] It is precisely its movement of vagary, the movement 'downward to darkness'[18] as a descent towards the insentience, the unconsciousness of sleep, classically associated with death, together with the opposite movement, in Vendler's fine phrase 'the compulsive image-making of the entranced imagination',[19] equally associated with the hypnagogic condition, that articulates the dynamics of the threshold. This is the movement of drifting down or away and, conversely, coming to, resurfacing; the abandonment of reality in favour of the unconscious, self-dissolution (Montaigne's already cited sense of 'oozing away so gently'), and also the return towards consciousness traversing the play and profusion of subconscious imagery, with an eventual return to the self, poised finally between sleep and waking.

I read the poem as constructing itself upon this shifting movement between sleep and waking: the 'drowsy numbness' (1)[20] of the opening stanza, and the descent 'Lethe-wards' (4), then refigured in the next stanza as an intoxication which will also enable the drift away from the world and its waking pain – 'That I might drink, and leave the world unseen, / And with thee fade away into the forest dim' (19–20). The movement is reiterated in the fourth stanza (and Vendler has emphasised in her reading the importance of the trope of reiteration in Keats's poetry) but here with the aspiration upwards, following the bird's flight, or more exactly that of its song, though only briefly, before the further lapse into 'verdurous glooms and winding mossy ways' (40) which will bring the sensuous fullness of the 'bower' of stanza five, sensuously imagined as it were with closed eyes, rather than wakefully seen. The sixth stanza identifies the lyric persona's hypnagogic condition – 'Darkling I listen' (51) – as replete with the sensory awareness best retained in the lapse towards sleep, hearing sustained where the other senses are occluded or abandoned, even as the traditional coupling of sleep and death is implicitly invoked, and the possibility of an absolute negation of consciousness and self is imagined. That move towards total unconsciousness is revoked, though, in favour of a further movement of imagination, rendering the sense of the transhistorical and the transmundane – the bird's song as timeless and the 'magic casements' (69) – almost proto-Mallarmean – opening into regions beyond place. Finally, with the echo of 'forlorn' (70), the last stanza brings the converse movement back towards the self, with paradoxically the implication that a kind of death (poetic death) will result from the return towards the waking individuated consciousness. 'Forlorn! The very word is like a bell / To toll me back from thee to my sole self.' (71–2) The final drift away is that of the imaginative faculty itself, figured in the bird's song, as the richly mobile awareness of the hypnagogic condition resolves into the conscious but unanswered self-interrogation – 'Do I wake or sleep?' (80)

This Romantic concern with the liminal condition between waking and sleeping is inherited by several of the the modernist writers of the earlier twentieth century. Joyce is one major example, as the close of the final story of *Dubliners*, 'The Dead', not to mention the whole project of *Finnegans Wake*, makes evident.[21] Indeed the canonical modernists all demonstrate in different ways a persistent concern with the threshold between waking and sleeping, even an anxiety focused on the hypnagogic state – Kafka, for instance, and Valéry, and notably the late modernist Beckett. (These are all writers who feature in the 'ongoing study' I referred to at the start of this essay.) Proust, whom I want to consider in the briefest coda here, is another example. The Proustian articulation of the vegetative consciousness, of the world of sleep,[22] remains exemplary – 'you cannot well describe the life of men if you don't have it bathe in sleep into which it plunges and which, night after night, winds around it as a peninsula is circled by the sea'.[23] That movement towards sleep is declared in the famous opening sentence – 'Longtemps je me suis couché de bonne heure'[24] – with its temporal uncertainty revealed in its curious grammatical construction (iterative adverb and perfect tense), which introduces the drama of the hypnagogic condition. A temporal and spatial indeterminacy, an unclarity of awareness, a lability of identity, infuse the opening pages on which the huge elaborate narrative edifice of *A la recherche* will construct itself.

> For a long time I used to go to bed early. Sometimes, when I had put out my candle, my eyes would close so quickly that I had not even time to say to myself: 'I'm falling asleep'. And half an hour later the thought that it was time to go to sleep would awaken me; I would make as if to put away the book which I imagined was still in my hands, and to blow out the light; I had gone on thinking, while I was asleep, about what I had just been reading, but these thoughts had taken a rather peculiar turn; it seemed to me that I myself was the immediate subject of my book: a church, a quartet, the rivalry between François I and Charles V. This impression would persist for some moments after I awoke; it did not offend my reason, but lay like scales upon my eyes and prevented them from registering the fact that the candle was no longer burning. Then it would begin to seem unintelligible, as the thoughts of a former existence must be to a reincarnate spirit; the subject of my book would separate itself from me, leaving me free to apply myself to it or not; and at the same time my sight would return and I would be astonished to find myself in a state of darkness, pleasant and restful enough for my eyes, but even more, perhaps, for my mind, to which it appeared incomprehensible, without a cause, something dark indeed.[25]

And rhythmically, persistently, through the novel, within and against its scrupulous delineation of the waking world, the world of sleep, more exactly of declension into and rising out of sleep, or of lapses from wakeful attention, will form material for description and reflection. The Proustian 'moments of happiness', such as the Madeleine episode, are construed as such lapses, a kind of inspiration associated with forgetting, with the loss of wakeful consciousness focused on the present, an inattentiveness proceeding out of the heart of the habitual. This has been well noted in an article by Jerry Aline Flieger. 'Like a Freudian slip – also called a lapse or parapraxis – the *moment bienheureux* is a lapse, a double movement involving both a break in the ongoing surface narrative, and a sudden, symptomatic intrusion of forgotten material into that narrative.'[26] As such it brings about the production, from revelation through digression and elaboration, of a discourse of figuration infusing and interrupting linear narrative. Flieger's reading of the Proustian text as divided between, on the one hand, a narrative discourse that is linear and horizontal, articulating itself metonymically, through continuity and contiguity of event, and on the other, metaphorically, figuratively, results perhaps in too simple a dichotomy, but may allow for the recognition of an interplay between a narrative mode that is, as it were, awake and extraverted, concerned with the social, with a realistically representable world, engaged with 'dailiness', and another mode that is engaged with a reiterated irruption of the figural, the metaphorical, a movement of verticality and profundity, associated with 'nightliness'.[27] Flieger notes perceptively Marcel's 'weaving' of his bedclothes and other 'diverse materials'[28] into the nest for peaceful sleeping[29] (comparable to aspects of the Keatsian 'bower'), and how this may be related to the insomniac Proust's own creation of his text, woven night after night, seeing the novel as 'less a product of insomnia than a certain creative sleepiness, a somnolence which favours the intrusion of dream material and dream "technique" onto wakeful consciousness'.[30] This 'intrusion' is essentially what I would describe as the motility of the hypnagogic process, alternating and interweaving the movements towards sleep and waking. The infusion of the hypnagogic into narrative results in a disturbance or diffusion of identity, of any singular and fixed perspective, of the established or assumed self, through blurring into plurality, the writing and written self as evoked through proliferation, intermittency, plasticity – a writing neither of the conscious or unconscious as distinct or autonomous modes, but of the interplay between them, evident in different articulations in all three of the writers I have been considering here.

Notes

1 Andreas Mavromatis, *Hypnagogia: The Unique State of Consciousness Between Wakefulness and Sleep* (London: Routledge and Kegan Paul, 1987). The classic and to date only major study of the topic.

2 Zechariah 4:10, quoted in Herbert Marks, 'The Twelve Prophets', in Robert Alter and Frank Kermode, eds, *The Literary Guide to the Bible* (Cambridge, Mass.: Belknap Press of the University of Harvard, 1987), 207–233 (226).

3 J. P. Fokkelman, 'Exodus', in Alter and Kermode, eds, *Literary Guide*, 56–65 (60).

4 Michel Covin, 'Un moment difficile à passer, mais vite oublié', in Michel Covin, ed., 'Visages du sommeil', special issue, *Revue des Sciences Humaines* 194 (1984): 7–30 (8).

5 Michel de Montaigne, 'On Practice', in *The Complete Essays*, ed. and trans. M. A. Screech (London: Penguin, 1991), 416–27. Quotations in English are from this edition, indicated by page numbers only in my text.

6 Michel de Montaigne, 'De l'exercitation', in *Essais*, 2 vols, ed. Maurice Rat (Paris: Garnier, 1962), 1:405–17. Quotations in French are from this edition, indicated by page numbers only in my text.

7 Montaigne, 'An Apology for Raymond Sebond', in *The Complete Essays*, 489–683 (674) / 'Apologie de Raymond Sebond', in *Essais*, 479–681 (672).

8 *The Works of George Herbert*, ed. F. E. Hutchinson (Oxford: Clarendon Press, 1941), 98.

9 Maurice Merleau-Ponty, 'Lecture de Montaigne', in *Signes* (Paris: Gallimard, 1960), 250–266 (251).

10 Ibid., 253.

11 René Descartes, *Meditations on First Philosophy: With Selections from the Objections and Replies*, trans. John Cottingham (Cambridge: Cambridge University Press, 1986), 13.

12 Ibid., 15.

13 Ibid., 19.

14 John Keats, *Sleep and Poetry*, in *The Poetical Works of John Keats*, ed. H. W. Garrod (Oxford: Clarendon Press, 1958), 51–61. Quotations marked by line numbers in my text.

15 John Keats, *Endymion*, in Garrod, ed., *Keats*, 63–188. Quotations marked by book and line numbers in my text.

16 The reference is to the lines from Yeats's poem 'Ego Dominus Tuus' – 'I see a schoolboy when I think of him, / With face and nose pressed to a sweet-shop window'. *The Collected Poems of W. B. Yeats* (London: Macmillan, 1963), 182.

17 Helen Vendler, *The Odes of John Keats* (Cambridge, Mass.: Belknap Press of the University of Harvard, 1983), 83.

18 Ibid., 84.

19 Ibid., 86.

20 John Keats, 'Ode to a Nightingale', in Garrod, ed., *Keats*, 257–260. Quotations marked by line numbers in my text.

21 See my essay 'Falling Asleep in the Wake: Reading as Hypnagogic Experience', in John Brannigan, Geoff Ward and Julian Wolfreys, eds, *Re: Joyce: Text Culture Politics* (London and New York: Macmillan, 1998), 163–81.

22 Marcel Proust, *Remembrance of Things Past*, 3 vols, trans. C. K. Scott-Moncrieff and Terence Kilmartin (London: Penguin, 1983), 2:787.

23 Ibid., 2:83.

24 Marcel Proust, *A la recheche du temps perdu*, 3 vols, ed. Pierre Clarac et André Ferré (Paris: Gallimard, 1954), 1:3.

25 Proust, *Remembrance of Things Past*, 1:3.

26 Jerry Aline Flieger, 'Proust, Freud, and the Art of Forgetting', *SubStance* 9, no. 4, issue 29 (1980): 66–82 (67).

27 Ibid., 70–72.

28 Proust, *Remembrance of Things Past*, 1:7.

29 Flieger, 'Proust', 69.

30 Ibid., 74.

Part Four

READING, WRITING, PLAYING, LISTENING

Chapter Eleven

READING ON THE THRESHOLD

Jason Scott-Warren

At some point in the mid-1990s, I bought a copy of Shakespeare's *Sonnets* in a second-hand bookshop in Cambridge. It was the long-outdated edition of W. G. Ingram and Theodore Redpath, published in 1964 by the University of London Press, in the second impression of 1967.[1] It must have sat in the publisher's warehouse for some time before it sold, since a sticker on the dust-jacket flap replaces the original price (35 shillings) with a new, decimalised and inflated figure (£3.45). My interest in the book begins, however, with the flyleaf, inscribed in blue biro, in a somewhat shaky hand:

To Ev,
with love,
From Robert. 13th March, 1977.

Lower down on the page, a little black-and-white photograph of the couple has been pasted in, subscribed: 'Us at Rhodes, / 1933.'

Many such gifts go unread, but this one did not. On the inside cover of the book, this time in Ev's hand, is a list of numbers – reading down, 116, 29, 91, 30, 53, 71, 25, 17. The list refers, of course, to individual sonnets, and it comes as no surprise that 116 ('Let me not to the marriage of true minds') should be in the vanguard – if Rhodes was perhaps the venue for a honeymoon, here is the poem of choice for weddings. The sonnet itself goes unmarked, but later items on the list receive explicit annotation. So 29 ('When in disgrace with Fortune and men's eyes'), which proclaims the transformative effects of 'thy sweet love rememb'red', prompts Ev to add: 'last two lines quite true of R. J. R. to me'. Beneath Sonnet 91, whose speaker proclaims that he is only wretched in that his beloved might withdraw his love 'and me most wretched make', Ev writes: 'No R. J. R. wont / he is true as steel', adding her initials, 'E R'. Sonnet 53 ('What is your substance, whereof are you made') is 'Quite true of R. J. R. to ev', while 25 ('Let those who are in favour with their stars') is annotated, simply, 'R. J. R and ev.' Just one more sonnet – a poem not on the initial list – receives annotation. Underneath 123 ('No, time, thou shalt not boast that I do change'), with its enigmatic reference to 'thy pyramids built up with newer might', we find a longer note: 'On seeing the Pyramids away back in time (1929) I thought of the slaves who carried the huge stones to build it [sic] – perhaps hungry weary. / E R. / 1978.'

Abrupt and naive as they are, these annotations offer a poignant example of reading as 'appropriation' – making a text one's own, or in this case perhaps two's own. The love-relationship that motivates the gift of the book becomes the explicit subject of the reading. Individual poems are either applied directly to that relationship or are criticised for their failure to capture its perfection. Accordingly, we find no annotations on the early sonnets, those that enjoin a young man to propagate his beauty by having children, or the poems towards the end of the sequence, with their fetid love-triangles and tortured sexual puns. This reader focuses on poems which speak of the trials of love – a love seemingly between men, but one which had been opened up for heterosexual reimagining as early as 1640, when John Benson's edition offered the *Sonnets* in radically new arrangements and amalgams, tricked out with generalised or blatantly boy-girl headnotes ('A Valediction', 'A request to his scornefull Love', 'Vpon the receit of a Table Booke from his Mistris').[2] Ev allows just one poem to escape the amorous frame: in her retrospection about Egypt she asserts herself ('I thought of the slaves') and draws attention to the gulf of time separating 1978 from 1929, a gulf dwarfed by the temporality of the pyramids.

Such annotations show up particularly starkly against the background of *this* edition. For the Ingram/Redpath *Sonnets* offers a scrupulously scholarly rendering of the text, with facing-page notes that are occasionally so full that they spill over onto subsequent pages. It is emphatically an edition for the formalist reader, which eschews any discussion of the identity of the 'Friend', the 'Dark Lady', 'Mr W. H.' and the 'Rival Poet' in favour of 'attention…to detailed meaning, and to the individual sonnets as works of art'. Although the preface recommends the book to the general reader, the text is ostentatiously learned, and does not begin to imagine the reading to which this particular copy was subjected.[3] Later gift-editions, festooned with emblematic illustrations (flowers, birds, hour-glasses) and Elizabethan portrait miniatures, would have been fitter for the purpose.[4]

As Ev's book suggests, reading is an affair of the threshold. The marks we make in our books cluster around their fronts and backs and edges. We inscribe our ownership or donorship on the front flyleaf or title-page, often with a date, sometimes with a place too. In this there is a sense of anticipation, of the pages that remain to be opened and the future in which our inscriptions will deepen in meaning. Philip Larkin's imagined widow, leafing through her old sheet music in 'Love Songs in Age', recalls 'that certainty of time laid up in store'; books help us to mark time, to demarcate the spaces of a life in which there are honeymoons and widowhoods to be had, thresholds of many kinds to be crossed.[5] The back of a book, meanwhile, is well-suited to preserving the fruits of reading – brief notes of points we might return to when we have left the immediate encounter behind us, signs that the text is slackening its grip. Then there are the margins and blank spaces, borderlands which will us to defy the soundless garrulity of the printed text, to release it from its rectilinear cage into the world of contention it claims to have left behind. Beneath the words, at the end of lines, across the visual surface of the letters if we are wielding a highlighter-pen, our marks articulate and animate our books, each one testifying to a meeting or a collision of minds, a movement across mental and material boundaries.

The threshold is also crucial to the way that books strive to make their claims upon readers – the prefaces, dust-jacket blurbs, notes, illustrations that surround the text and exert a subtle but pervasive influence on the way we read it. Gérard Genette, who gave these elements of the book an over-arching name in his *Paratexts: Thresholds of Interpretation* (1987; English translation 1997), has to count as one of the greatest 'thinkers on the threshold', even if his study at times looks more like a Borgesian mock-catalogue of literary curios (many of them discovered 'by the luck of the stepladder') than a contribution to theory or poetics.[6] The paratext is for Genette 'a transitional zone between text and beyond-text' (407), a repertoire of customary practices that serve to present the text and to make it present in the world (1), 'a "vestibule" that offers the world the possibility of either stepping inside or turning back' (2). Often it is a border-zone between the everyday and the extraordinary (think, perhaps, of the notes to *The Waste Land*), a 'fringe at the unsettled limits that encloses with a pragmatic halo the literary work'.[7] If it is true that a text changes when the world around it changes, then the paratext is often the index of such change, since it functions visibly as an 'instrument of adaptation' (408) to a new cultural environment. By surveying the rise and fall of particular paratextual fashions – the epigraph, say, beloved of nineteenth-century novelists and twentieth-century radicals (159–60); or the dedication, deemed obsolete in its 'supplicant' form since the invention of authorial royalties (131) – we gain some insight into 'the customs and institutions of the Republic of Letters' (14).

Although that phrase has a Swiftian ring (and the rigmarole of prefaces, epigraphs and dedications does begin to look absurd in Genette's account), this threshold is in practice nothing if not enigmatic. The paratext has its own erotics. Like clothing, layers of commentary or stylish dust-jackets are an invitation to unwrapping. They can play coquettish games with the reader, or they can go pimping; Genette quotes Antoine Furetière's pronouncement that 'A lovely title is a book's real procurer' (91). We might recall Shakespeare's play of diseased pandering, *Troilus and Cressida*, prefaced in some printed copies by an unsigned epistle from 'A never writer, to an ever reader', which tried to cajole that reader into buying it.[8] But a book's body-language is made up as much by what it doesn't say as what it does – by the noble abstention of a Gallimard volume from back-cover verbiage (26), or the fact that a poem 'is presented in isolation on the otherwise blank page, surrounded by what Eluard called its "marges de silence"' (34). The paratext is diaphanous, the more so because only a part of the paratext (the 'peritext', as Genette christens it) is materialised in the book we hold in our hands. The rest (the 'epitext') floats freely in the world, in the form of publishers' advertisements, authorial letters and interviews, even bits of gossip that circulate around the text and influence its interpretation. People who know about Proust's part-Jewish ancestry and his homosexuality read his work differently from those who do not, and 'anyone who denies the difference is pulling our leg' (8). What is more, even those elements of the paratext which form part of the book are apt to be elusive. '"The paratext," properly speaking, does not *exist*; rather, one chooses to *account in these terms* for a certain number of practices or effects' (343). How does a footnote (seemingly part of the paratext) change if the author turns it into a parenthesis in the text? What do we do with a text such as Sterne's *Tristram Shandy*, which subsumes into itself numerous paratexts, right down to the marbled paper that ought to be pasted inside the binding? Only a fully-qualified 'paratextologist' (40) can answer such thorny questions.

Perhaps the most startling feature of Genette's thinking on the threshold is the prominence it accords to the author. The point of any paratext, he states in conclusion, is 'to ensure for the book a destiny consistent with the author's purpose' (407). These words are carefully chosen, in the awareness that 'the author's purpose' usually stops short of specifying a typeface, format, and paper-stock, and may have little to do with dump-bins, promotional tours and magazine interviews. Nobody could accuse Genette of naivety about the role of publishers and other agents in the shaping of a book's presentation to the world. Still, the question of how far a work's paratexts might be constituted in its reception is left unbroached. An author's anticipation of criticism, and his inclusion of a prefatorial 'lightning rod' (208) to deflect it, counts; so too does an author's response to criticism (354–6). But what of that criticism itself, and its power to transform the public perception of a text? Here, Genette is silent. The reader is the vanishing point of his study. Everything in the paratext is directed towards readers, actual or potential, but the agency of those readers goes unexamined. We are left forever on the brink.

To push the question a stage further, we might ask: what of individual readers? Could Ev's responses to Shakespeare, however humble, however resistant to the learned editors' designs, be considered a paratext? If an *author* inscribes a copy of her book, Genette's ear pricks up: 'it is unnecessary to add how valuable for each work an itemised account of all its inscriptions would be' (140–1). But such an account would work to efface the particular copy, rediscovering the 'constitutive ideality' (35) of the literary text and with it the traditional business of criticism. Yet, while texts cannot (like paintings or sculptures) be identified with their material instantiations, they cannot be apprehended unless they take material forms; and literary critics have recently begun to be interested in what readers have made of those forms – in the fate, that is to say, of the individual book. To take such an interest requires some adjustments. For, just as we idealise the text, so too we often tend to think of reading, at its most meaningful, as an essentially private activity, an affair between an individual and a text, conducted in solitude, silence and mental space (certainly, this is how it is often depicted in art).[9] We can be fully aware of the many social and sociable aspects of reading, and of its multifarious concretions, its places and paraphernalia, and still cling to the post-romantic fallacy.[10] The illusion is sustained by the fact that, in the modern world, books come to us as finished articles which do not prompt us to acts of creativity that leave a trace. Even the act of writing in a book is frequently proscribed by modern pedagogy. Things have not always been this way.

* * *

In the late eighteenth century, the relationship between readers and texts was opened up to new forms of inventive play. In the wake of the Reverend James Granger's *Biographical History of England* (1769), the fashion for cutting, pasting, tipping-in and souping-up books with images of all kinds reached pandemic levels. Granger's work, essentially a bibliography of engraved portraits accompanied by historical anecdotes relating to the figures they depicted, focused a well-established humanist/antiquarian interest in collecting images of the illustrious, enriched by the burgeoning of physiognomy and of a desire for more intimate histories of the past.[11] The result was a craze for 'heads' which could be incorporated, with snippets of Granger's text, into lavish volumes which would display the collector's wealth, leisure and connoisseurship. In one of the most extensive of these 'extra-illustrated' or 'grangerised' texts, the Whig MP Richard Bull turned the comparatively modest (and itself unillustrated) *Biographical History* into a behemoth in 19 large-folio volumes, supplemented by sixteen additional volumes that carried the viewer forward from the Glorious Revolution (where Granger broke off) to the reign of George III.[12] Such an elephantine project required a belief in the malleability of books – of *these* books, which Bull was creating, but also of the numerous titles which were being destroyed in the process. Many of the images in a collection like this came from frontispieces, which underwent a 'mad spoliation' at the hands of the extra-illustrators. A satirical poem of 1813 lamented that Granger's 'biographic page' was 'so much the rage' that 'scarce one book its portrait graces, / Torn out alas! each author's face is'.[13] The contribution of 'Anti-Guillotine' to the *Gentleman's Magazine* of 1802 compared portrait print collectors with French republicans, 'so eager are they to take of[f] the heads of persons eminent for rank'. Although the motives of genteel head-collectors were in reality profoundly conservative, there was some truth in the charge that the grangerisers were decapitating books; Granger himself objected to Bull's tendency to discard useful bibliographical information as he discarded the volumes from which his images were taken.[14] But perhaps the head contained all the information one needed. Tellingly, the word 'frontispiece' derives from the medieval Latin *frontispicium*, the act of 'looking at the forehead' in the science of metaposcopy, 'the art of judging character or telling a person's fortune from the forehead or face'.[15] One of the many peripheral paratexts of the printed book, the means by which the author (as it were) steps over the threshold to greet the reader, the portrait frontispiece was given a new weight in these collections. Where Ben Jonson had enjoined readers of the 1623 Shakespeare folio to 'looke / Not on his Picture, but his Booke', the extra-illustrators privileged the visual as a means of enlivening knowledge traditionally conveyed in words.[16]

The fashion for grangerising was predicated upon a conception of the book as a vehicle for social display rather than private communion. Richard Bull's folios were pieced together with a strong sense of showmanship, each page striving to impress. As a result they enjoyed a rich social life, travelling frequently by coach 'for the entertainment of Granger and other interested parties'.[17] What, one wonders, did early viewers make of the spectacle? As modern commentators have noted, the sheer profusion of images on each page of such collections frequently threatens to upset their controlling aesthetic; for us, part of the fascination of the genre is its visual *in*coherence. Inevitably, when images are drawn from many different periods and places, a sense of temporal dislocation sets in.[18] A copy of George Gascoigne's *The noble art of venerie or hunting* (1611), extra-illustrated by Joseph Haslewood with around fifty hunting pictures from *The British Sportsman* (1798–99), offers a good example: the rough woodcuts of the original publication look like barbarous relics of a pagan past when set alongside the ultra-civilised and sentimentalised inserts.[19] Yet, for all its visual confusion, Haslewood's book (like Bull's) opens up a shareable, sociable space: these pictures might just as well be hanging on the huntsman's walls as nestling within his books.

Books also began to turn into art galleries in the hands of George C. George of Penryn in Cornwall, discussed by Stuart Sillars in his account of the extra-illustration of Shakespeare's plays.[20] Interlarding Shakespeare's works with engravings and watercolours, George's books prompt the familiar sense of profligacy. The over-abundance here is again temporal – George's volumes are 'a visual variorum, valuable in instantly displaying changing tastes in selection of scenes and styles of depiction' – but it is also intellectual, part and parcel of an approach to Shakespeare's plays which reads them as continuous with the histories they depict. Portraits, historical engravings, illustrations of the play imagined and of the play staged; all are thrown together in an 'apparently random mingling of forms'. Sillars believes it was this profusion that made the books work as a spur to polite conversation (about 'which of the images was the most effective, the truest to the play's progression, or…the most effective at showing the characters' emotions').[21] Such projects flourished because of the social games they made possible.

The extra-illustrated book was often intended to be a shared intellectual resource, customised by one for the benefit of many. An exemplar of Sir James Ware's history of the Bishops of Ireland comes densely annotated (with many notes drawn from other copies in the scholarly domain), and interleaved with illustrations, periodical and newspaper cuttings, pamphlets, letters, and documents.[22] Numerous instances of this kind of collaborative antiquarian collection survive in libraries today. There they are ghosted by less rational collections that contain a premonition of the internet in their manically associative mode. A grangerised copy of Thomas Mathias's satire on contemporary authors, *Pursuits of Literature, or, What you will* (1812) feels like hypertext, with any reference to a person or a place (however fleeting) requiring its own disruptive illustration. The poem begins to be crowded out by the pictures, as if it had only been composed as a pretext for an extravagant visual feast.[23]

First prize for strangeness in this genre goes to a vamped-up book that combines elements of the intellectual resource and of the surfable miscellany. It began life as a heraldry manual. Augustine Vincent's *A discoverie of errours* (1622) was a contribution to the print-war between the York herald, Ralph Brooke, and the historian William Camden; it went through the presses of William Jaggard at the same time as the 1623 Shakespeare folio, and seems to have attracted some of the same readers.[24] In this copy, the text has been thickly annotated by a seventeenth-century antiquary – as yet unidentifed, but a serious player with access to the public records. The book took a new turn in the late eighteenth or early nineteenth century, when (divided into two volumes) it fell victim to a series of cutting and pasting exercises, all of them focused on the text's readerly thresholds. In the first place, a set of frontispieces

Figure 7. Extra-illustration in a copy of Augustine Vincent, *A Discoverie of Errours in the First Edition of the Catalogue of Nobility*, 1622. Image © The British Library Board.

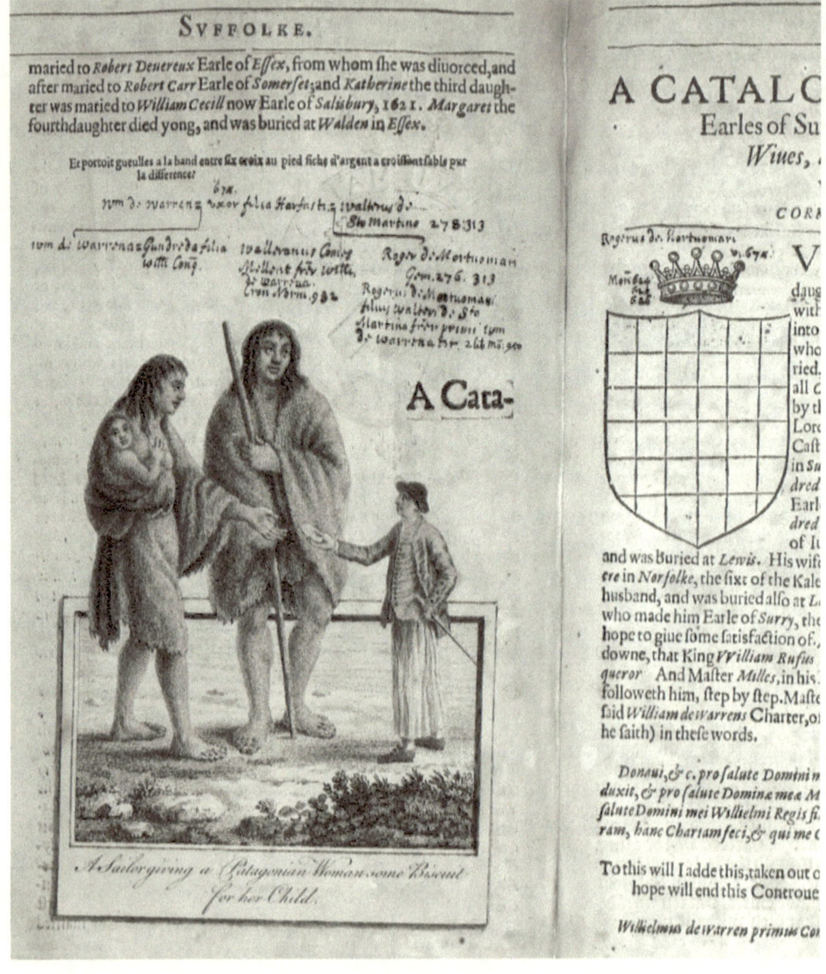

and tailpieces was stuck in, apparently to celebrate the joy of heraldry. A number of the engravings present visual allegories, the original meanings of which are utterly obscure, though all have been graced with handwritten Latin epigraphs which claim them as commentaries on nobility. The most brazen manuscript additions are, however, those made to a tipped-in portrait of Edward Cave, founder of the *Gentleman's Magazine*, engraved in 1754 after a painting of 1740.[25] In this book the image has been doctored so that it now purports to represent Augustine Vincent; his name appears on a letter in the sitter's hand, and the book beside him is not the *Gentleman's Magazine* but the 'Catal[ogue] / of / Nobilit[y]'. The forgery continues on into the small print – the tiny 'F. Worlidge pinx[it] 1754' at the foot of the engraving has been altered so that the date reads '1621'.

But the weirdest elements in this bibliographic confection are the pasted-in engravings at the end of each section of the text. Some are of birds set pertly on twigs, others of scenes that might be read as symbols of mortality (the tomb of Cestius in Rome, overgrown with weeds; a Cupid sitting on a classical pediment in a landscape of ruins). But many depict flora and fauna from the Old World, the New World, and the even newer worlds of the Pacific. Here are armadillos, Californian goats, even (peering up beneath an account of Thomas Howard, fourth Duke of Norfolk) a 'Patagonian Pinguin'.[26] Others present foreign lands and peoples. Beneath an account of the earldom of Suffolk, a well-dressed sailor offers a Patagonian giantess 'some Biscuit' for her child (Figure 7). The entry on the earls of Sussex is preceded by 'A New Zealand Warrior in his proper Dress, compleatly Armed, according to their Manner.' Finally, there is at least one semi-pornographic image, a picture of 'The Kitchen where the Poor Girls were employed & often whipped & tortured', showing a woman naked but for her stockings and shoes, her clothes strewn around her, tied by her arms to a rope in the ceiling as she awaits her fate.[27] The deployment of such disparate and far-flung materials (most of them culled from the *Gentleman's Magazine*) to decorate the fringes of a cherished heraldic compendium suggests how the act of reading breaches the boundaries between radically different cultural spheres.[28] Just as Ev reads her own relationship directly against the love delineated in Shakespeare's *Sonnets*, so this earlier reader saw no clash between Vincent's woodcut shields and the engravings of global curiosities dished up in eighteenth-century periodicals. Both volumes speak of historical divides, yet readers cross these thresholds at a leap.

* * *

The vogue for extra-illustrating might be taken to be a cul-de-sac of book history, a collective collecting mania that (like the cabinets of curiosities of an earlier period) appears bizarre only in retrospect. But it is also possible to view it as the last great expression of the *ancien régime* of print. For, before the arrival of the pre-bound book in the second quarter of the nineteenth century, a significant proportion of books were offered for sale unbound, openly inviting creative appropriation by the purchaser.[29] Paratextual decisions that are now made by the publisher were the province of the reader. What combination of paper, wood and leather to use in the binding (if it was to be bound at all); how to decorate it; whether to interleave it with blank pages for notetaking or to set it alongside other books related in content, or perhaps just in size – all of these choices were the consumer's. Authors, concomitantly, were freer to particularise their books (copies of which they often received from the publisher as part-payment for their labours), and sometimes fashioned individual copies for individual readers.[30]

In this *ancien régime*, it was common for books to burst their boundaries in ways that prefigure grangerisation. Bindings made a public statement: they could be ostentatiously plain, declaring the owner's seriousness and sobriety; or they could be gaudy, demonstrating social distinction quite as clearly as clothing. The flamboyant aristocrat Richard Sackville, Earl of Dorset, had eight large folios bound in crimson satin, gold-blocked with the letters 'R E D' – his initials, his identity, but also the colour of the plush covering.[31] A reader could encode coy messages into a binding, as when Sir Richard Browne (father-in-law to John Evelyn) had his gilded monogram surrounded by the 's-clavo', a slashed-'s' that hinted that Browne was a 'slave' to love.[32] Or the binding could proclaim one's ambitions and achievements. In the early seventeenth century, one 'M^RS^ ELIZABETH COLLES' had her name tooled onto a sparkling binding which gathered together a Latin dictionary and two introductions to Latin grammar, letting everyone know about her plans to intrude on traditionally male linguistic territory.[33] A decade or two earlier, the court composer John Bull stamped his name on a volume containing a debate about the merits of plainchant and polyphony, a collection of lute music by Anthony Holborne, and a French treatise on dancing.[34] The result was a shimmering vade mecum to catch the eye of Elizabeth I.

Early printers often conceived of their publications as pamphlets or 'separates' which could be bound together with other texts in a kind of literary pick-and-mix.[35] In this they followed expectations created by the (almost entirely bespoke) culture of manuscript, and many such miscellanies or *sammelbände* must have put printed and handwritten texts together, although centuries of rebinding and reclassifying have made it hard to identify such volumes today. Compilations of certain kinds of printed text do survive. More's *Utopia* and Erasmus's *Praise of Folly* often turn up in the company of educational treatises, handbooks of rhetoric or letter-writing, and orations, all of them trumpeting the new humanist education. Some books from this period seem scarcely to have existed as coherent entities. The poems of Samuel Daniel and of Edmund Spenser were published in numerous small units that were assembled into 'Collected Works' by booksellers or readers, creating nightmares for modern cataloguers.[36]

As well as determining how a book would be composed, *ancien régime* readers also attempted to influence interpretation. The early modern textual marketplace was a scarcity economy, in which much sharing and loaning took place. And, for a variety of reasons, 'reading' frequently meant shared reading, reading aloud. In such circumstances, it made sense to stamp judgements on books.[37] The title-page or frontispiece, the book's forehead, was the place to plant such judgements, like horns on the brow of the cuckold. That was where Edward Coke wrote his damning verdict on Francis Bacon's *Instauratio Magna* (1620): 'It deserveth not to be read in schooles / but to be fraughted in the ship of fooles'.[38] It was also where the Elizabethan recusant-hunter Richard Topcliffe re-christened Cardinal William Allen's *True, Sincere and Modest Defense*, branding it 'A false, sediccoos, & immodest offense: sett out by English traytors abroade (& summe at home) Groaning for the Gallows'.[39] In 1545 William Cecil (later one of the architects of the Topcliffe's Protestant England) signed the title-page of a Catholic treatise and indicated his approval on the facing flyleaf. 'Although this work may seem long to you at first glance, Reader, nevertheless I hope you will not give up on reading it carefully. For if you finish it, you will I hope be well strengthened and armed against the unholy deceptions of the Sacramentarians. Farewell'.[40] Stephen Alford, in his biography of Burghley, guesses that these words were penned when Cecil made a gift of the book, perhaps to his alma mater, St John's College, Cambridge.[41] But, given the currency of 'reader paratexts' in the period, they could be an admonition to all who would encounter the text in this copy. Books deemed seriously misleading required more vigorous rebuttal. Confronted with the writings of the Portuguese bishop Osorius, the civil lawyer Walter Haddon scattered insults ('you lie, sycophant!') throughout the margins.[42]

The community of readers for such threshold commentary extends through time as well as space. Indeed, the archetypal form of such inscriptions may be the notes on births and deaths that traditionally adorn the spare leaves of family bibles. Such notes are a safely Protestant version of the moving formulae found in many medieval and early modern books, requesting prayers for the owner's soul. These are most at home in devotional works such as Books of Hours, where they range from the highly formal (professional scribal additions, painted images of the owner at prayer) to crudely scratched inscriptions.[43] But such prayers also turn up in secular books. A printed copy of Chaucer's works informs us on a title-leaf that 'Walter Blownt ys oner of this boke' and asks: 'thow blissed [sic] mother of god praye for me . they [sic] sarvant', while a fifteenth-century husbandry manual enjoins, 'Sir Everard Digby bought this book; pray for him and his parents'.[44] As objects that go on speaking even in silence, as heirlooms that might survive into a future we will not see, books make useful substitutes for mass-priests and tombstones.

Any essay which claims, as this does, that our relationship with print has become far less physical over the course of the last two centuries is duty-bound to end by speculating about how all this will change thanks to the advent of the internet. This essay, however, means to resist any such predictable conclusion. Instead, I offer you, my reader, a space in which you are free to write or draw or press or paste anything you like. Let us hope that no two copies of *Thinking on Thresholds* will ever be the same again.

Notes

1 *Shakespeare's Sonnets*, ed. W. G. Ingram and Theodore Redpath (London: University of London Press, 1964).

2 *Poems: Written by Wil. Shake-speare. Gent.* (London: John Benson, 1640), D2r, D6v, E6r. See further Margreta de Grazia, 'The First Reader of *Shake-speares Sonnets*', in Leonard Barkan, Bradin Cormack and Sean Keilen, eds, *The Forms of Renaissance Thought* (Basingstoke: Palgrave, 2009), 86–106.

3 Ingram and Redpath, eds, *Sonnets*, ix–x, xii.

4 See for example William Shakespeare, *The Sonnets*, illustrated by Ian Penney (London: Barrie and Jenkins, 1988).

5 Philip Larkin, *Collected Poems* (London: Faber and Faber with The Marvell Press, 1988), 113.

6 Gérard Genette, *Paratexts: Thresholds of Interpretation*, trans. Jane E. Lewin (Cambridge: Cambridge University Press, 1997), 217. Genette's work was originally published as *Seuils* (Paris: Seuil, 1987). Further references to it are incorporated in parentheses in the main text.

7 This formulation of Genette's is quoted by Richard Macksey in his forward to *Paratexts*, xvii.

8 William Shakespeare, *The Famous Historie of Troylus and Cresseid* (London: R. Bonian and H. Walley, 1609), ¶2r.

9 Garrett Stewart, *The Look of Reading: Book, Painting, Text* (Chicago: University of Chicago Press, 2006), 175–86.

10 A powerful case for the social nature of reading in the 'romantic period' itself is made by H. J. Jackson, '"Marginal Frivolities": readers' notes as evidence for the history of reading', in Robin Myers, Michael Harris and Giles Mandelbrote, eds, *Readers, Annotators, and the Signs of Reading* (London: British Library, 2005), 137–51; idem, *Romantic Readers: The Evidence of Marginalia* (New Haven: Yale University Press, 2005).

11 Marcia Pointon, *Hanging the Head: Portraiture and Social Formation in Eighteenth-Century England* (New Haven: Yale University Press, 1993), 53–78; Lucy Peltz, 'Facing the Text: the amateur and commercial histories of extra-illustration, c. 1770–1840', in Myers et al., eds, *Readers*, 91–135.

12 Pointon, *Hanging*, 70–2; Peltz, 'Facing the Text', 102–7; see further Lucy Peltz, 'Engraved Portrait Heads and the Rise of Extra-Illustration: The Eton Correspondence of the Revd James Granger and Richard Bull, 1769–1774', *Journal of the Walpole Society* 66 (2004): 1–162.

13 Pointon, *Hanging*, 59–60.

14 Peltz, 'Engraved Portrait Heads', 8, 22–3.

15 OED, 'frontispiece, *n.*'; 'metaposcopy, *n.*1'. On the relationship between head-collecting and physiognomy, see Peltz, 'Facing the Text', 122.

16 William Shakespeare, *M[r] William Shakespeares Comedies, Histories, & Tragedies* (London: William Jaggard, 1623), facing title-page.

17 Peltz, 'Engraved Portrait Heads', 32.

18 Pointon, *Hanging*, 71–2, 75. On 'polytemporality' and material culture, see Jonathan Gil Harris, *Untimely Matter in the Age of Shakespeare* (Philadelphia: University of Pennsylvania Press, 2009).

19 George Gascoigne, *The noble art of venerie or hunting* (London: Thomas Purfoot, 1611); Cambridge University Library (hereafter 'CUL'), Syn.7.61.238.

20 Stuart Sillars, *The Illustrated Shakespeare, 1709–1875* (Cambridge: Cambridge University Press, 2008), 214–51.

21 Ibid., 222, 226. Compare Peltz, 'Engraved Portrait Heads', 33–4.

22 Sir James Ware, *The whole works of Sir James Ware concerning Ireland* (Dublin: 'For the Author', 1739–46); CUL Adv.c.95.2. Additions to this volume were made by J. H. Todd (1805–1869), founder of the Irish Archaeological Society (ODNB).

23 Thomas James Mathias, *The pursuits of literature: a satirical poem in four dialogues, with notes*, 16th edition (London: Becket and Porter, 1812); CUL LE.11.87.

24 Augustine Vincent, *A Discoverie of Errours in the First Edition of the Catalogue of Nobility* (London: William Jaggard, 1622), British Library (hereafter 'BL'), 607 l 15. For the printing, see Peter Blayney, *The First Folio of Shakespeare* (Washington: Folger Shakespeare Library, 1991), 24–5; Edward Dering's 'Booke of Expences', 1617–28 (transcription by Laetitia Yeandle online at http://www.kentarchaeology.ac/authors/020.pdf (accessed 26 June 2010)), 34v, 41r.

25 A version of this engraving accompanies the entry on Cave (1691–1754) in ODNB.

26 Vincent, *Discoverie*, fols ¶7r, G3v, 2Y3v.

27 Ibid., fols 2S4v, 3X4v, 4E4v.

28 Several of the engravings are found in the *Gentleman's Magazine* for 1783–4, although others date back to 1767. The penguin may come from the *Universal Magazine of Knowledge and Pleasure* 45 (1769), 150–1, while the whipping image fits with an 'Abstract of the Tryal of the Brownriggs for the Murder of Mary Clifford, their Apprentice Girl', *London Magazine* 36 (1767): 477–81, although I have been unable to trace a precise source. On the various 'Destruction Rooms' that extracted and sold old journal illustrations in this period, see Peltz, 'Facing the Text', 91–3.

29 David Pearson, *English Bookbinding Styles 1450–1800: A Handbook* (London: British Library, 2005), 1.

30 For an example, see Jason Scott-Warren, *Sir John Harington and the Book as Gift* (Oxford: Oxford University Press, 2001).

31 Frederick A. Bearman, Nati H. Krivatsy and J. Franklin Mowery, *Fine and Historic Bookbindings in the Folger Shakespeare Library* (Washington D. C.: Folger, 1992), 139; Richard Almack, 'Queries: Richard Sackville, Earl of Dorset', *Notes and Queries* 3rd ser., 7 (1865): 7.

32 M. M. Foot, 'An Englishman in Paris: John Evelyn and his Bookbindings', in Anne De Coster and Claude Sorgeloos, eds, *Bibliophilies et reliures* (Brussels: Tulkens, 2006), 231–45 (234).

33 CUL Rel.d.61.2. Colles was probably the Somersetshire gentlewoman whose will is National Archives, PCC PROB 11/165 [15 May 1634]).

34 CUL Rel.c.56.4. For Bull (1559x63–1628), see ODNB.

35 Alexandra Gillespie, *Print Culture and the Medieval Author: Chaucer, Lydgate, and their Books 1473–1557* (Oxford: Oxford University Press, 2006), esp. 72–6.

36 A. C. Hamilton, ed., *The Spenser Encyclopedia* (London: Routledge, 1990), 259.

37 Elspeth Jajdelska, 'Pepys in the History of Reading', *Historical Journal* 50 (2007): 549–69 (552–6); Jason Scott-Warren, 'News, Sociability and Bookbuying in Early Modern England: The Letters of Sir Thomas Cornwallis', *The Library* 7th ser., 1 (2000): 381–402 (384–5).

38 Francis Bacon, *Instauratio Magna* (1620), copy at Holkham Hall, Norfolk; reproduced in Jason Scott-Warren, *Early Modern English Literature* (Cambridge: Polity, 2005), 133.

39 William H. Sherman, *Used Books: Marking Readers in Early Modern England* (Philadelphia: University of Pennsylvania Press, 2007), xvii–xx.

40 'G C Lectori // Quanquam opus hoc grande tibi videri possit Lector / consultum tamen tibi velim ut in perlegendo non / desistas. Nam si hunc assecutus fueris satis strenuum / ac armatum fore adversus impias sacramentariorum sy= / cophantias spero. vale'; in Bishop John Fisher, *De Veritate Corporis et Sanguinis Christi in Eucharistia* (Cologne: Peter Quentell, 1527), CUL Rel.d.52.17. Thanks to Margaret Meserve for assistance with this translation.

41 Stephen Alford, *Burghley: William Cecil at the Court of Elizabeth I* (New Haven: Yale University Press, 2008), 28.

42 CUL Adv.c.8.1, fol. C1v ('Mentiris sycophanta'). On adversarial annotation, see William H. Sherman, *John Dee: The Politics of Reading and Writing in Early Modern England* (Amherst: University of Massachusetts Press, 1995), 65–75.

43 Eamon Duffy, *Marking the Hours: English People and their Prayers 1240–1570* (New Haven: Yale University Press, 2006), 23–52.

44 BL 644.M.1, Chaucer, *The Workes of Geffray Chaucer* (London: Wyllyam Bonham, 1545(?)), fol. 2A1r; CUL Inc.3.F.2.2 [3197], Petrus de Crescentiis, *Liber ruralium commodorum* (Louvain: Johannes de Paderborn, n.d.); 'Dominus Everardus digbii comparavit hunc librum Orate pro eo et pro suis parentibus'.

Chapter Twelve

WHEN I BEGIN I HAVE ALREADY BEGUN[1]

Gabriel Josipovici

I remember reading a series of interviews with Karlheinz Stockhausen.[2] This was in the eighties, when the composer was at the height of his fame. I was particularly struck by his account of a visit to Japan, which made a deep impression on him. The Japanese, he noted, did not have the same sense of time as we have in the West. For them time was either something that passed extremely swiftly or extremely slowly, and the large middle range we inhabit did not seem to exist. An example of this was Sumo wrestling. The two enormous combatants, artificially fattened for years for this sport, would size each other up in total stillness for what seemed an eternity, and then suddenly, almost before the spectator could see it, one had thrown the other out of the ring. Stockhausen, whose own music had from the start followed a route far removed from the major traditions of the West, was enchanted. He was also much taken by the Japanese attitudes to space. He grew fascinated by the Japanese use of sliding doors and windows, which had the effect, he said in the interview, of blurring the threshold between inside and outside, an effect heightened in many of the temples by the winding and labyrinthine paths which led to them, so that as one approached one felt oneself to be sometimes almost on top of them and then, seconds later, as far away as ever.

For reasons I did not understand, these remarks of Stockhausen's excited me, and led, eventually, to my writing a little story called 'Second Person Looking Out'. I decided to write a story about a rather formal party in a house with sliding doors and windows, in which the protagonist is at times approaching the house, at times within it, and at times departing from it. I thought I would write the story in nine parts, in the past, present and future, and in the first, second and third persons. In the end I realised that it only needed three parts, in the first, second and third person, each part involving a protagonist who was approaching, within, and departing from the house, and therefore moving between past, present and future. Here is an extract from the start of the second section, in the third person:

> He has walked through the seventeen rooms. He has talked to many of the guests as well as to his host. At times he has stopped alone in front of a window and stared out at the landscape.
>
> It has been explained to him that the house is approached by numerous paths, some of which, he has been told, will be closed when he leaves, with a bamboo stick laid across the path, but, by following those stones which have a piece of string tied round them and fastened in a triple knot he will be able to find his way out again.
>
> 'How much further is it?' he asks his guide.
>
> 'Not much further,' the man says, hurrying ahead.
>
> They round a hillock, and there is the house ahead of them.
>
> 'There are seventeen rooms in the house,' the guide explains. 'Each room has three windows, which can be moved to any position on the walls or covered over if necessary.'
>
> His host has moved away from him and wandered into the next room. The young lady to whom he has just been introduced asks him: 'Is this a temple or something?'
>
> 'No. Just a private house.'
>
> 'It reminds me of a temple,' she says.
>
> They are standing in the fourteenth room. The three windows all face the tall trees at the back of the house. The light from the downstairs rooms illuminates the lawn, but that only serves to make it darker under the trees. His host, in answer to a question, explains: 'The windows are always moved once a guest has looked through them.'
>
> 'That must be disconcerting for the guest,' he says.
>
> 'It is the custom,' his host says, standing beside him in the dark.
>
> He advances slowly, feeling each step ahead of him for fear of treading on a bamboo stick laid across his path.[3]

Why had reading the interview with Stockhausen excited me and led me to the writing of this story? Probably because I too, without quite realising it, had been as unhappy with the narrative traditions I had inherited as Stockhausen had been with the musical ones; because I too was looking for ways of escaping from the beginning, middle and end form which seemed to be the only way to write narrative, as it seemed to be the only way to compose music. Those novels and stories which began, like *David Copperfield*, with 'I was born on…' or 'I was born at…' or 'Had you been in such and such a place at such and such a time you would have seen…', while they might be the only way of writing narrative, did not, I obscurely felt, correspond at all to how I felt in my own life. There I could find no beginnings and no ends but rather obscure correspondences, repetitions and foldings, which nevertheless demanded to be explored in a narrative mode – but where was that mode to be found?

As I discovered, narratives did exist which corresponded to my secret intuitions, but though they were hardly marginalised – they were among the most famous works of literature in the Western canon – they seemed to lead their lives in a parallel universe, not impinging on the tradition of the novel which had become, in the West, the dominant narrative tradition. When I came across them my heart leapt and I obscurely knew that these were the narratives for me:

Nel mezzo del cammin di nostra vita
  mi ritrovai per una selva oscura
  che la diritta via era smarrita.
Ah quanto a dir qual era e cosa dura
  esta selva selvaggia e aspra e forte
  che nel pensier rinova la paura!…
Io non so ben ridir com'io v'entrai
  tant'era pieno di sonno a quel punto
  che la verace via abbandonai.
Ma poi ch'i'fu al pie d'un colle giunto,
  la dove terminava quella valle
  che m'avea di paura il cor compunto,
guardai in alto, e vidi le sue spalle
  vestite gia de'raggi del pianetta
  che mena dritto altrui per ogni calle.
Allor fu la paura un poco queta
  che nel lago del cor m'era durata
  la notte ch'i' passai con tanta pieta. (lines 1–6, 10–21)

[In the middle of the journey of our life I came to myself within a dark wood where the straight way was lost. Ah, how hard a thing it is to tell of that wood, savage and harsh and dense, the thought of which renews my fear!… I cannot rightly tell how I entered there, I was so full of sleep at that moment when I left the true way; but when I reached the foot of a hill at the end of that valley which had pierced my heart with fear I looked up and saw its shoulders already clothed with the beams of the planet that leads men straight on every road. Then the fear was quieted a little which had continued in the lake of my heart during the night I had spent so piteously…][4]

So begins Dante's *Commedia.* Though the poem is regarded as one of the four or five classics of European civilisation, when I first read it I sensed at once that it was quite different from Virgil's *Aeneid* or Milton's *Paradise Lost,* in that it did not require a great effort of the historical imagination, or great erudition, to enter into it, as those two works did, but spoke to me directly and immediately. Of course it is rich in learning, richer perhaps than those other poems, and the commentaries on every canto are so numerous that no-one but a dedicated scholar could read them all; but that does not alter the fact that it is possible to read the poem as, somehow, telling one's own story and telling it in a way which, for me at any rate, made immediate sense.

Someone has been lost in a dark wood and now emerges into an open valley to see, touching the mountains that tower above, the first beams of the rising sun. But this narrator, unlike the first person narrators of nineteenth-century novels, is quite ready to confess that he does not know how he got into the wood, how his way was lost. Everything in those opening lines (and the opening is not over) speaks of renewal, of emergence from darkness and confusion, but we do not know if wood and valley and rising sun are metaphor or reality, and *it does not matter.* For all reading is in a sense the reading of metaphor, making mine what the writer has put out there, what the protagonist is experiencing. We open the book, we start to read. What happened before the book starts is lost precisely because there were no words for it; or, to put it another way, the beginning of words is the beginning of a coming to consciousness. Time and space have lost their rigidity, and when we begin to read we are straight away inside something whose threshold we have not consciously crossed because, in a sense, when the poem begins it has already, long ago, begun. Partly this is a function of Dante's way with language: 'In the middle of *our* life, *I* found myself…' That the narrator's life and mine share a basic structure is attested by the 'one' – the middle of *our* life, thirty-five by the biblical reckoning; that one element in this structure concerns finding again what was lost is brought out by the next phrase: '*mi ritrovai*', '*je me suis retrouvé*' as the French would put it (English, lacking the reflexive, has to opt for the clumsy: 'I found myself' or the too specifically psychological: 'I came to'). I was lost in a dark wood but now I begin to find my way again; I was lost to myself, but now, as I start to read, I begin to find myself again. And in the third line of this extraordinary first tercet (a three-line stanza invented by Dante for the occasion, which is not quite a *stanza,* a (closed) *room*, since it links with the next in a chain ababcbcdc, each line consisting of 11 syllables), *diritta* and *smarritta* – straight and lost or confounded – echo ironically one with the other, forcing us, as we read, to recognise how easily that which is straight can be lost but, by the same token, how easily that which is lost can be recovered, made straight (how, at the level of speech production, even internal speech production, the complicated tongue and lip movement which produces the hissing of '*sma*' can relax into the easy '*di*').

Did Proust know Dante? It would be surprising if he didn't, but there are no references in the letters or in *A la recherche* (which has such extended passages on Giotto, on Saint Mark's in Venice, and on medieval French cathedrals) to show that Proust had actually read Dante. Perhaps he had not and it was simply that he and Dante were working the same seams, that led him to find, after much patient labour, testified by the number of drafts we have for the opening pages, a first sentence that blurs all thresholds and also hinges on a reflexive: 'Longtemps, je me suis couché de bonne heure'.[5] As numerous commentators have pointed out, it is impossible to translate this sentence, for what exactly is the force of that *longtemps* which will find its echo in the last word of the massive work, many thousands of pages later… *temps*? And how to translate *je me suis couché*? 'I went to bed' or 'I used to go to bed' or 'I laid me down' are all impossibly wordy or archaic. The sentence leads into an extended meditation on how fluid the border is between sleep and waking: having finally managed to get to sleep, the narrator is woken by sounds of the city coming to life at dawn, only to realise that it is in fact the night watchman in the hotel doing his rounds, putting out the lights at midnight; he then meditates on how, in sleep, we hold within us, like Adam, all the innumerable possibilities of the human race and how, on waking, we have to revert to the one possibility which is the life we actually have, a life which is partially given and partially chosen. In the course of this meditation Proust/Marcel passes in lightning review all the rooms in which he has slept and which we will come to know in the pages that follow, rather as a Mozart overture compresses all the major themes of the opera to follow in music which seems so carefree, so intent only on its own inner logic, that these overtures are often performed by themselves. The effect of this is that when we do meet those rooms later we sense that we have already been there. Once again, it seems that in order for the story to begin it must, in a sense, have already begun.

Eliot, of course, did know Dante, and references to Dante in his great later poems, like *Ash Wednesday* and *Four Quartets*, are explicit and unironic, in contrast to *The Waste Land*, where the distance between Dante's Europe and the Europe of the years immediately after World War I is highlighted. In the later poetry what is important is similarity, not difference. As in Dante and Proust, the first lines of *Burnt Norton*, the first of the *Four Quartets*, convey the impression that the poem has started long before its actual start. As in those other two works it manages to do this because the poet has found a series of very specific and local ways of conveying a radical vision. After a few lines which do not so much convey information about time and eternity as establish a mood (which I tend to think of as the mood in which, unable to sleep, at four in the morning, we talk to ourselves and imagine that what we are saying has enormous profundity – and perhaps it has, but by morning that profundity has evaporated), the poem takes a new turn, one which is, as with Dante and Proust, both surprising and somehow long-predicted. In fact, this much shorter work retains from first to last the sense that it is both a narrative and a commentary on how this narrative has come into being, maintains itself, and arrives at its end:

Time present and time past
Are both perhaps present in time future
And time future contained in time past.
If all time is eternally present
All time is unredeemable.
What might have been is an abstraction
Remaining a perpetual possibility
Only in a world of speculation.
What might have been and what has been
Point to one end, which is always present.
Footfalls echo in the memory
Down the passage which we did not take
Towards the door we never opened
Into the rose-garden. My words echo
Thus, in your mind.
But to what purpose
Disturbing the dust on a bowl of rose-leaves
I do not know.
Other echoes
Inhabit the garden, shall we follow?
Quick, said the bird, find them, find them,
Round the corner. Through the first gate.
Into our first world shall we follow
The deception of the thrush? Into our first world.
There they were, dignified, invisible,
Moving without pressure, over the dead leaves…[6]

The world of memory and of the imagination, like the world of the unconscious as Freud described it, does not know the meaning of the word 'no'. So 'footfalls echo in the memory / Down the passage which we did not take', and that passage leads us into a rose-garden (the definite article before 'passage' and 'rose-garden' helps persuade us that there was one and only one passage, one and only one rose-garden; but note also the tact whereby what starts as only a sound, the echo of feet, turns into a passage and then into a door and then into what is to be found beyond the door). And so, as we read the poem, the magic is worked and we *are* in that rose-garden, where the rest of this opening section takes place.

The echoes are not only of Dante but of *Alice in Wonderland* and Frances Hodgson Burnett's *The Secret Garden*, which suggests that the Victorians and Edwardians, particularly in their children's books, tapped unconscious material which the official culture tended to repress, so that what the first wave of Modernist authors such as Eliot and Joyce and Conrad and Forster could be seen to be doing is only making that material explicit. Like the narrator of *A la recherche*, 'more destitute', as he wakes up, 'of human qualities than the cave-dweller', but for whom then 'the memory, not yet of the place in which I was, but of various other places where I had lived, and might now very possibly be, would come like a rope from heaven to draw me up out of the abyss of not-being, from which I could never have escaped by myself';[7] like Dante the pilgrim emerging from the dark wood into the valley still bathed in shadow, but the peaks of whose surrounding mountains the rays of the rising sun are already striking, the narrator of *Four Quartets* is somehow given the opportunity, by the words that have gone before, to hear the footfalls and to follow them in memory or imagination (remember that what is Marcel's memory is Proust's and the reader's imagination) down a passage never taken and then open a door never opened so as to emerge into a garden that is somehow familiar. The poem has only just begun but it has already, we feel, been going on for a long time, has been going, in fact, for all our lives.

We all know how, in our own lives, decisions are not taken strictly on their merits, but largely because of who and what we are, and who and what we are is something mysterious to us, but is clearly made up of genetic, social and other factors, which include all the decisions we have and have not made in the years we have lived. We know too how dreams and involuntary, chance memories, memories triggered by smells or tastes or perhaps something felt or half-seen, suddenly put us in touch with areas of ourselves we did not know were there, had lost touch with, and how important these seem to us to be. The classic novel, good as it is in dealing with some things, seems not to know how to deal with these, or perhaps can only deal with them in very indirect ways. What my reading of Proust, Dante and Eliot gave me, and what reading those interviews with Stockhausen helped me articulate, was that there are other ways of writing narrative, as of conceiving of space and time, which, to me at any rate, seemed more true and more rewarding: ways that glide easily across thresholds unknown and remembered, with dim but intuitive recognition.

It might be thought that traditional cultures, those with a strong sense of the importance of thresholds, of rites of passage, would have been inimical to such modes of narration, but the opposite is true. As the case of Dante might have suggested, these modes are actually closer to the ways of thinking of traditional societies than is the classic novel, and a little thought might suggest why this should be so. Traditional societies have a strong sense of the porousness of individuals, of how we each of us merge into others and into the community at large. It is the novel which sets the individual as a closed vessel, up against society, and makes a fetish of individual freedom and success. Those rites of passage which clearly mark at least birth, puberty, marriage and death in traditional societies also clearly mark the places where the individual joins the group: in baptism or circumcision in Christianity and Judaism, at the start; in the first communion and the *bar mitzvah* which scholars believe was modelled on it, since it is not attested before the later middle ages, when the individual is deemed old enough to acknowledge for him or herself a membership of that community; in marriage where the joining of two families is seen as sanctioned by God in both Christianity and Judaism; and in death, when the individual is recognised by the community he or she has left behind as now entering that larger communion of the dead. These thresholds, being communal, bring the individual in touch with the larger group. This means that they are moments when the individual is helped to escape the narrow unfolding of his or her unique life, made to see that 'io' and 'nostra vita' are forever conjoined, and that the recovery of the 'I', 'mi ritrovai', is one with the recognition that it is not only my life but our life. It is as though the threshold between the various aspects of one life are the moments when we can recognise this, and it suggests that in my three examples what the authors have attempted is in a sense to naturalise the sacramental: this is how our lives are, not as Balzac and Stendhal depict it. Let me give just three examples of the porousness of thresholds in the great monotheistic cultures, so as to bring home the perhaps surprising closeness between radical modernism and ancient tradition.

Monotheism, it is sometimes claimed, brought with it a new sense of the historical: in the place of the cyclical world-view of the irrigation-based and sedentary cultures of the Ancient Near East, Egypt and Mesopotamia, the Israelites, a nomadic people, brought the idea of a God who created the world once and for all and acted in it at decisive moments, notably in the freeing of the Chosen People from enslavement in Egypt. But this is not, as Protestant theologians sometimes take it to be, the moment of a clear transition from repetition to linearity, from cultures whose rituals are based on the annual cycle to ones which recognise the decisive intervention of God in history in a unique moment. At least that is not how the Jews themselves, the descendants of the biblical Israelites, chose to see it. That once-and-for-all moment in which God acted in history is recalled and symbolically repeated every year at Passover, when the participants in the Passover meal are enjoined to see what happened then as happening now, and those who experienced those events in the past not as 'them' but as 'us'. A similar paradox pertains, of course, to the Easter ceremonies of the Catholic and Orthodox Churches, and indeed, to the daily celebrations of the Mass in those two Churches. When one grasps this one can see that one of the things Dante is trying to do is to make of his poem a parallel both to the Easter liturgy and to the Mass. And the parallels one finds between Dante and Proust and Eliot would then suggest that these modern writers have only found ways of extending the life of these ancient rituals, both Christian and Jewish, and in a sense naturalising the sacraments.

My second example has to do not with the Israelites but with later Jewish commentary on the Bible. The first sentence of Genesis is familiar to nearly everyone: 'In the beginning God created the Heaven and the Earth' – in the Hebrew: *bereshit bara elohim et ha-shamayim va-et ha-aretz*. There are as many difficulties with this opening sentence as there are with Proust's, but for our purposes what is important is that first word, *bereshit*. The word derives from *rosh*, head. The letter B with which, in this form (in-the-beginning) it starts, is written, in Hebrew, thus: ב. It is called *bet*, which means a house, and it is the second letter of the Hebrew as of the English alphabet. The rabbis argued that it is not by chance that the Bible begins not with the first but with the second letter, and that this second letter has the shape it has. As it is open on the left and closed on the right (remember that Hebrew is written from right to left), what follows, i.e. the whole Bible, is open to examination, but what precedes is closed off. That is, we must not ask what came before, we must simply start. One does not search for origins, for these can never be found (to imagine one can find them is to usurp the place of God); one starts somewhere and gradually finds oneself and one's subject. This is precisely what the implicit argument is in Dante, Proust and Eliot.

My third example comes from Islam and it demonstrates a lack of concern with thresholds as decisive transitions, this time not in the realm of time or text but of space and architecture. Visitors to the great ninth-century mosque of Ibn Tulun in Cairo can make their way to the roof of the building (Figure 8). From there they will look down on a vast courtyard with an elaborate well in the centre, from which four grooves lead to the four corners of the building which surrounds the yard (not shown on the diagram). These symbolise the four rivers of Paradise. All round the courtyard are arcades, which, seen from ground level, are found to be two deep on three sides and five deep on one, but this is not visible from the roof, where the four sides appear uniform, as in the cloister of a medieval cathedral. But the crucial difference is that the cloister is only an adjunct to the cathedral, an ambulatory area distinct from the sacred area which is entered through the imposing doors in the Western façade, which often themselves lead only to an antechamber which then leads into the main body of the Church (two superb and very different examples are New College chapel in Oxford and the Romanesque church of Vézelay in France). In the mosque of Ibn Tulun, by contrast, *there are no doors, because there are no walls*. The *mihrab* and *minbar*, the prayer niche and pulpit, which are aligned towards Mecca, and which are what define the communal focus of the building, are to be found in the side of the courtyard where the arcades are five columns deep, and the floor there is covered with carpets. But that is all. Like the other three sides enclosing

Figure 8. Floor Plan of the Mosque of Ibn Tulun, Cairo.

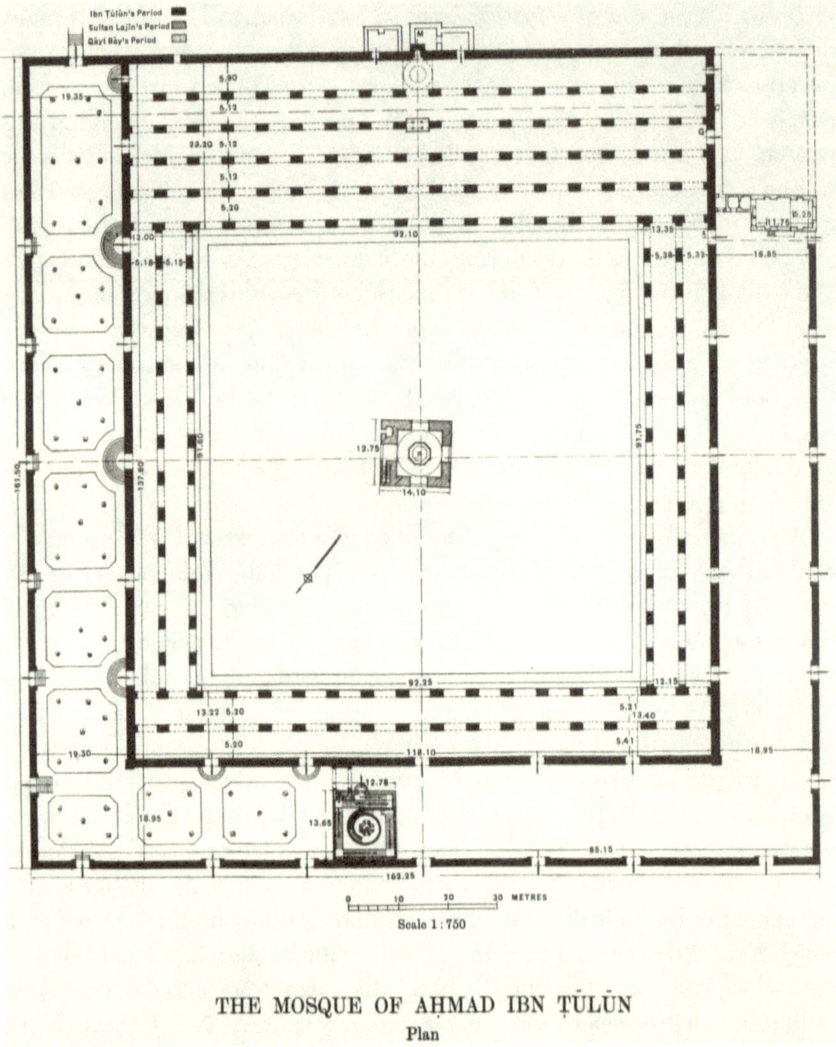

Scale 1 : 750

THE MOSQUE OF AḤMAD IBN ṬŪLŪN
Plan

the central courtyard, it is only separated from the courtyard by the pillars which form the arcades. This is a huge shock to the Westerner. What, he asks, is inside, what out? Like Stockhausen's Japanese temples, this sacred edifice has no clear inside and outside, only degrees of innerness and outerness.

What is the explanation for this? At one level there is a simple historical reason why early mosques were often like Ibn Tulun: they were built on the model of Mohamed's house in Mecca. In regions where the distinction is not between cold (outside) and warmth (round a fire, inside), but between sun and shade, there is much less reason to build walls and doors. What you need is protection from the sun, not from the cold. But this, like the nomadic origins of the Israelites, has a profound effect on the religious practices and perceptions of the inhabitants of the region: inner and outer are not shut off from one another, nor the individual from the community; not only are thresholds porous, they are almost non-existent.

These three examples suggest that the great monotheistic religions of the world, while recognising the importance of thresholds and of rites of passage, also see the individual as far more open, far more a part of a larger community than does the post-Enlightenment West. Only the High Priest could enter the Holy of Holies in the Israelite Temple, the place where the Ark of the Covenant was kept, but the Ark itself was a portable house, so to speak, and the God of the Israelites had expressly forbidden David to build him a temple, since he dwelt everywhere and nowhere, and no merely human building could ever house him. It was perhaps in response to some such imperative that Stockhausen, no less than Dante, Proust and Eliot, was drawn to the creation of works which do not so much have beginnings, middles and ends as move forward in circular fashion towards an end which, when it is eventually reached, is discovered to be the true beginning:

We shall not cease from exploration
And the end of all our exploring
Will be to arrive where we started
And know the place for the first time.
Through the unknown, remembered gate
When the last of earth left to discover
Is that which was the beginning;
At the source of the longest river
The voice of the hidden waterfall
And the children in the apple-tree
Not known, because not looked for
But heard, half-heard, in the stillness
Between two waves of the sea.[8]

Notes

1 *This essay is dedicated to the memory of Stephen Medcalf.*
2 Jonathan Cott, *Stockhausen: Conversations with the Composer* (London: Robson Books, 1974).
3 Gabriel Josipovici, 'Second Person Looking Out', in *In the Fertile Land* (Manchester: Carcanet, 1987), 15–21 (18–19) (modified).
4 Dante Alighieri, *The Divine Comedy of Dante Alighieri*, 3 vols, trans. and ed. John D. Sinclair, revised edition (London: John Lane, 1948), 1:22–3.
5 Marcel Proust, *A la recherche du temps perdu*, 3 vols, ed. Pierre Clarac et André Ferré (Paris: Gallimard, 1954), 1:3.
6 T. S. Eliot, 'Burnt Norton', in *Collected Poems 1909–1962* (London: Faber and Faber, 1974, repr. 2002), 177–183 (177–8).
7 Marcel Proust, *Swann's Way*, trans. by C. K. Scott Moncrieff (London: Penguin, 1957), 12.
8 T. S. Eliot, 'Little Gidding', in *Collected Poems*, 201–209 (209).

Chapter Thirteen

THRESHOLDS IN IMPROVISATION: FREEDOM, THE ETERNAL PRESENT, AND THE DEATH OF JAZZ

Rick Foot

they live forever who live in the present[1]

There are several elements present in improvised music which seem to distinguish it from music of other kinds. The inherent process of becoming, the unrealised nature of the music, its ephemerality and air of revelation, the lack of any document outside of the instant in which it happens: all these point towards the way in which the act of improvising and the result are inextricably tangled. There is no separation of the act of performing from the music performed – there is only the process. Successful improvisation involves a continual hovering in the doorway, a pointing at a landscape, a set of possibilities, rather than the representation of the landscape that is the through-composed work. The fragility of that extended moment is the substance of such music: it is by definition poised on the threshold of realisation.

This essay will be particularly concerned with why it is that the recording process seems so inadequate a representation of an improvised performance – why so little of the experience, both from performers' and audience's point of view, seems to survive the transfer to tape or disc. Indeed, if recording is found lacking in this respect, to treat it as the necessary and sufficient documentation may be damaging to the development and survival of the music itself. This, in turn, would go some way towards explaining the intuitive sense that jazz, that most thoroughly documented of improvised musical forms, is somehow worked through, exhausted – a completed art form. My argument will be based less on what ought to happen than on what actually happens in practice: it will offer gestures towards a phenomenology of improvisation.

The Temporal Threshold

Every form of music exists only in the moment, on the threshold between past and future, balanced perfectly on the cusp. But there is a critical difference in improvised music. In playing a composition the performer walks a tightrope of sense and time: there is a single linear thread connecting past and future and going through the threshold of the present, and the player either negotiates it successfully, or falls off if the execution fails. There is a harking back even in the moment of performance, a long lingering gaze back to the composer. The best the performer can aspire to is the more or less perfect representation of someone else's thought.[2] When improvising, however, the musician is surrounded by a fuzzy cloud of possibility, and there is no single correct thread to choose from – an indefinite unrealised collection of potential routes extends like a cone into the future. The waveform of possibilities collapses into a linear thread as the performance progresses.

In recording, all that is registered on tape is the collapsed line – the intimation of possible states cannot survive now that the moment has passed – so the performance moves from the fluid present into the fixed past, a change of state that renders it as a two dimensional object, a slice through the original presented as though on a slide for later scrutiny. As Alain Danielou puts it, 'Of the living music in which improvisation plays an essential part, a gramophone record gives us only a frozen or fixed moment, like a photograph of a dancer.'[3] Composition is, after all, closure – the end of a process. Improvisation is the opening of a doorway. It is not through having executed the piece that perfect expression is achieved, but through the continual process of hovering on the brink of execution. It is that threshold experience that distinguishes, precisely, the improvised from the composed. The aim is not even to produce a piece of music – the 'piece of music' which is a composition does not exist here. It is just to find emotional affect, immediate sense, to perpetuate the flow of ideas. The musicians, the space, the audience are all inside a bubble of context, part of a musical language game in the Wittgensteinian sense; this context is what gives the music its meaning. Divorced from this environment by the recording process, the work is flattened out: it cannot make sense of the same kind. The recording is still music, but it is now a document to be pondered and analysed and re-read. Some of the context survives the transfer to disc, as a silhouette retains an object's outline, but the aspects lost are precisely those which make the improvisation what it is – in the transfer it is reduced to the status of a written piece. All its inadequacies as a composition will be laid bare, a peculiarly fruitless exercise as it was never intended to be treated as composition in the first place. As the composer and improviser Cornelius Cardew describes this,

> Documents such as tape-recordings of improvisation are essentially empty… What a recording produces is a separate phenomenon, something really much stranger than the playing itself, since what you hear on tape or disc is indeed the same playing, but divorced from its natural context. What is the importance of this natural context? The natural context provides a score which the players are unconsciously interpreting… [a score] that co-exists inseparably with the music, standing side by side with it and sustaining it.[4]

On the Brink of New Terrain

The purest example of music in its 'natural context' is free improvisation – that is, improvising with no predetermined formal constraints. The form creates itself in performance. When free music is completely successful, it attains a continually self-renewing momentum. The music takes on its own life, seems to grow unbidden from a central position between the musicians. From the performers' perspective, the sense is not that there is instant composition going on, but quite the reverse: the collective sound seems to dictate the course of the piece, independent of and somewhere above the supporting roles of the players and the collective will of the group. A landscape appears, a whole unexpected inexplicable territory ready to be explored, and the musicians hover on its threshold – they can gaze at it from the periphery, may have the chance to explore a path or two before the piece reaches its natural conclusion, but the ephemeral nature of the music means that the landscape vanishes at the end of the performance. This experience of the unaligned centre of the music being somewhere else, and visible through a window, is available even to the solo performer: rather than playing what one hears, it is as though one's fingers are doing the hearing – a loss of self in the music.

As an instrumentalist this is a strange and magical state to find oneself in – a transcendent moment outside time, where the music flows through the fingers and instrument in an uninterrupted stream, with one's self-consciousness reduced to the role of delighted spectator: a stretching out of the cusp of the present into a timeless perfection. If the self is a fiction designed to account for the delusion that our lives have a narrative, then the timelessness of this state represents the perfect release from this delusion – plucked from the narrative and lost in the eternal present.

In practice, the intent of free music to reveal new landscapes with every performance is unworkable – it is an ideal state to aim for, rather than a guaranteed presence. The strain of seeking new ground in preference to the immensely easier option of revisiting old territory may lead the musicians to fall back on familiar devices. Any free group begins to develop its own vocabulary, its own preferred methods, and as the music drifts towards predictable processes, old landscapes are re-explored – the threshold is breached. When the landscape is stepped into and explored, the magic dies.

Between Performer and Audience

It is tempting to suggest that a further threshold is present in performance between the musicians and the audience – a doorway or opening that can be widened or shut altogether according to the mood of either of the parties. One of theatre's most persistent issues is the view that it represents a barrier: the desire to break through the fourth wall between stage and audience is implicit in most modernist drama – an idea addressed by Jean Chothia's essay in this volume.[5]

The audience for improvisation has a privileged position. As Derek Bailey observes, 'to improvise and not to be responsive to one's surroundings is a contradiction… the audience for improvisation, good or bad, active or passive, sympathetic or hostile, has a power that no other audience has. It can affect the creation of that which is being witnessed. And…has a degree of intimacy with the music that is not achieved in any other situation.'[6]

Despite the difficulty and abstraction of much free improvising, the issues discussed in Milton Babbitt's essay 'Who cares if you listen?'[7] where he argues that contemporary music will be incomprehensible to anyone not intimately involved in the genre, are marginally alleviated by the immediacy of the process. In a way the audience are already past the most awkward barrier to their understanding of proceedings. There is the opportunity to get inside the music in the instant of creation – and as Stanley Cavell has pointed out, this is revelatory: 'we may find ourselves *within* the experience of such compositions, following them; and then the question whether this is music and the problem of its tonal sense, will be – not answered or solved, but rather…will disappear, seem irrelevant'.[8]

It might be thought that this picture is artificial – do we really respond differently to improvisations? Is music not there, as sound in the room, to move us or not according to its own intrinsic qualities? For the sound in the room to be considered music at all, it must be meant – there must be an active intention involved – and while this essay lacks the scope to address issues of intention in art, it is possible to draw attention to the attitude we have to improvised music by looking at cases of deception.

Consider, for example, a situation common in improvised performance, when the musicians emerge suddenly from a long passage of increasingly fragmented senselessness into an emphatic piece of unison playing, granting the illusion of satisfying structure to the formless noise that has preceded it, a retrospective sense imprinted on the past. For the audience, and indeed the musicians for they are part of the audience too, this spontaneous resolution can be thrilling, cathartic, a kind of magic. Here we have something that only makes sense once its process of becoming is over. It is only its echo in the memory that seems coherent. But it may be that there is a disguised map being followed by the performers here, and that the seeming revelation is a trick, preplanned. And this would make the performance a different kind of object. Similarly, if we see the same band on successive nights and discover that what appeared to be spontaneous creation is prewritten, that solos have been worked out in advance, we feel let down, slightly cheated. Why is it important to know what is improvised and what predetermined? Clearly we respond differently to each, but why? Is it the mysticism of the act of creation? Here we are, little gods, making sense from the void… thus we present ourselves. To be told the sense was in fact prewritten would be to face a significant disappointment, just as it would be similarly deflating to discover that the pyrotechnical vocal gymnastics being apparently performed in one's presence are in fact merely being mimed to a backing tape. Though it may be the same performers on the prerecorded tape, still as audience we feel cheated – there is deceit, something inauthentic here. As an audience we seek out the intimacy, the direct affect described by Derek Bailey above – and that we can respond as we do to moments we sense to be inauthentic is enough to indicate that there is a distinctive, authentic experience to be grasped.

Jazz 1: Continual Revolution[9]

What we have, then, is a model of improvisation in practice: an unrecordable process of continuous flux, balanced on the threshold of the moment, offering potential revelation of new worlds, and having an intimate engagement with its audience. The history of jazz can be viewed as a struggle to keep these elements in play.

The formal essence of jazz is improvisation over a predetermined structure – most usually song form. In the natural development of the music – and no musical form has evolved so rapidly – there is a continual pressing against the boundaries that define the form itself, an ever-present urge to move on, evolve, transcend. Progress has been through an expansion of the vocabulary, or a development of process – a move into new territory where the threshold experience, the hovering on the brink of discovery, can be maintained. Charlie Parker did this through harmonic expansion, and the adoption of hectic tempi; Ornette Coleman through abandoning the song form as the basis for improvisation; Charles Mingus through the spontaneous extension of form in performance; Miles Davis by a succession of moves from bebop through cool jazz, modal jazz, a hypermodern harmonic and rhythmic approach with the classic quintet with Wayne Shorter et al., and ultimately by embracing amplification and the possibilities offered by rock and funk. But in all these cases, the overarching substance of the music remains unchanging: it still sounds like jazz.

Listening now to the revolutionary music Ornette Coleman was playing in 1959 – *Change of the Century*, *The Shape of Jazz to Come* – it is hard to hear just what is so extraordinary about his approach. We can listen to John Coltrane's *Giant Steps*[10] – the last step down the road of increasing harmonic complexity begun by Charlie Parker and Dizzy Gillespie in the bebop revolution fifteen years earlier – and be unable to distinguish its approach from Ornette's entirely different tack. *Giant Steps* still follows the standard jazz blueprint, which takes the harmonic structure of the opening and closing theme and uses this as the repeating structure over which the musicians improvise. Ornette Coleman's approach, while still bookending performances with a theme, makes a radical move beyond song form into improvisation on mood, taking the theme at the start as no more than an indicator of an emotive area to explore. For contemporary audiences, he offered exactly that threshold experience discussed earlier: his vision of a new world opening out through his playing was interpreted by his enthused supporters as a radical refreshing of the music, a whole new wonderland of freedom to explore; and by his detractors as a window on to an awful formless void, chaos, the abyss. It is curious that we can barely catch an echo of this now. Though some of what followed in the free jazz movement he inspired can still seem shocking, Ornette in this period can sound quaint, cheerful, harmless.[11] This must in part be due to the inadequacies of recording as a medium, a point I will return to. But there is another issue here: we have heard so much music since 1959 that our ability to hear has been corrupted by it all. Contemporary notions of dissonance and consonance are radically different from those of fifty or a hundred or three hundred years ago. And just as what has been seen cannot be unseen (an inevitable effect of the internet), so what has been heard cannot be unheard. We can no longer listen to Bach or Monteverdi or even Wagner or Britten without the filter of all the subsequent developments in music which we have been unable to avoid, all the weary noise of the twentieth century since the advent of recording and endless unavoidable regurgitation.

So, to attempt to recreate the music of, say, the Baroque period by using period instruments may have some legitimacy, but to suggest that through such a process we are revealing how the music sounded at the time is patently nonsense. Even if we were able to slip back in time and listen to a period performance, we would still be condemned to hear that performance through the perceptual filter of all the music which has succeeded it. The neoclassical approach to jazz, treating the past forms of the music with reverence, stumbles against this inevitability. Our ears hear differently – that is the further threshold at which sense and affect must be negotiated. The ear, indeed, is as much of a threshold here as it is in the experience of listening to poetry – the process Angela Leighton explores in her essay in this volume.

Jazz 2: The Audience as Obstacle

The audience for improvisation has a unique effect, both in shaping the results, determining a significant part of the environment within which the performance takes place, and on occasion providing an obstacle that must be overcome. The need for affect, something that will move, and be sufficiently entertaining to keep the majority involved in the process, can lead to trickery, the invocation of learned devices – a bit of smoke and mirrors in lieu of real engagement to achieve the desired result.

Alternatively, one can simply turn one's back.[12] In many performances at the more modern end of the jazz spectrum, the musicians seem to be merely entertaining themselves – their engagement with anything outside the confines of the group is so minimal that one might feel that the same performance would result whether anyone else was in the room or not. It is as though the performers have retreated behind a smooth, unbreachable wall. One might, indeed, assert after Babbitt[13] that in these circumstances it is only the musicians who will know when the doorway of revelation is open, where the threshold into a new world is present; but such an assertion offers a model of performance so caught up in itself, so narcissistic that it risks disappearing into solipsism.

One way to avoid this self-absorption would be to employ a singer – not that this has ever been adopted as a serious solution. Many jazz musicians are instrumentalists who abhor the idea of jazz as a vocal form, and despite or because of the example of those rare singers who have gained wholehearted acceptance within the jazz world, they resent the common view that the legacy of Sinatra, Ella Fitzgerald and others sits beneath the jazz umbrella at all. Yet the difficulties such musicians have with engaging with an audience – though the refusal to make this engagement may be seen more as wilful resistance than difficulty – can be almost entirely overcome by adding a vocalist to the ensemble. The singer reaches across the divide, creates an opening in the wall, a threshold through which the audience can attain at least partial glimpses of the sense of what the musicians on the far side are up to, a bridge across the gulf between language and music.

The need for such a bridge is increasingly apparent now that so much music is available through the proliferation of media, and so much of it is listened to in a casual and unengaged way. Jazz can have a ragged sound, uncomfortable and slightly ugly to the ear – which is irrelevant when the listener is caught up in the process, and can sit inside the music. But where music is consumed differently, as background or mood-setter, only the lusher and less abrasive strands of jazz will survive; and then only for the quality of their surface. And here, it is the audience who refuse to cross the threshold and engage with the music as it was (presumably) intended – sitting resolutely, instead, with their backs to the window.

Jazz 3: Documentation

There is no document in improvisation – but in jazz, documents abound. Everything we know about the history of the music relates to landmark recordings – from the Armstrong Hot Fives and Sevens through Parker's recordings for Dial and Savoy, Ornette Coleman's early forays on Atlantic, Coltrane on Atlantic, then Impulse; to the point in the early sixties when to know which record label an artist was on was enough to give one a reasonable idea of their pedigree and style – Blue Note, Riverside, Jasmine: all had their stable of players and their house style.

This points to a significant problem for musicians and for their music. Jazz and recording technology evolved simultaneously. Of course it is enormously useful to be able to listen to an established figure's work over and over again, analyse it and emerge with a better theoretical understanding – from the earliest days of the genre[14] every jazz musician of significance will have spent time analysing the recorded output of the players they admire. But when an improvised form perpetuates itself through recordings, and an essential part of the music can never be captured on record, what is perpetuated is in danger of being something less, or at least other than, the music in its original form. Jazz has become an over-analysed music, so that it is now widely taught in music colleges and elsewhere – and what tends to be taught is a set of rules and processes of dubious value to the improviser.

Jazz theory is a necessary part of the musician's armoury – no player can reliably expect to negotiate a set of changes to, say, a Wayne Shorter tune without a grasp of the theory underlying the harmonies. But to describe a tune like Shorter's *Wild Flower*[15] as an exploration of phrygian maj6 harmonies (mode II of the melodic minor), while it allows you to play something acceptably musical or at least consonant over the chords, is insufficient to an understanding of what it is to improvise over the tune. That seizing of the moment, its expansion, or the sense of theatre caught in an eternal present, is not contained in the information offered about which notes are legitimate over a Dsus b9 or a C7 lydian dominant chord. The very idea of legitimacy and illegitimacy is challenged by the improviser's art. What is caught in the recording process is not the players' perspective as they hover on the threshold, with a glimpse of new landscape beyond, but the landscape itself.

When Miles Davis released *Kind of Blue*, modal jazz was in its infancy. Remarkable as the recording is, it lends itself far too easily to analysis. For example, the opening tune has a structure based on two dorian scales a semitone apart; the complete form for *Flamenco Sketches* consists of playing a sequence of scales in order, moving from one to the next ad lib; the Miles solo on *So What* has become so famous that not only could two out of three jazz musicians you stopped in the street sing you at least the opening eight bars, but the solo itself has been orchestrated for big band, by George Russell and others, and been quoted by numerous musicians in their own solos.[16] The original glimpse of a magical new landscape afforded by modal albums such as *Kind of Blue* and Coltrane's *A Love Supreme* has led, not to other equivalent threshold experiences, but to a very thorough and uninspiring exploration of the terrain, trampling it into a muddy wasteland.[17]

The Death of Jazz

The death of jazz has been announced with wearying regularity from early in its history, usually as a result of a revolution which is said to have killed the essence of the music. But it is precisely these revolutions which have kept the music alive, maintaining its fragile position on the threshold of new territory. The neoclassical approach to jazz, with its reverence for past documentation and its emphasis on the exploration of old landscapes, condemns the music to suffocate in its own stasis. Saxophonist Steve Lacy describes a point of inertia reached in the 1950s:

> [T]hat's where the music always has to be – on the edge – in between the known and the unknown and you have to keep pushing it towards the unknown otherwise it and you die… in the '50's jazz was no longer on the edge. When you reach what was called 'hard bop' there was no mystery any more… for me playing with the accepted people never worked out. Simply because they knew all the patterns and I didn't… when Bud Powell made them, fifteen years earlier, they weren't patterns. But when somebody analysed them and put them into a system it became a school and many players joined it… Jazz got so that it wasn't improvised any more.[18]

He goes on to illustrate the development of jazz by taking a line through successive trumpeters:

> [J]azz, from the time it first began, was always concerned with degrees of freedom. The way Louis Armstrong played was 'more free' than earlier players. Roy Eldridge was 'more free' than his predecessors, Dizzy Gillespie was another stage and [Don] Cherry was another. And you have to keep it going otherwise you lose that freedom. And then the music is finished. It's a matter of life and death. The only criterion is: – 'Is this stuff alive or is it dead?'[19]

If we agree with Lacy that jazz progresses by the relentless pursuit of freedom, there is an inevitable end point. We can ask, who was more free than Don Cherry? The answer is, no one. The boundaries of the music – the formal constraints which define it as jazz – were pushed outwards to the point where the free jazz movement emerged into a space with no constraints whatsoever. Musicians in this space have two choices: they can accept the territory of free music, a wider and non-idiomatic form; or they can turn back into the idiom of jazz, and re-explore old territory. In the former case they must abandon jazz altogether; in the latter they are faced with the absence of those threshold elements that keep the music alive.

Even if we reject Lacy's concern with freedom, it is clear that by concentrating on its recorded history at the expense of its improvisatory essence, jazz has moved in an arc from 'the sound of surprise' to a nostalgic recycling of its past.[20]

Coda: Improvisation in Interpretation, and the Composer as Improviser

I have tried to indicate that improvisation is not composition in the moment: that it is a different process entirely, and with a different aim. I will conclude by looking at a couple of instances in which composition and improvisation seem to meet each other on a middle ground.

The first example is György Ligeti's second string quartet, a transcendently beautiful and difficult piece that seems in part to work better on paper than in performance. There are any number of contemporary compositions that call for improvisation; what is remarkable about Ligeti's work is that it is ostensibly through-composed, yet reaches out towards the immediacy of the improvised. Parts of the score are so detailed that it is impossible to grasp their substance in the moment.[21] The second movement starts with a kind of canon of precise technique, where a succession of exactly articulated devices, indicating on which string and with what articulation each note is to be played, is passed from player to player. Though the detail of this is manifest in the score, it is far harder to convey, or grasp, in performance. But there is also the general comment: 'a few extremely fast metronome markings represent the ideal tempo; the real tempo has to approach the given values as closely as possible'; repeated exhortations to play particular sections 'as though crazy'; and at a passage of absurdly fast cadenza-like figures, the instruction, 'the figuration is played as fast as possible, independent of the metre and the bar boundaries, and also independent of the other instruments... Depending on the difficulty of execution, change of register etc., play in a virtuoso "hazardous" manner.'[22] In performance this will become an ad hoc chaos of notes, a gesture in the moment, aiming at an intent – here the music opens out into something spontaneous, ephemeral and gripping.

The second example is the music of the double bassist and composer Charles Mingus. The stamp of Mingus's personality is all over his music, even when backing a soloist in full flight, and even on albums such as *Oh Yeah*[23] where he leaves Doug Watkins with the unenviable task of filling the bassist's role while he cajoles and hollers and boots the ensemble along from the piano... In the boiling chaos of his most compelling pieces, he seems to give his sidemen the freedom to do anything – provided that what they choose to do is exactly what he wants.[24] For much of his career he refused to let his musicians write anything down, preferring to teach his pieces by playing or singing lines to the band, often shouting a new counter-line to the horn section in mid performance – nothing too fixed, nothing tied down, a chaos of intent – giving an immediacy of affect, a striking example of creation in the moment. His band was often billed as the Charles Mingus Jazz Workshop – Mingus music was ever a work in progress. Mingus was a prodigiously talented improviser, but what makes his music exceptional is his use of the medium. Jazz musicians tend to enjoy the restrictive nature of the form of the music they play even though, as discussed above, the music is most potent when those restrictions are being stretched. What Mingus achieved was to pick up the medium in both hands and bend it to his will. He not only played bass or piano, but played the entire band – using it as an instrument on which to compose in the moment.

Both these examples represent music as risk taking, where the 'hazardous' nature of the enterprise is in the foreground. They point towards possible ways in which the composed and the improvised can form a synthesis: music that exists on the threshold between the two.

Notes

1 'Wenn man unter Ewigkeit nicht unendliche Zeitdauer, sondern Unzeitlichkeit versteht, dann lebt der ewig, der in der Gegenwart lebt.' [If we understand eternity to mean not time without end, but timelessness, then they live forever who live in the present.] Ludwig Wittgenstein, *Tractatus Logico-Philosophicus* (Frankfurt: Edition Suhrkamp, 1963), 6.4311. My own translation.

2 'There is a crucial difference [between interpretation and improvisation] in terms of the way in which performers approach music. If you are playing in a symphony orchestra or if you are playing a piece of chamber music, you are trying, often against fairly heavy odds, to find out what somebody has meant when they said something. And I think that a jazz player, for example, is saying what is in him. He puts very much more of his total personality into what he does. I think he's a much happier individual in many ways.' Anthony Pay, quoted in Derek Bailey, *Improvisation: Its Nature and Practice in Music* (Derbyshire: Moorland Publishing, 1980), 87.

3 Alain Danielou, quoted in Bailey, *Improvisation*, 123.

4 Cornelius Cardew, 'Towards an Ethic of Improvisation' (1971), in *Cornelius Cardew: A Reader*, ed. Edwin Prévost (Harlow, England: Copula, 2006), 125–134 (127–128).

5 Consider Stoppard's Rosencrantz and Guildenstern, themselves shut off from the play, which happens elsewhere; or Clov in *Endgame*, turning his telescope on the audience: 'I see…a multitude…in transports…of joy. That's what I call a magnifier.' Samuel Beckett, *Endgame* (London: Faber and Faber, 1958), 25.

6 Bailey, *Improvisation*, 61.

7 Milton Babbitt, 'Who cares if you listen?' *High Fidelity* 8, no. 2 (February 1958): 38–40. It is rumoured that the magazine's editor chose to replace the less contentious title ('The Composer as Anachronism') with an invention of his own – unfortunately for Babbitt, who is now remembered more as the author of this than for any of his music. His argument – that just as advancements in physics and mathematics would make lectures in those subjects incomprehensible to the uninformed public, so contemporary music had advanced to the point where the issues of concern to the composer were beyond the reach of a lay audience – has tended to get lost in the furore surrounding the piece's title.

8 Stanley Cavell, 'Aesthetic Problems of Modern Philosophy', in *Must We Mean What We Say?* (Cambridge: Cambridge University Press, 1976), 73–96 (84). Italics in original.

9 There is almost no decent criticism on jazz – no body of writing to compare to Adorno, Hans Keller et al. In *But Beautiful* (London: Jonathan Cape, 1991), perhaps the only truly brilliant piece of writing about jazz, Geoff Dyer observes that jazz is its own best critic – the music itself in its headlong self-referential development provides its own commentary and exposition (165–172). In addition to Dyer's book, the reader interested in jazz revolutions is referred to Valerie Wilmer's book about the free jazz movement, *As Serious as your Life* (London: Allison and Busby Ltd, 1977).

10 Ornette Coleman, *The Shape of Jazz to Come*, Atlantic LP 1317, 1959 and *Change of the Century*, Atlantic LP 1327, 1959, released 1960; John Coltrane, *Giant Steps*, Atlantic LP 1311, 1959, released 1960.

11 Compare the devastating noise of Albert Ayler's 'Ghosts' from *Spiritual Unity*, ESP Disk ESP1002–2, 1964 with any of Ornette Coleman's early recordings.

12 Miles Davis, never one to pander to his audience's desires, took exactly this step in the mid-1950s and never really turned to face them again.

13 Babbitt, 'Who cares if you listen?'

14 That is, after the New Orleans scene of the early 1900s. Buddy Bolden never recorded; the trumpet players who followed him, however – King Oliver, Louis Armstrong and others – all did.

15 Recorded on Wayne Shorter, *Speak No Evil*, Blue Note BLP 4194, 1965.

16 To give one example – the tenor solo on Branford Marsalis's 'Ballad of Chet Kincaid' from *Crazy People Music*, Columbia CK-46072, 1990 quotes extensively from it amid much studio hilarity.

17 Miles Davis, *Kind of Blue*, Columbia CK-64935, 1959; John Coltrane, *A Love Supreme*, Impulse! GRD155, 1965.

18 Quoted in Bailey, *Improvisation*, 71–2.

19 Quoted in Bailey, *Improvisation*, 73.

20 Whitney Balliett, *The Sound of Surprise – Forty-Six Pieces on Jazz* (New York: Dutton, 1959); and cf. Bailey, *Improvisation*, 65: 'Each successive jazz revival leaves the music more firmly established as a bulwark of the nostalgia industry.'

21 Evan Parker has suggested that composing on paper belongs more in the realm of literature than in music: '[I]f the score represents some kind of ideal performance why does it ever have to be performed? Surely it would be better for the music-lover to read the score, alone or with others, conducted or unconducted as his preference dictates? If it is objected that this attitude is too unemotional, then I would reply that the score is itself too unemotional; and since it concerns itself with the description rather than the emotions themselves it would be more appropriate to consider score-making as an esoteric branch of the literary arts with its own criteria rather than as anything to do with music.' Quoted in Bailey, *Improvisation*, 96.

22 György Ligeti, *String Quartet no. 2* (1968) (Mainz: Schott, 1971).

23 Charles Mingus, O*h Yeah*, Atlantic LP 1377, 1961.

24 Cf. Dyer, *But Beautiful*, 97.

Chapter Fourteen

THRESHOLDS OF ATTENTION: ON LISTENING IN LITERATURE

Angela Leighton

And what do I point to by the inner activity of listening? To the sound that comes to my ears, and to the silence when I hear nothing? – Wittgenstein

I am sitting on a terrace in Sicily, listening to the sound of the sea breaking on the rocks below.

That statement, in the present, is not quite true of course, at least no longer quite true, because the time of sitting, and even the time of writing that 'I am sitting', have already slipped into some future, anytime, anywhere, of the reader who reads it, and who, in a kind of reverse action, then understands that 'I am sitting', but also, with luck, imagines that he or she might also be sitting, 'listening to the sound of the sea'. Writing plays lovely tricks on our willing ears. But it reminds us, too, that in order to read with attention we must cross all sorts of time-barriers and place-barriers, journeying across varieties of half-truths, like 'I am sitting', which we have mostly learned to cross by convention, but which the literary text asks us to cross again in imagination.

And much of this activity happens in the ear, that subtle, often underrated organ, which is itself composed of a series of halls and obstacles which transmit sound waves to the brain. First of all, there is not one ear, but three: in medical terminology, the outer, the middle, and the inner ear. Within these three lies a complex architecture of parts, not only the drum-like mechanism of the eardrum and the shell-shaped whorls of the cochlea, for instance, but also the threshold areas of the 'oval window', the 'round window' and the 'two-chambered vestibule'. As sound waves are passed through this complex organ, causing fine hairs, fluids, membranes and small bones to vibrate on the way, they send messages to the brain which sorts them into sense. That sound waves travel, not only outside us but also through our ears, suggests the extent to which movement, time, alterability, variation, are basic to the act of hearing. But the human ear itself can only go so far in detection of sound. Beyond what is technically called 'the threshold of audibility' lies the unheard 'sound-shadow' of noises which lie outside its range. Thresholds are a limit as well as an opening. When thinking about the complexities of listening to and in literature, the notion of thresholds as places of passage and blockage, rooms and doors, might offer a suggestive, working metaphor for the varieties of attention demanded by the literary text.

On that terrace in Sicily I found myself listening constantly to the sea. The sea, when it breaks on rocks, is an ever varying sound, rhythmic but never regular, repetitive but never the same, with a vocabulary of whisperings, hissings, sighings, rushings, which suggests a creature of diverse moods and vast potential. At night I could hear it through the open window, amplified by quiet, clarified by space, a cradle of lulling sibilants to the ear. In storms, however, it would come rushing and crashing, breaking against the breakwater, its volume swelling as each wave heaved a massive shoulder, and retreated in sheetfalls of whisper. And the lightning, that sudden tuning-fork in the sky, would crack, and pause – a split-second, maybe, or a long moment – before its thunderous growl travelled outwards in altering registers.

It is a strange concert, that of sea and storm, thrilling in its mix of rage and restraint, percussion and pause, in its play of sound and after-sound, – itself a reminder of the complex physics of aurality. Living on the edge of that sea was like turning an ear to something, not easily predictable or interpretable but, like literature, enticing, versatile, on the move – something constantly challenging the ear's own thresholds of attention.

* * *

With this memory in mind, I'd like to probe the idea of listening in literature, and not only as a writerly or readerly activity, but also as an event in the text, a kind of stage-direction calling attention to an act we tend to take for granted. As has often been pointed out,[1] our critical metaphors: vision, insight, form or imagination, are predominantly eye-based, obscuring the activity of the ear. There are no such equivalents for what the ear can do, no word for innerly hearing to match vision or insight. The advantage, however, is that ear-based metaphors retain the surprise of unfamiliarity; they have not yet set into conceptual categories or critical shorthand. They are therefore often dear to writers. 'But take breath and read it with the ears',[2] writes Hopkins, letting us hear what a breath-taking activity this might be. Robert Frost constantly rings the changes on what the ear can do: he writes of 'the hearing ear', 'the imagining ear', 'the observing ear', 'the summoning ear';[3] Joyce relishes the inventions of the ear which 'seehears',[4] W. S. Graham, of 'the mind's ear',[5] Seamus Heaney, the 'deep ear'.[6] The ear has thresholds and depths, metaphorical as well as literal, which writers themselves constantly explore. It can imagine, observe, summon, even see or think. Its synaesthetic possibilities are particularly attractive to writers who, after all, need us to read all eyes and ears at once, seeing words on the page but simultaneously hearing what they sound like. On the whole, however, seeing is easy. It is listening which touches on the hard work of understanding what we read, since listening is an attention to the changing, harmonic depths of language, its constantly altering sea-sounds.

This yoking of the ear and the understanding has always been common in writings about music. Daniel Barenboim, for instance, recently described music as 'the wisdom that becomes audible to the thinking ear'.[7] It is a surprising sentence, which reminds us that we might think through listening. That phrase, 'the thinking ear', puts two irreconcilables together and asks us to rethink both thought and ear. The 'wisdom that becomes audible to the thinking ear' might not be wisdom *about* anything, but a form of knowledge which is always still only *becoming* audible. The question of how the ear might think, or how thinking might listen, lies at the heart of this paper, even if it poses, like Barenboim's sentence, a clash of categories which will not quite resolve into a thought we can easily think.

So let me turn to literature, and to one of those iconic passages which seems to elude thought, yet resonates powerfully in the ear. It is from that most ear-minded of writers, Walter Pater, and it's a sentence from the 'Giorgione' chapter of *The Renaissance* – the chapter in which he frets about art's aspiration to music. He writes:

> In these, then, the favourite incidents of Giorgione's school, music or the musical intervals in our existence, life itself is conceived as a sort of listening – listening to music, to the reading of Bandello's novels, to the sound of water, to time as it flies.[8]

As always with Pater, his thinking is caught on the hoof, in the twists and turns of his syntax, in his timing, his calculated pauses and punctuation, and especially in his use of the dash. The dash is an extraordinarily resourceful mark, being a crossing point between two phrases which also holds them apart. On the one hand it is a finish, completing a syntactical unit, and on the other it is a pointer to something more, a kind of after-thought or after-sense, which remains optional, tendentious. So here, the phrase: 'life itself is conceived as a sort of listening –' marks an end, rounds up a point, and leaves 'listening' hanging intransitively, without any focussing object. But it also signals one of those moments of hesitation, a pause for thought and a change of tack. A 'sort of listening', the gerund, becomes, on the other side of the dash, a present participle, 'listening to'. Pater writes: 'a sort of listening – listening to music, to the reading of Bandello's novels, to the sound of water, to time as it flies'. It is a curious list of randomly specific examples, as if he were trying out this and that, reaching casually for what comes to hand. For what, one might ask, does 'time as it flies' sound like, if listened to? That 'time flies' is an easy cliché, but 'time as it flies', with its slightly long-drawn-out timing, as if the phrase were taking its own time, certainly exercises the listening ear. The effect of that last item on the list, then, is to keep us, all ears, still listening hard at the end of the sentence: to 'time as it flies'. Pater may not have given any useful definition of 'life', but his sentence has whetted, without entirely satisfying, our appetite to listen. It is as if he were asking us to listen to sounds in the sound-shadow, to sounds increasingly just out of hearing's range.

Meanwhile, he is also asking us to listen to the sentence itself: its hesitancy, its rhythm, its peculiar listening attention to words which will not quite do, and finally, its attempt to prolong a listening which stays just short of its object, if only by the length of a dash: 'a sort of listening –'. Pater, then, lets us hear how 'a sort of listening' remains larger than any object, unsatisfied by the list of sounds which follows, and how it might go on in time, even in time as it flies, beyond the end of its own sentence. Pater's 'listening', even his 'listening to', is never quite convinced by what it might hear. Wishfully intransitive, it remains poised on a threshold of attention, like a cocked ear, set to catch what might pass while also letting it pass.

Hearing and listening – those verbs differ, as they do in French: *entendre/écouter*, or in Italian: *sentire/ascoltare*, for instance. Moreover, in English the extra emphasis of listening is signalled by the preposition. 'To hear' takes a direct object, leading quickly into what is heard: 'I hear you', while to listen requires another word: I listen *to* you. And of course, there are many alternatives: I can listen to, or for, or out for, or in – even, perhaps, listen up or over or beyond. In each of these, the activity of the verb is redirected, and the object set at a more effortful distance. It is this, perhaps, that creates its appeal for the writer. Listening reaches towards its object, but does not need it.

Here, for example, is Wallace Stevens, bringing out the difference between the two in his essay 'The Noble Rider and the Sound of Words'. He writes: 'The deepening need for words to express our thoughts and feelings…makes us listen to words when we hear them, loving them and feeling them, makes us search the sound of them.'[9] Poetry 'makes us listen to words when we hear them'. To hear is quick and easy; to listen comes after, later, and involves a revision and intensification of hearing. It might also involve loving, feeling, searching 'the sound of them'. To 'search the sound' of words is not necessarily to find it, but to hope to find it. Everything in this sentence conspires to make listening a labour, an effort. To 'listen to words when we hear them' is to take them again, to re-hear, to 'search the sound' more thoroughly, with a kind of extra, caressing attention of the ear. The task of the poet, then, is not simply to write, but to 'listen…when we hear'.

When I began searching for philosophical or theoretical accounts of listening I was interested to find how few they seem, and how incidental, mostly tucked away like asides or afterthoughts. For example, Heidegger takes time out from analysing thinking in poetry to reflect on the topic in his essay, 'Poetically Man Dwells'. Here, he passingly wonders about listening as the source of human speech, and then as the gift that marks out the poet. 'The more poetic a poet is…' he writes, 'the greater is the purity with which he submits what he says to an ever more painstaking listening.'[10] Here it is again, listening as re-hearing. The poet speaks, then listens, with a more 'painstaking' attention. Like Stevens, Heidegger makes listening take pains, somehow pause and reassess what, before, was merely said or heard.

Gaston Bachelard's *The Poetics of Space*, which is mostly dedicated to sight and visual structure, also gestures briefly, but suggestively, towards the ear. Quoting René Daumal, he declares at one point: 'Another poet teaches us, if one may say this, to hear ourselves listen'.[11] If Wallace Stevens makes us 'listen…when we hear', Bachelard makes us 'hear ourselves listen'. Both are turning an ear on the act, exploiting the difference between hearing and listening, to suggest that the reader of poetry enters an arena of doubly effortful attention and self-attention. Like Pater's favourite intransitive constructions which leave the verb hanging: 'a sort of listening –', Bachelard too suggests that 'to hear ourselves listen' might be to hear nothing except the sound of listening. What the poet gives us is a space in which to pay attention to our own attention – like putting an ear to a shell. A little earlier he had written that the poet knows 'how to make us listen, not to say, super-listen'.[12] He needs that new word, 'super-listen', to convey the extra intensity of the act, whether over and above, or somehow superlatively. Either way, the verb remains intransitive. The poet does not make us listen *to* anything, necessarily, but merely tunes up our ears to listen better, or more, or more listeningly.

Roland Barthes' lovely little essay, 'Listening', which defines three types of the verb, is one of the most suggestive accounts of this complex act. The 'first listening', he writes, 'might be called an *alert*. The second is a *deciphering*.'[13] So, first we are alerted by a sound, and second, we want to decipher that sound. The sensory '*alert*' of the ear is thus kept separate from the thinking-deciphering work of the mind. Barthes almost forgets to suggest a third till, a few pages later, almost by the by, he writes: 'But also, listening is *taking soundings*.'[14] Like Stevens' to 'search the sound of them', Barthes remembers that listening is not just about pricking up your ears and deciphering meanings; it's also about sounding sounds. '*taking soundings*' takes us into the whole area of linguistic noise, of poetry's deep-sea undertow of aural effects. This third kind of listening trawls for noises. The pun on sounding, meaning to sound out, to search for, and also to dive deep, helps describe the way that listening is not an automatic sensory reflection, but a hard-working exploration. It is as if this verb were always something more than what it hears, always a listening out for sounds beyond sounds, as if, from its threshold, set to catch what lies outside our immediate range.

In all these examples, then, there is a sense that learning to listen is what literature might teach – teach by a kind of shared activity, a mutual, ongoing apprehension. 'The ear is the only true writer and the only true reader',[15] writes Frost, as if the work required for both were the same. Those moments when writers make special calls on our ears, often by planting an oddly-angled listener in the text, are moments when listening becomes as much an object as the means of finding an object. In such moments, we listen to ourselves listening, and therefore to the space of listening which opens up in the curious, imagining ear of the text itself.

Here, for example, is a little poem by Christina Rossetti called 'A Green Cornfield'. This seems to be in a familiar Romantic tradition, the singing bird, a model for the poet and an object of aspiration. But in fact, as you'll hear (if you listen), Rossetti turns away from this tradition in a surprising, distinctly gendered move:

The earth was green, the sky was blue:
  I saw and heard one sunny morn
A skylark hang between the two,
  A singing speck above the corn;

A stage below, in gay accord,
  White butterflies danced on the wing,
And still the singing skylark soared,
  And silent sank and soared to sing.

The cornfield stretched a tender green
  To right and left beside my walks;
I knew he had a nest unseen
  Somewhere among the million stalks:

And as I paused to hear his song
  While swift the sunny moments slid,
Perhaps his mate sat listening long,
  And listened longer than I did.[16]

This beautifully orchestrated little verse turns on pauses: first the pauses of the 'singing skylark' who falls silent and soars to sing, then the pause of the speaker who 'paused to hear his song', then the long, continuing pause of what in fact she hears. She stops paying attention to the old songs of the poets, Shelley's in particular, and listens instead to a quietness in which 'Perhaps his mate sat listening long, / And listened longer than I did.' At the point where the poem should end, Rossetti keeps us listening. How long is 'long', or even 'longer'? The speaker does not know if there is a bird on a nest, yet she still listens for that listening, which in turn, she imagines, listens for hers. The sense of the animal attention, the fearful wariness of the nesting bird, gives to that listening pause a wonderful, inscrutable depth. It also creates a listening space in which all sorts of listenings meet, the speaker's, the bird's, the reader's. 'Another poet teaches us', Bachelard writes, 'to hear ourselves listen.' What we hear in this poem is the sound of listening, somehow turned up to high volume, as if it were the object that listening listens for.

This attention at the threshold, which may be a threshold onto nothing, is also evoked in Wallace Stevens' 'The Snow Man'. This seems to be a poem about looking, about the sheer blank dazzle of the snow; but it too contains a hidden listener. In the last two stanzas there's a sound:

> Which is the sound of the land
> Full of the same wind
> That is blowing in the same bare place
>
> For the listener, who listens in the snow,
> And, nothing himself, beholds
> Nothing that is not there and the nothing that is.[17]

The brilliant metaphysical conundrum of that last line, which depends on seeing, beholding, has tended to obscure something else going on, not in the eye but the ear: 'the sound of the land', the sound of 'the same wind' and of 'the same bare place'. That they are all 'the same' seems boring, monotonous, and yet 'For the listener, who listens in the snow' it is sound that matters, even the same sound coming again and again. So the ear of the poem is at cross purposes with its eye. Here is a figure, or at least an activity, which seems to go on, somehow irrespective of anything it might listen *to*. Stevens' line, with its intransitiveness, its tautology, its pausing commas, opens up another of those odd spaces for listening, which never quite finds an object. This may, certainly, just be an evocation of the hush of snow. Or it may be that, like Rossetti, Stevens is asking the reader to listen more than to look, to notice how there might always be something more, a something or nothing more, to listen *for*. He too puts an ear in the poem which, oddly angled, not quite assimilated, gives us an indeterminate threshold from which to pay attention, to something or even just to itself – to make us listen to listening. It is often the strangest object in poetry.

This is related, of course, to something critics have always noted: that the sound-effects of poems are part of what they are about. Garrett Stewart's *Reading Voices* has recently highlighted this '*challenge* of sound to sense', what he calls the 'churn of wording beneath and between the chain of words'.[18] His attention to the phonotext in the text, the 'errancy' of sound in 'the errand of meaning',[19] is a way of reminding us to use ears as well as eyes, to let the musical side of the brain be switched on. Indeed, understanding literature might come precisely from detaching the churn, the errancy of language, from the drive to make sense, and thus of course to confront a different sort of sense. To replace the idea of understanding with the idea of listening might then be to accept that what literature offers is not something understood; it is something listened to. We tend to say of difficult contemporary poetry, for instance, 'I don't understand it' when, perhaps, we should say: 'I don't know how to listen to what I am hearing.' Very often, in time, we *learn* to listen, by attending to the poet's own listening techniques which are written into the text. When applied to literature, understanding asks to be re-routed through the ear.

In his recent book, *Music, Language, and Cognition*, Peter Kivy proposes an interesting formula: that there might be 'cognition without content'.[20] Spelling it out, he writes that 'cognition without content' would amount to 'hearing *that* certain musical things are going on, and, the while, thinking about these goings on and about your hearing them'.[21] So understanding music comes round to an old circularity: 'hearing…and, the while, thinking…about your hearing'. It is an anti-utilitarian form of 'cognition', which turns the ear on the ear, hearing on hearing, to suggest that such cognition is its own end. Like many writers before him, Kivy tries to define cognition in the arts of sound as hearing rather than something heard, as verb rather than noun, as labour rather than achievement.

When it comes to literature, this sense of labour is everywhere evident in writers' own descriptions of the ear. There is a fascinating sentence in one of Robert Frost's *Notebooks* which suggests how we might listen to literature. He writes: 'The best place to get the abstract sound of sense is from voices behind a door that cuts off the words.'[22] It is a sentence which performs what it describes: it sets us listening, and listening not directly *to* but *for* something, round or through or beyond the obstacle of that 'door'. In order to make sense of this sentence we must listen 'behind a door', to the somehow interrupted wavelengths of words: 'voices behind a door that cuts off the words.' Perhaps what Frost is also saying is that doors, the blocking devices to easy meaning, are as important in literature as the words and the voices. It is the door which makes us 'super-listen', with that extra effort of not being quite sure we can hear what we should be hearing. When Seamus Heaney, in an essay called 'Sounding Auden', proposes to 'listen in to some passages of Auden's work',[23] he lets us hear the door which makes Auden *sound*. To 'listen in' is to be an outsider, to know the text as a house or room to which we have no direct admittance, but on whose threshold we might stand. With its hint of overhearing or eavesdropping, of putting an ear to a wall or a door, the phrase, 'I shall listen in', lets us hear that listening to poetry must overcome a difficulty. When Joyce writes in the 'Sirens' chapter of *Ulysses*, 'My ear against the wall to hear',[24] he too might be thinking of those walls and doors which make literary language difficult, oblique, a 'sound of sense', rather than just sense.

And of course it is Joyce who relishes such indirections of the ear. His short story, 'The Dead', is a text full of doors and walls and windows, through which we, like the hero, must learn to listen. Joyce, here, seems to be trying out something he will become a master of: that is, writing listenings. His brother Stanislaus once asked: 'I wonder will any scruffy old professor recognise Jim's ability to write general noise on paper'.[25] Learning to 'seehear'[26] the written noises in Joyce is to cultivate an 'eyed ear',[27] – that very Joycean synaesthesia of the reading act, as Matthew Bevis points out. Like all writers, Joyce is concerned to train us to listen, and to listen differently, not only setting ear against eye, but also taking us far into the listening spaces of the text, spaces full of 'earie' noises, blocked by doors.

Now listen to the listenings in this passage from the 'Sirens' episode of *Ulysses*. It is that crucial moment when Lydia puts the sea-shell to the ear of George Lidwell:

> To the end of the bar to him she bore lightly the spiked and winding seahorn that he, George Lidwell, solicitor, might hear.
>
> – Listen! she bade him…
>
> Ah, now he heard, she holding it to his ear. Hear! He heard. Wonderful. She held it to her own and through the sifted light pale gold in contrast glided. To hear.
>
> Tap.
>
> Bloom through the bardoor saw a shell held at their ears. He heard more faintly that that they heard, each for herself alone, then each for other, hearing the plash of waves, loudly, a silent roar.
>
> Bronze by a weary gold, anear, afar, they listened.[28]

So Joyce plays his own variations on the ear which hears, setting ear-rhymes against eye-rhymes, and constantly repeating the verb, as if the reader, like everyone, were trying to hear better: 'that he…might hear… Ah, now he heard…his ear. Hear! He heard… To hear… their ears. He heard…they heard…hearing… anear, afar'. The luck of English is that the ear rhymes with what it does. Meanwhile the shell, that old poetic trope, plays the same echoey game. It gives out a mysterious, half-rhyming 'roar', which might be the sea, or the blood going round, or just the sound of listening trapped in its hold. Joyce then adds to the fun by first asking us, with George Lidwell, to 'Listen!' then, with Bloom, to hear 'through the bardoor'. Bloom in fact doesn't hear anything at all, not literally, because he is observing the whole scene through glass. And yet, perhaps precisely because of those various obstacles: the shell, Lydia, Lidwell, the bardoor, he does also succeed in 'hearing…loudly, a silent roar'. That it is 'loudly, a silent roar' makes it a wild imagination of hearing, a something and nothing, a contradiction of sound to which we, like the shell-hearers, still want to attend – perhaps precisely because it is most like hearing nothing.

If hearing enjoys its rhyming echoes, listening, in this passage, enjoys the mystery of intransitiveness: 'Bronze by a weary gold, anear, afar, they listened.' A couple of pages later, Joyce is still harping on it: 'Listen. Bloom listened. Richie Goulding listened. And by the door deaf Pat, bald Pat, tipped Pat, listened.'[29] The presence of Pat, who is 'hard of hear by the door',[30] sets the whole of this chapter in context. Ulysses' men may have blocked their ears with wax to avoid hearing the sirens, but in Joyce's version, it is the deaf and door-blocked who in fact listen hardest and best. Pat, who is deaf, and stands 'by the door', on his own doubly blocked threshold of deafness, is the one who listens most continuously; who super-listens. 'deaf Pat, bald Pat, tipped Pat, listened.' As Pat listens, intransitively, to nothing he can hear, so the act, as in so many of these texts, opens a wide radius. What does it mean to listen, without hearing, and therefore with a kind of unfinished expectation? Perhaps that is exactly what is required of us, readers of texts: to listen 'behind a door', through the difficulties and obstructions of language; and not just listen to, but for, or through, or in, or out for. It is, to return to Pater, who also lies behind this whole chapter, 'a sort of listening – ' followed by a long, pausing dash.

So Joyce redirects sound through the imagined deafness of his waiting waiter. Meanwhile, the phrase 'tipped Pat' reminds us of another sound which has sounded throughout, and which signals something else on Bloom's mind. 'tipped Pat' condenses to 'Tap.' That is the sound of the blind piano tuner, whose 'tap' interrupts the whole episode, whose cane taps along the pavement at the end, and whose tapped tuning-fork sets everyone listening in the first place:

> From the saloon a call came, long in dying. That was a tuningfork the tuner had that he forgot that he now struck. A call again. That he now poised that it now throbbed. You hear? It throbbed, pure, purer, softly and softlier, its buzzing prongs. Longer in dying call.[31]

In Joyce's wonderful concert of words, attention is set by the deaf, and pitch by the blind. Both figures insist on strange listenings – listenings which must get past all the intervening doors, internal and external, of what cannot easily be heard: the sound of the sea in the sea-shell. 'a call came, long in dying.' 'Longer in dying call', Joyce writes of the tuning-fork, working all the puns on 'long in' and 'longing', on 'dying call', with its Tennysonian fall, and the urgent joke that in 'dying' we might 'call'. The tap of the tuning-fork, and the tap of the cane, re-heard in 'tipped Pat', is one way of keeping at the back of our ears a sound that strikes the key pitch of this extraordinary ear-text.

If Joyce keeps us listening, 'anear, afar', to all the virtuosic ear-play of his words, this is only an extreme example of what all writers do. Literature offers a threshold of listening, and makes us pause there. It stops us going straight over into sense and comprehension. Like 'tipped Pat', or like Bloom, we stand at a door, which may be a place of blockage or may be a threshold of extra attention, or may, indeed, be both. From there we strain to listen to the imaginable anti-sense that literature gives us: 'the plash of waves, a silent roar'.

One last example comes from the opening paragraph of Elizabeth Bishop's short story 'In the Village'. It contains, like Joyce's chapter, its own regulating, rather frightening tuning-fork:

> A scream, the echo of a scream, hangs over that Nova Scotian village. No one hears it… The scream hangs like that, unheard, in memory – in the past, in the present, and those years between. It was not even loud to begin with, perhaps. It just came there to live, forever – not loud, just alive forever. Its pitch would be the pitch of my village. Flick the lightning rod on top of the church steeple with your fingernail and you will hear it.[32]

This is a story which plays round the harrowing sound-memory of the mad mother's scream. That first paragraph gives us the sound of it, or the 'echo' of it, or the 'unheard' sound of it, or at least 'the pitch' of it, struck like a note. Visually, Bishop hangs the scream like a sword of Damocles over the village. But in fact it hangs in her ears, neither past nor present, neither loud nor soft, neither heard nor remembered, until it is flicked. That flick is the flicker of a lightning set deep in her imagination; it is also the regulating pitch of a tuning-fork. When Bishop as a young woman once developed a serious infection of the ear, she spent weeks in hospital and became fascinated by what she called 'All the physics of sound and balance, such fancy bones, and tuning forks'.[33] The autobiographical scream of her short story is a deep-set tuning-fork, which sets the pitch of much of her life's work. 'Flick the lightning rod…with your fingernail and you will hear it', she advises the reader, letting the imaginary touch, of fork or lightning (or forked lightning), reproduce the same note that might be tapped deep in the story of her own life.

While that scream of maternal insanity is the sound that sets 'the pitch' of all Bishop's subsequent verbal music, it is also, in this story, a way to tune the ears of the reader to many other sounds, both real and make-believe: to the child playing hairpin music in her grandmother's hair; to her aunt playing the piano while the pig is butchered; to her grandfather's talk, when she is not 'listening to what he is saying', but 'listening for sounds from upstairs';[34] to the 'Clang'[35] of Nate the blacksmith, who shapes and holds the blocked-out scream on his anvil, and even to the 'ears' of the shoeing horse, which are, Bishop writes, 'secret entrances to the underworld'.[36] Listening, in this story, may be a cover-up, an imaginary artistic adornment, a controlled, useful work, or a threshold to another place, another life: an entrance 'to the underworld', from where terrible sounds emerge. It is as if she were suggesting an awful, existential reality at the heart of things: a sort of Munsch scream that is the first premise of her own ear-minded aesthetic. She, like Joyce, uses the tuning-fork image to set the 'pitch' of what she writes, and so set the reader listening for all the roundabout, repressed, discrepant sounds that follow.

In all these examples, then, writers might be elaborating, in practice, a theory of what literary language is about. It is not just that literature takes us by the ear, making us hear its rhythms, its pauses, its underground noises, and it is not just that the act of listening may be written in as part of the story; it is also that the text works by becoming a listening space, a hold which holds us attentive to words, especially words which have suffered the lovely deflection, estrangement and blockage of what we call the literary. 'The ear', writes Frost, 'is the only true writer and the only true reader.' The ear trains us to listen in to the art of the literary, which is also the art of understanding by ear. It may, then, be time to put an ear back into our critical writings, even if there are no hard-and-fast rules about how it works – even if what the ear might hear is nothing but itself, on its own, open threshold of attention, still listening…

Notes

1 See, for instance, Martin Jay, *Downcast Eyes: The Denigration of Vision in Twentieth-Century French Thought* (Berkeley, L.A.: University of California Press, 1993), 1–3. Increasingly, philosophers and critics have bewailed the domination of the visual in our thought: see, especially, Don Ihde, *Listening and Voice: A Phenomenology of Sound* (Athens, Ohio: Ohio University Press, 1976), 6-12; Casey O'Callaghan, *Sounds: A Philosophical Theory* (Oxford: Oxford University Press, 2007), 4–8; and Marjorie Perloff and Craig Dworkin, eds, *The Sound of Poetry / The Poetry of Sound* (Chicago: University of Chicago Press, 2009), esp. 1–9.

2 *The Letters of Gerard Manley Hopkins to Robert Bridges*, ed. Claude Colleer Abbott (London: Oxford University Press, 1935; repr. 1955), 79.

3 Robert Frost, *Collected Poems, Prose, and Plays*, sel. Richard Poirier and Mark Richardson (New York: The Library of America, 1995), 682, 687, 675.

4 James Joyce, *Ulysses*, ed. Jeri Johnson (Oxford: Oxford University Press, 1993), 271.

5 W. S. Graham, *The Nightfisherman: Selected Letters of W. S. Graham*, ed. Michael and Margaret Snow (London: Oxford University Press, 1999), 162.

6 Seamus Heaney, 'Sounding Auden', in *The Government of the Tongue* (London: Faber and Faber, 1988), 109–28 (109).

7 Daniel Barenboim, *Everything is Connected: The Power of Music* (London: Weidenfeld and Nicholson, 2008), 3.

8 Walter Pater, *The Renaissance: Studies in Art and Poetry*, ed. Adam Phillips (Oxford: Oxford University Press, 1986), 96.

9 Wallace Stevens, 'The Noble Rider and the Sound of Words', in *Wallace Stevens: Collected Poetry and Prose*, ed. Frank Kermode and Joan Richardson (New York: The Library of America, 1997), 643–65 (662).

10 Martin Heidegger, 'Poetically Man Dwells', in *Poetry, Language, Thought*, trans. Albert Hofstadter (New York: Harper and Row, 1971), 213–29 (216).

11 Gaston Bachelard, *The Poetics of Space*, trans. Maria Jolas (Boston, Mass.: Beacon Press, 1994), 181; originally published as *La Poétique de l'espace* (Paris: Presses universitaires de France, 1958).

12 Ibid., 178.

13 Roland Barthes, 'Listening', in *The Responsibility of Forms: Critical Essays on Music, Art, and Representation*, trans. Richard Howard (Oxford: Basil Blackwell, 1986), 245–60 (245).

14 Ibid., 250.

15 Frost, *Collected Poems, Prose, and Plays*, 677.

16 *The Complete Poems of Christina Rossetti: A Variorum Edition*, 3 vols, ed. R. W. Crump (Baton Rouge: Louisiana State University Press, 1979–90), 1:197.

17 Stevens, 'The Noble Rider and the Sound of Words', 8.

18 Garrett Stewart, *Reading Voices: Literature and the Phonotext* (Berkeley, L.A.: University of California Press, 1990), 25.

19 Ibid., 27.

20 Peter Kivy, *Music, Language, and Cognition: And Other Essays in the Aesthetics of Music* (Oxford: Clarendon Press, 2007), 223.

21 Ibid., 231.

22 Frost, *Collected Poems, Prose, and Plays*, 664.

23 Heaney, 'Sounding Auden', 109.

24 Joyce, *Ulysses*, 270.

25 In Harry White, *Music and the Irish Literary Imagination* (Oxford: Oxford University Press, 2008), 153.

26 Matthew Bevis, *The Art of Eloquence: Byron, Dickens, Tennyson, Joyce* (Oxford: Oxford University Press, 2007), 252.

27 Ibid., 263–69.

28 Joyce, *Ulysses*, 269.

29 Ibid., 272.

30 Ibid., 262.

31 Ibid., 253.

32 Elizabeth Bishop, 'In the Village', in *The Collected Prose*, ed. Robert Giroux (New York: Farrar, Straus, and Giroux, 1984), 251–74 (251).

33 Quoted in Brett Millier, *Elizabeth Bishop: Life and the Memory of It* (Berkeley, L.A.: University of California Press, 1993), 94.

34 Bishop, 'In the Village', 271.

35 Ibid., 252.

36 Ibid., 257.

SELECT BIBLIOGRAPHY (INCLUDING DISCOGRAPHY)

Alford, Stephen. *Burghley: William Cecil at the Court of Elizabeth I.* New Haven: Yale University Press, 2008.

Almack, Richard. 'Queries: Richard Sackville, Earl of Dorset'. *Notes and Queries* 3rd ser., 7 (1865): 7.

Alter, Robert, and Frank Kermode, eds. *The Literary Guide to the Bible.* Cambridge, Mass.: Belknap Press of the University of Harvard, 1987.

Andalzùa, Gloria. *Borderlands/La Frontera: The New Mestiza.* San Francisco: Aunt Lute, 1987.

Anderson, Benedict. *Imagined Communities: Reflections on the Origin and Spread of Nationalism.* London: Verso, 1983.

Anonymous. 'Abstract of the Tryal of the Brownriggs for the Murder of Mary Clifford, their Apprentice Girl'. *London Magazine* 36 (1767): 477–81.

———. *The Travels of Hildebrand Bowman.* London: W. Strahan and T. Cadell, 1778.

———. *A Warning for Fair Women.* Ed. Charles Dale Cannon. The Hague: Mouton, 1975.

Antoine, André. *Mes Souvenirs sur le Théâtre Libre.* Paris: Fayard, 1921.

———. *Le Théâtre Libre.* Paris: 1887; 1887–90; May 1890; October 1891; 1893–4.

Appel, Alfred. *Nabokov's Dark Cinema.* New York: Oxford University Press, 1974.

Armstrong, Isobel. *Victorian Glassworks: Glass Culture and the Imagination 1830–1880.* Oxford: Oxford University Press, 2008.

Auerbach, Erich. *Mimesis: The Representation of Reality in Western Literature.* Trans. Willard R. Trask. Princeton, N.J.: Princeton University Press, 1953.

Ayler, Albert. 'Ghosts'. In *Spiritual Unity.* ESP Disk ESP1002–2. 1964.

Babbitt, Milton. 'Who cares if you listen?' *High Fidelity* 8, no. 2 (February 1958): 38–40.

Bachelard, Gaston. *The Poetics of Space.* Trans. Maria Jolas. Introd. John Stilgoe. Boston, Mass.: Beacon Press, 1994. Originally published as *La Poétique de l'espace.* Paris: Presses universitaires de France, 1958.

Bailey, Derek. *Improvisation: Its Nature and Practice in Music.* Derbyshire: Moorland Publishing, 1980.

Balliett, Whitney. *The Sound of Surprise – Forty-Six Pieces on Jazz.* New York: Dutton, 1959.

Balta, Evangelia. *Karamanlidika Additions: Bibliographie analytique (1584–1900).* Athens: Centre d'Études d'Asie Mineure, 1987.

———. *Karamanlidika Nouvelles additions et compléments: Bibliographie analytique.* Athens: Centre d'Études d'Asie Mineure, 1997.

———. *Karamanlidika XXe siècle: Bibliographie analytique.* Athens: Centre d'Études d'Asie Mineure, 1987.

Barbour, Stephen, and Cathie Carmichael, eds. *Language and Nationalism in Europe*. Oxford: Oxford University Press, 2000.

Barenboim, Daniel. *Everything is Connected: The Power of Music*. London: Weidenfeld and Nicholson, 2008.

Barthes, Roland. *Camera Lucida*. Trans. Richard Howard. London: Vintage, 2000.

———. *The Responsibility of Forms: Critical Essays on Music, Art, and Representation*. Trans. Richard Howard. Oxford: Blackwell, 1986.

Baxandall, Michael. *Painting and Experience in Fifteenth-Century Italy*. Oxford: Oxford University Press, 1988.

Bearman, Frederick A., Nati H. Krivatsy and J. Franklin Mowery. *Fine and Historic Bookbindings in the Folger Shakespeare Library*. Washington D. C.: Folger, 1992.

Beckett, Samuel. *Endgame*. London: Faber and Faber, 1958.

Benjamin, Walter. *The Arcades Project*. Trans. Howard Eiland and Kevin McLaughlin. Cambridge, Mass.: Harvard University Press, 1999, repr. 2002.

———. *Reflections: Essays, Aphorisms, Autobiographical Writings*. Ed. Peter Demetz. New York: Schocken, 1987.

Bevis, Matthew. *The Art of Eloquence: Byron, Dickens, Tennyson, Joyce*. Oxford: Oxford University Press, 2007.

Bishop, Elizabeth. *The Collected Prose*. Ed. Robert Giroux. New York: Farrar, Straus, and Giroux, 1984.

———. *The Complete Poems 1927–1979*. London: Chatto and Windus, 1983.

Biswas, Moinak, ed. *Apu and After: Revisiting Ray's Cinema*. London: Seagull Books, 2006.

Blackburn, Simon. *Truth*. London: Penguin, 2006.

Blayney, Peter. *The First Folio of Shakespeare*. Washington: Folger Shakespeare Library, 1991.

Bloom, Gina. *Voice in Motion: Staging Gender, Shaping Sound in Early Modern England*. Philadelphia: University of Pennsylvania Press, 2007.

Boswell, James. *The Life of Samuel Johnson, LL.D.* Ed. R. W. Chapman. Oxford: Oxford University Press, 1980.

Brentano, Clemens. *Godwi*. In *Werke*, Vol 2. Munich: Carl Hanser Verlag, 1963.

Bronte, Emily. *Wuthering Heights*. Ed. Hilda Marsden. Oxford: Clarendon Press, 1976.

Butler, Judith. 'Merleau-Ponty and the Touch of Malebranche'. In Taylor Carman and Mark B. N. Hansen, eds, *The Cambridge Companion to Merleau-Ponty*. Cambridge: Cambridge University Press, 2005, 181–205.

Campbell, I. C. *'Going Native' in Polynesia: Captivity Narratives and Experiences from the South Pacific*. Westport, Conn.: Greenwood Press, 1998.

Cardew, Cornelius. 'Towards an Ethic of Improvisation'. 1971. In *Cornelius Cardew: A Reader*, ed. Edwin Prévost. Harlow, England: Copula, 2006, 125–134.

Carroll, David. *Paraesthetics: Foucault, Lyotard, Derrida*. New York: Methuen, 1987.

Cavarero, Adriana. *For More Than One Voice: Toward a Philosophy of Vocal Expression*. Trans. Paul A. Kottman. Stanford: Stanford University Press, 2005.

Cave, Terence. 'Lapin ou canard? Essai sur les binômes littéraires'. In Delphine Denis, Mireillel Huchon, Anna Jaubert, Michael Rinn and Olivier Soutet, eds, *Au corps du texte: hommage à Georges Molinié*. Paris: Champion, 2010, 257–66.

———. 'Mignon's afterlife in the fiction of George Eliot'. *Rivista di letterature moderne e comparate* 56 (2003): 165–82.

———. *Mignon's Afterlives: Crossing Cultures from Goethe to the Twenty-First Century*. Oxford: Oxford University Press, forthcoming in 2011.

———. 'Singing with tigers: recognition in *Wilhelm Meister*, *Daniel Deronda* and *Nights at the Circus*'. In Philip F. Kennedy and Marilyn Lawrence, eds, *Recognition: The Poetics of Narrative: Interdisciplinary Studies on Anagnorisis*. New York: Peter Lang, 2009, 115–34. Reprinted in slightly modified form in Terence Cave, *Retrospectives: Essays in Literature, Poetics and Cultural History*, ed. Neil Kenny and Wes Williams. Oxford: Legenda, 2009, 168–85.

———. 'Written on the scroll: Diderot, Goethe and Blixen'. *Oxford German Studies* 33 (2004): 51–69.

Cavell, Stanley. 'Aesthetic Problems of Modern Philosophy'. In *Must We Mean What We Say?* Cambridge: Cambridge University Press, 1976, 73–96.

Chatterjee, Partha. *The Nation and Its Fragments: Colonial and Postcolonial Histories*. Delhi: Oxford University Press, 1994.

Chattopadhyay, Swati. *Representing Calcutta: Modernity, Nationalism and the Colonial Uncanny*. London: Routledge, 2005.

Chaucer, Geoffrey. *The Workes of Geffray Chaucer*. London: Wyllyam Bonham, 1545(?).

Chaudhurani, Indira Debi, ed. *Puratani*. Kolkata: Indian Associated Publishing Company, 1957.

Chaudhuri, Supriya. 'A Sentimental Education: Love and Marriage in *The Home and the World*'. In Datta, ed., *A Critical Companion*, 45–65.

Chekhov, Anton. *The Cherry Orchard*. In *The Oxford Chekhov*, ed. and trans. Ronald Hingley, vol. 3. London: Oxford University Press, 1964.

Clendinnen, Inga. *Dancing with Strangers*. Cambridge: Cambridge University Press, 2005.

———. 'Who Owns the Past?' *Quarterly Essay* 23 (2006).

Coetzee, J. M. *Foe*. London: Penguin, 1988.

Coleman, Ornette. *Change of the Century*. Atlantic LP 1327. 1959, released 1960.

———. *The Shape of Jazz to Come*. Atlantic LP 1317. 1959.

Coltrane, John. *Giant Steps*. Atlantic LP 1311. 1959, released 1960.

———. *A Love Supreme*. Impulse! GRD155. 1965.

Conrad, Joseph. *Nostromo: A Tale of the Seaboard*. Ed. Jacques Berthould and Mara Kalnins. Oxford: Oxford University Press, 2007.

Cott, Jonathan. *Stockhausen: Conversations with the Composer*. London: Robson Books, 1974.

Covin, Michel. 'Un moment difficile à passer, mais vite oublié'. In Michel Covin, ed., 'Visages du sommeil'. Special issue, *Revue des Sciences Humaines* 194 (1984): 7–30.

Crescentiis, Petrus de. *Liber ruralium commodorum*. Louvain: Johannes de Paderborn, n.d.

Dabney, Stuart. *Nabokov: The Dimensions of Parody*. Baton Rouge: Louisiana State University Press, 1978.

Dante Alighieri. *The Divine Comedy of Dante Alighieri*. 3 vols. Trans. and ed. John D. Sinclair. Revised edition. London: John Lane, 1948.

Datta, P. K., ed. *Rabindranath Tagore's 'The Home and the World': A Critical Companion*. Delhi: Permanent Black, 2003.

Davies, R. T., ed. *Medieval English Lyrics*. London: Faber and Faber, 1963.

Davis, Miles, *Kind of Blue*. Columbia CK-64935. 1959.

de Grazia, Margreta. 'The First Reader of *Shake-speares Sonnets*'. In Leonard Barkan, Bradin Cormack and Sean Keilen, eds. *The Forms of Renaissance Thought*. Basingstoke: Palgrave, 2009, 86–106.

———. *'Hamlet' Without Hamlet*. Cambridge: Cambridge University Press, 2007.

Dening, Greg. *Mr Bligh's Bad Language*. Cambridge: Cambridge University Press, 1992.

Dering, Edward. 'Booke of Expences'. 1617–28. Transcription by Laetitia Yeandle online at http://www.kentarchaeology.ac/authors/020.pdf (accessed 26 June 2010).

Derrida, Jacques. *Aporias*. Trans. T. Dutoit. Palo Alto: Stanford University Press, 1993.

———. *Of Hospitality: Anne Dufourmantelle invites Jacques Derrida to respond.* Trans. Rachel Bowlby. Palo Alto: Stanford University Press, 2000.

———. 'How to Avoid Speaking: Denials'. Trans. Ken Friedren. In *Derrida and Negative Theology*, ed. Harold Coward and Toby Foshay. Albany: State University of New York Press, 1992, 73–142.

Descartes, René. *Meditations on First Philosophy: With Selections from the Objections and Replies.* Trans. John Cottingham. Cambridge: Cambridge University Press, 1986.

Dessen, Alan C., and Leslie Thomson. *A Dictionary of Stage Directions in English Drama, 1580–1642.* Cambridge: Cambridge University Press, 1999.

Diderot, Denis. *La Religieuse.* In *Œuvres romanesques*, ed. H. Bénac. Paris: Garnier, 1962.

Dolar, Mladen. *A Voice and Nothing More.* Cambridge: MIT Press, 2006.

Doyle, Arthur Conan, Sir. *The Edge of the Unknown.* London: John Murray, 1930.

Dubrow, Heather. '"They took from me the use of mine own house": Land Law in Shakespeare's *Lear* and Shakespeare's Culture'. In Dennis Kezar, ed., *Solon and Thespis: Law and Theater in the Renaissance.* Notre Dame: University of Notre Dame Press, 2007, 81–98.

Duffy, Eamon. *Marking the Hours: English People and their Prayers 1240–1570.* New Haven: Yale University Press, 2006.

Dyer, Geoff. *But Beautiful.* London: Jonathan Cape, 1991.

Eliot, T. S. *Collected Poems 1909–1962.* London: Faber and Faber, 1974, repr. 2002.

Ellis, William. *Polynesian Researches.* 2 vols. London: Fisher and Jackson, 1830.

Elsaesser, Thomas, ed. *The BFI Companion to German Cinema.* London: British Film Institute, 1999.

Feigel, Lara, and Alexandra Harris, eds. *Modernism on Sea: Art and Culture at the British Seaside.* Oxford: Peter Lang, 2005.

Field, Andrew. *Nabokov: His Life and Art.* London: Hodder and Stoughton, 1967.

Fisher, Bishop John. *De Veritate Corporis et Sanguinis Christi in Eucharistia.* Cologne: Peter Quentell, 1527.

Flieger, Jerry Aline. 'Proust, Freud, and the Art of Forgetting'. *SubStance* 9, no. 4, issue 29 (1980): 66–82.

Fokkelman, J. P. 'Exodus'. In Alter and Kermode, eds, *The Literary Guide to the Bible*, 56–65.

Foot, M. M. 'An Englishman in Paris: John Evelyn and his Bookbindings'. In Anna De Coster and Claude Sorgeloos, eds, *Bibliophilies et reliures.* Brussels: Tulkens, 2006, 231–45.

Forster, E. M. *Abinger Harvest.* London: Andre Deutsch, 1996.

Forster, Georg. *A Voyage Round the World.* 2 vols. London: White, 1777.

Forster, Johann Reinhold. *Observations Made during a Voyage Round the World.* Ed. Nicholas Thomas, Harriet Guest, and Michael Dettelbach. Honolulu: University of Hawai'i Press, 1996.

Foucault, Michel. 'Of Other Spaces'. Trans. Jay Miskowiec. *Diacritics* 16, no. 1 (1986): 22–7. Originally published in French as 'Des espaces autres: Une conférence inédite de Michel Foucault'. *Architecture-Mouvement-Continuité* (October 1984): 46–49. Online: http://foucault.info/documents/heteroTopia/foucault.heteroTopia.en.html (accessed 26 June 2010).

———. *The Order of Things: An Archaeology of the Human Science.* London: Tavistock Publications, 1970.

Freud, Sigmund. 'The Uncanny'. In *The Standard Edition of the Complete Psychological Works of Sigmund Freud*, ed. and trans. James Strachey. Vol. 17. London: Hogarth, 1955, 219–252.

———. *'The Wolfman' and Other Cases*. Ed. Gillian Beer. London: Penguin, 2003.

Frost, Robert. *Collected Poems, Prose, and Plays*. Sel. Richard Poirier and Mark Richardson. New York: The Library of America, 1995.

Gascoigne, George. *The noble art of venerie or hunting*. London: Thomas Purfoot, 1611.

Gaskell, Elizabeth. *Mary Barton*. The Knutsford Edition: London: Smith, Elder, 1906.

Genette, Gérard. *Paratexts: Thresholds of Interpretation*. Trans. Jane E. Lewin. Cambridge: Cambridge University Press, 1997. Originally published as *Seuils*. Paris: Seuil, 1987.

Gillespie, Alexandra. *Print Culture and the Medieval Author: Chaucer, Lydgate, and their Books 1473–1557*. Oxford: Oxford University Press, 2006.

Goethe, Johann Wolfgang. *Wilhelm Meisters Lehrjahre*. Ed. Erich Schmidt. Frankfurt am Main: Insel Taschenbuch, 1980.

Golston, Michael. *Rhythm and Race in Modernist Poetry and Science: Pound, Yeats, Williams, and Modern Sciences of Rhythm*. New York: Columbia University Press, 2008.

Goutsos, Dionysis, and Marilena Karyolemou. 'Introduction'. *International Journal of the Sociology of Language* 168 (2004): 1–17.

Graham, W. S. *New Collected Poems*. Ed. Matthew Francis. London: Faber and Faber, 2004.

———. *The Nightfisherman: Selected Letters of W. S. Graham*. Ed. Michael and Margaret Snow. London: Oxford University Press, 1999.

Greenblatt, Stephen. *Hamlet in Purgatory*. Princeton: Princeton University Press, 2002.

Grenville, Kate. *The Secret River*. Melbourne: The Text Publishing Company, 2005.

Gubbins, Paul, and Mike Holt, eds. *Beyond Boundaries: Language and Identity in Contemporary Europe*. Clevedon, England: Multilingual Matters, 2002.

Guha, Ranajit. *Dominance without Hegemony: History and Power in Colonial India*. Cambridge, Mass.: Harvard University Press, 1997.

Guthrie-Smith, Herbert. *Tutira: The Story of a New Zealand Sheep Station*. Edinburgh and London: William Blackwood, 1969.

Hake, Sabine. *The Cinema's Weird Machine: Writing on Film in Germany, 1907–1933*. Lincoln: University of Nebraska Press, 1993.

Hall, N. J. *Max Beerbohm: A Kind of Life*. New Haven: Yale University Press, 2002.

Hamilton, A. C., ed. *The Spenser Encyclopedia*. London: Routledge, 1990.

Hardy, Thomas. 'The Dorsetshire Labourer'. *Longman's Magazine*, July 1883, 252–69. Collected in *Thomas Hardy's Personal Writings*, ed. Harold Orel. London: Macmillan, 1967, 178–9.

Harris, Jonathan Gil. *Untimely Matter in the Age of Shakespeare*. Philadelphia: University of Pennsylvania Press, 2009.

Heaney, Seamus. 'Sounding Auden'. In *The Government of the Tongue*. London: Faber and Faber, 1988, 109–28.

Heidegger, Martin. 'Poetically Man Dwells'. In *Poetry, Language, Thought*. Trans. Albert Hofstadter. New York: Harper and Row, 1971, 213–29.

Heller-Roazen, Daniel. *The Inner Touch: The Archaeology of a Sensation*. New York: Zone Books, 2007.

Hennique, Léon. *Jacques Damour*. Paris: Charpentier, 1887.

Herbert, George. *The Works of George Herbert*. Ed. F. E. Hutchinson. Oxford: Clarendon Press, 1941.

Hill, Geoffrey. *Collected Poems*. London: Penguin, 1959, repr. 1985.

Hopkins, Gerard Manley. *The Letters of Gerard Manley Hopkins to Robert Bridges*. Ed. Claude Colleer Abbott. London: Oxford University Press, 1935, repr. 1955.

Hutson, Lorna, ed. 'Forum: Fifty Years of the King's Two Bodies'. Special issue, *Representations* 106 (Spring 2009).

Ihde, Don. *Listening and Voice: A Phenomenology of Sound*. Athens, Ohio: Ohio University Press, 1976.

Irigaray, Luce. 'The Power of Discourse and the Subordination of the Feminine'. In Margaret Whitford, ed., *The Irigaray Reader*. Oxford: Blackwell, 1991, repr. 1995, 108–32.

Issacharoff, Michael. *Discourse as Performance*. Stanford: Stanford University Press, 1989. Originally published as *Le Spectacle du discours*. Paris: Librairie José Corti, 1985.

Jackson, H. J. '"Marginal Frivolities": readers' notes as evidence for the history of reading'. In Myers et al., eds, *Readers, Annotators, and the Signs of Reading*, 137–51.

———. *Romantic Readers: The Evidence of Marginalia*. New Haven: Yale University Press, 2005.

Jajdelska, Elspeth. 'Pepys in the History of Reading'. *Historical Journal* 50 (2007): 549–69.

Jameson, Fredric. *The Political Unconscious*. 1981; London: Routledge, 2002.

———. *Signatures of the Visible*. New York: Routledge, 1992, 2007.

Jay, Martin. *Downcast Eyes: The Denigration of Vision in Twentieth-Century French Thought*. Berkeley, L.A.: University of California Press, 1993.

Johnson, Samuel. *A Journey to the Western Islands of Scotland*. Ed. Mary Lascelles. New Haven: Yale University Press, 1971.

Josipovici, Gabriel. *In the Fertile Land*. Manchester: Carcanet, 1987.

Joyce, James. *Ulysses*. Ed. Jeri Johnson. Oxford: Oxford University Press, 1993.

Jullien, Jean. *Le Théâtre vivant*. Paris: Charpentier, 1892.

Kalush, William, and Larry Sloman. *The Secret Life of Houdini: The Making of America's first Superhero*. New York: Atria Books, 2006.

Kames, Henry H., Lord. *Sketches of the History of Man*. 4 vols. London: W. Strahan and T. Cadell, 1778.

Kantorowicz, Ernst H. *The King's Two Bodies*. Princeton: Princeton University Press, 2007.

Karoulla-Vrikki, Dimitra. 'Language and Ethnicity in Cyprus under the British: A Linkage of Heightened Salience'. *International Journal of the Sociology of Language* 168 (2004): 19–36.

Keats, John. *The Poetical Works of John Keats*. Ed. H. W. Garrod. Oxford: Clarendon Press, 1958.

Kivy, Peter. *Music, Language, and Cognition: And Other Essays in the Aesthetics of Music*. Oxford: Clarendon Press, 2007.

Kizilyürek, Niyazi, and Sylvaine Gautier-Kizilyürek. 'The Politics of Identity in the Turkish Cypriot Community and the Language Question'. *International Journal of the Sociology of Language* 168 (2004): 37–54.

Kottman, Paul A. *Tragic Condition in Shakespeare*. Baltimore: Johns Hopkins University Press, 2009.

Lacan, Jacques. 'The Mirror Stage as Formative of the Function of the *I*'. In *Écrits: A Selection*, trans. Alan Sheridan. London: Routledge, 1989, 1–8.

Lakoff, George. *Women, Fire, and Dangerous Things: What Categories Reveal about the Mind*. Chicago and London: Chicago University Press, 1987.

Lane, Jeremy. 'Falling Asleep in the Wake: Reading as Hypnagogic Experience'. In John Brannigan, Geoff Ward and Julian Wolfreys, eds, *Re: Joyce: Text Culture Politics*. London and New York: Macmillan, 1998, 163–81.

Larkin, Philip. *Collected Poems*. London: Faber and Faber with The Marvell Press, 1988.

Le Loyer, Pierre. *A Treatise of Specters*. London: Val. S., 1605.

Leighton, Angela. *On Form: Poetry, Aestheticism, and the Legacy of a Word*. Oxford: Oxford University Press, 2007.

Lévi-Strauss, Claude. *Myth and Meaning*. London: Routledge and Kegan Paul, 1978.

———. *Structural Anthropology*. Trans. Claire Jacobson. New York: Basic Books, 1963.

Lewis, Geoffrey. *The Turkish Language Reform: A Catastrophic Success*. Oxford: Oxford University Press, 1999.

Ligeti, György. *String Quartet no. 2*. 1968. Mainz: Schott, 1971.

Lukács, Georg. 'Tagore's Gandhi Novel'. In *Reviews and Articles for Die Rote Fahne*. Trans. Peter Palmer. London: Merlin Press, 1983, 8–11.

Lustig, T. J. *Henry James and the Ghostly*. Cambridge: Cambridge University Press, 1994.

Mackridge, Peter. *Language and National Identity in Greece 1766–1976*. Oxford: Oxford University Press, 2009.

MacPherson, Malcolm, ed. *The Black Box: All-New Cockpit Voice Recorder Accounts of In-Flight Accidents*. New York: Quill, 1998.

Maning, F. E. *Old New Zealand*. London: Smith Elder, 1863.

———. *Old New Zealand and Other Writings*. Ed. Alex Calder. Leicester: Leicester University Press, 2001.

Manocci, Lino. *The Annunciation: Lino Mannocci*. London: Curwen Gallery, 1992.

Mantel, Hilary. 'Dreams & Duels of England'. *New York Review of Books*, 22 October 2009, 8–12.

Marks, Herbert. 'The Twelve Prophets'. In Alter and Kermode, eds, *The Literary Guide to the Bible*, 207–233.

Marsalis, Branford. *Crazy People Music*. Columbia CK-46072, 1990.

Mathias, Thomas James. *The pursuits of literature: a satirical poem in four dialogues, with notes*. 16th edition. London: Becket and Porter, 1812.

Maude, H. E. *Of Islands and Men: Studies in Pacific History*. Oxford: Oxford University Press, 1968.

Mavromatis, Andreas. *Hypnagogia: The Unique State of Consciousness Between Wakefulness and Sleep*. London: Routledge and Kegan Paul, 1987.

McKeon, Michael. *The Secret History of Domesticity: Public, Private and the Division of Knowledge*. Baltimore: Johns Hopkins University Press, 2005.

Menninghaus, Winfried. *Schwellenkunde: Walter Benjamin's Passage des Mythos*. Frankfurt am Main: Suhrkamp, 1986.

Merleau-Ponty, Maurice. 'Lecture de Montaigne'. In *Signes*. Paris: Gallimard, 1960, 250–266.

———. *The Visible and the Invisible*. Trans. A. Lingis. Evanston: Northwestern University Press, 1968.

Mieszkowski, Jan. 'Art Forms'. In David S. Ferris, ed., *The Cambridge Companion to Walter Benjamin*. Cambridge: Cambridge University Press, 2004, 35–53.

Milcairns, Susan. *Native Strangers*. Auckland: Penguin, 2007.

Millier, Brett. *Elizabeth Bishop: Life and the Memory of It*. Berkeley, L.A.: University of California Press, 1993.

Mingus, Charles. *Oh Yeah*. Atlantic LP 1377. 1961.

Montaigne, Michel de. *Essais*. 2 vols. Ed. Maurice Rat. Paris: Garnier, 1962.

———. *The Complete Essays*. Ed. and trans. M. A. Screech. London: Penguin, 1991.

Mosnier, Charles. *André Antoine*. 7 vols. Ms. Bibliothèque de l'Arsenal, Paris, n.d.

Mulvey, Laura. 'Visual Pleasure and Narrative Cinema'. *Screen* 16, no. 3 (1975): 6–18.

Murphy, Daniel J., ed. *Lady Gregory's Journals*. 2 vols. Smythe: Gerrards Cross, 1978–1987.

Myers, Robin, Michael Harris and Giles Mandelbrote, eds. *Readers, Annotators, and the Signs of Reading*. London: British Library, 2005.

Nabokov, Vladimir. *The Enchanter*. 1986; London: Penguin, 2009.

———. *King, Queen, Knave*. London: Harmondsworth, 2001. Originally published in Russian, 1928.

———. *Laughter in the Dark*. London: Penguin, 2001. Originally published in Russian as *Kamera Obskura*, 1933.

———. *Lolita*. 1959; Harmondsworth: Penguin, 2000.

———. *Mary*. London: Penguin, 2009. Originally published in Russian, 1926.

———. *The Real Life of Sebastian Knight*. 1941; London: Penguin, 2001.

Nichols, Tom. *Tintoretto: Tradition and Identity*. London: Reaktion, 1999.

Nicholson, John. *White Chief: The Colourful Life and Times of Judge F. E. Maning of the Hokianga*. Auckland: Penguin Group, 2006.

Norman, Will and Duncan White. *Transitional Nabokov*. Oxford: Peter Lang, 2009.

O'Callaghan, Casey. *Sounds: A Philosophical Theory*. Oxford: Oxford University Press, 2007.

Orlin, Lena Cowen. *Private Matters and Public Culture in post-Reformation England*. Ithaca: Cornell University Press, 1994.

Pasolini, Pier Paolo, dir. *Teorema* (Theorem). 1968; Koch Lorber Films, 2005.

Pater, Walter. *The Renaissance: Studies in Art and Poetry*. Ed. Adam Phillips. Oxford: Oxford University Press, 1986.

Pearson, David. *English Bookbinding Styles 1450–1800: A Handbook*. London: British Library, 2005.

Peltz, Lucy. 'Engraved Portrait Heads and the Rise of Extra-Illustration: The Eton Correspondence of the Revd James Granger and Richard Bull, 1769–1774'. *Journal of the Walpole Society* 66 (2004): 1–162.

———. 'Facing the Text: the amateur and commercial histories of extra-illustration, c. 1770–1840'. In Myers et al., eds, *Readers, Annotators, and the Signs of Reading*, 91–135.

Perloff, Marjorie, and Craig Dworkin, eds. *The Sound of Poetry / The Poetry of Sound*. Chicago: University of Chicago Press, 2009.

Phillips, Adam. *Houdini's Box: On the Arts of Escape*. London: Faber and Faber, 2002.

Pifer, Ellen. *Nabokov and the Novel*. Massachusetts: Harvard University Press, 1980.

Pinero, Arthur Wing. *The Second Mrs Tanqueray*. 1893. In *Arthur Wing Pinero: Three Plays*, ed. Stephen Wyatt. London: Methuen, 1985.

Pointon, Marcia. *Hanging the Head: Portraiture and Social Formation in Eighteenth-Century England*. New Haven: Yale University Press, 1993.

Poovey, Mary. *A History of the Modern Fact*. Chicago: Chicago University Press, 1998.

Proust, Marcel. *A la recherche du temps perdu*. 3 vols. Ed. Pierre Clarac et André Ferré. Paris: Gallimard, 1954.

———. *Remembrance of Things Past*. 3 vols. Trans. C. K. Scott-Moncrieff and Terence Kilmartin. London: Penguin, 1983.

———. *Swann's Way*. Trans. by C. K. Scott Moncrieff. London: Penguin, 1957.

Ramadan, Adam. 'The Guest's Guests: Palestinian Refugees, Lebanese Civilians, and the War of 2006'. *Antipode* 40, no. 4 (2008): 658–77.

Rassundari Debi. *Amar jiban* (My Life). In N. Jana et al., eds, *Atmakatha* (Autobiographies). 5 vols. Kolkata: Ananya Prakashan, 1981–86, 1 (1981): 1–81.

Rilke, Rainer Maria. *Duino Elegies*. Ed. and trans. J. B. Leishman and Stephen Spender. London: Hogarth Press, 1963.

Robinson, Andrew. *Satyajit Ray: The Inner Eye*. Delhi: Oxford University Press, 2004.

Rosetti, Christina. *The Complete Poems of Christina Rossetti: A Variorum Edition*. 3 vols. Ed. R. W. Crump. Baton Rouge: Louisiana State University Press, 1979–90.

Ruskin, John. *Works of John Ruskin*. 39 vols. Ed. E. T. Cook and Alexander Wedderburn. London: George Allen, 1903–1912.

Said, Edward. *Beginnings*. London: Granta, 1998.

———. 'Secular Criticism'. In *The World, Text and the Critic*. Cambridge, Mass.: Harvard University Press, 1983, 1–30.

Salaville, Sévérien, and Eugéne Daleggio. *Karamanlidika: bibliographie analytique d'ouvrages en langue turque imprimés en caractères grecs*. 3 vols. Athens: Institut français d'Athènes, 1958–1974.

Salmond, Anne. *The Trial of the Cannibal Dog*. London: Allen Lane, 2003.

Sarkar, Tanika. 'Many Faces of Love: Country, Woman and God in *The Home and the World*'. In Datta, ed., *A Critical Companion*, 27–44.

———. *Words to Win: The Making of 'Amar Jiban': A Modern Autobiography*. New Delhi: Kali for Women, 1999.

Scolnicov, Hanna. *Women's Theatrical Space*. Cambridge: Cambridge University Press, 1994.

Scott-Warren, Jason. *Early Modern English Literature*. Cambridge: Polity, 2005.

———. 'News, Sociability and Bookbuying in Early Modern England: The Letters of Sir Thomas Cornwallis'. *The Library* 7th ser., 1 (2000): 381–402.

———. *Sir John Harington and the Book as Gift*. Oxford: Oxford University Press, 2001.

Shakespeare, William. *The Famous Historie of Troylus and Cresseid*. London: R. Bonian and H. Walley, 1609.

———. *The First Folio: Norton Facsimile*. New York: Hamlyn, 1968.

———. *Hamlet*. Ed. G. R. Hibbard. Oxford: Oxford University Press, 1987.

———. *Mr William Shakespeares Comedies, Histories, & Tragedies*. London: William Jaggard, 1623.

———. *Poems: Written by Wil. Shake-speare. Gent.* London: John Benson, 1640.

———. *The Riverside Shakespeare*. Ed. G. Blakemore Evans. Boston: Houghton Mifflin, 1974.

———. *Shakespeare's Sonnets*. Ed. W. G. Ingram and Theodore Redpath. London: University of London Press, 1964.

———. *The Sonnets*. Illustrated by Ian Penney. London: Barrie and Jenkins, 1988.

Shamir, Milette. *Inexpressible Privacy: The Interior Life of Antebellum American Literature*. Philadelphia: University of Pennsylvania Press, 2006.

Shelley, Mary. *Frankenstein: or, The Modern Prometheus*. London: Colburn and Bentley, 1831.

Sherman, William H. *John Dee: The Politics of Reading and Writing in Early Modern England*. Amherst: University of Massachusetts Press, 1995.

———. *Used Books: Marking Readers in Early Modern England*. Philadelphia: University of Pennsylvania Press, 2007.

Shorter, Wayne. *Speak No Evil*. Blue Note BLP 4194. 1965.

Sillars, Stuart. *The Illustrated Shakespeare, 1709–1875*. Cambridge: Cambridge University Press, 2008.

Silverman, Kaja. *The Threshold of the Visible World*. New York: Routledge, 1996.

Steedman, Carolyn. *Strange Dislocations: Childhood and the Idea of Human Interiority, 1780–1930*. London: Virago Books, 1995.

Stevens, Wallace. 'The Noble Rider and the Sound of Words'. In *Wallace Stevens: Collected Poetry and Prose*, ed. Frank Kermode and Joan Richardson. New York: The Library of America, 1997, 643–65.

Stewart, Garrett. *The Look of Reading: Book, Painting, Text*. Chicago: University of Chicago Press, 2006.

———. *Reading Voices: Literature and the Phonotext*. Berkeley, L.A.: University of California Press, 1990.

Stewart, Susan. *Poetry and the Fate of the Senses*. Chicago: University of Chicago Press, 2002.

Straumann, Barbara. *Figurations of Exile in Hitchcock and Nabokov*. Edinburgh: Edinburgh University Press, 2008.

Strindberg, August. *Strindberg Plays: One*. Trans. Michael Meyer. London: Methuen, 1976.

Tagore, Abanindranath. *Apan Katha* (My Story). Kolkata: Ananda Publishers, 2005.

Tagore, Rabindranath, articles, February 1907 to September–October 1908: 'Byadhi o Pratikar', *Prabasi*, Shravan 1314; 'Path o Patheya', *Bangadarshan*, Jyaishtha 1315; 'Samasya', *Prabasi*, Asharh 1315; 'Sadupay', *Prabasi*, Shravan 1315; 'Deshahit', *Bangadarshan*, Ashvin 1315.

———. *Ghare Baire*. Kolkata: Vishva Bharati, 1994.

———. Presidential address delivered to the Pabna Pradeshik Sammilani (February 1907). *Prabasi*, Phalgun 1314.

Templar, Marcus A. 'Tasting the Bitter *Pekmez*: Causes of Turkey's Instability'. *Journal of Global Change and Governance* 1, no. 2 (2008). Online: http://dga.rutgers.edu/JGCG/vol_I_2.html (accessed 26 June 2010).

Thomas, Keith. *The Ends of Life: Roads to Fulfillment in Early Modern England*. Oxford: Oxford University Press, 2009.

Thomas, Nicholas. *In Oceania: Visions, Artifacts, Histories*. Durham: Duke University Press, 1997.

———. '"On the Origin of the Human Species": Forster's Comparative Ethnology'. In Forster, *Observations Made during a Voyage Round the World*, xxiii–xl.

Toker, Leona. *Nabokov: The Mystery of Literary Structures*. Ithaca: Cornell University Press, 1989.

Tomlinson, Charles. *Annunciations*. Oxford: Oxford University Press, 1989.

Trudgill, Peter. 'Greece and European Turkey: From Religious to Linguistic Identity'. In Stephen Barbour and Cathie Carmichael, eds, *Language and Nationalism in Europe*. Oxford: Oxford University Press, 2000, 240–63.

Vasudevan, Ravi. 'Nationhood, Authenticity and Realism in Indian Cinema: The Double-Take of Modernism in Ray'. In Moinak Biswas, ed., *Apu and After: Revisiting Ray's Cinema*. London: Seagull Books, 2006, 80–115.

Vendler, Helen. *The Odes of John Keats*. Cambridge, Mass.: Belknap Press of the University of Harvard, 1983.

Vincent, Augustine. *A Discoverie of Errours in the First Edition of the Catalogue of Nobility*. London: William Jaggard, 1622.

Ware, Sir James. *The whole works of Sir James Ware concerning Ireland*. Dublin: 'For the Author', 1739–46.

Wedekind, Frank. *Erdgeist*. In *Werke*, vol. 3, ed. Hartmut Vinçon. Darmstadt: Häusser, 1996.

Wheeler, Roxann. *The Complexion of Race*. Philadelphia: University of Pennsylvania Press, 2000.

White, Harry. *Music and the Irish Literary Imagination*. Oxford: Oxford University Press, 2008.

Wilmer, Valerie. *As Serious as your Life*. London: Allison and Busby Ltd, 1977.

Wittgenstein, Ludwig. *Philosophische Untersuchungen (Philosophical Investigations)*. With translation by G. E. M. Anscombe. Oxford: Blackwell, 1953.

———. *Tractatus Logico-Philosophicus*. Frankfurt: Edition Suhrkamp, 1963.

Wood, Michael. *Literature and the Taste of Knowledge*. Cambridge: Cambridge University Press, 2005.

Woolf, Virginia. *Mrs. Dalloway*. London: Chatto and Windus, 1968.

Wyllie, Barbara. *Nabokov at the Movies*. Jefferson: McFarland and Co., 2003.

Yashin, Mehmet. *Don't go back to Kyrenia.* Trans. Taner Baybars. London: Middlesex University Press, 2001.

———, ed. *Step-mothertongue: From Nationalism to Multiculturalism: Literatures of Cyprus, Greece and Turkey*. London: Middlesex University Press, 2000.

———. *Toplu Şiirler (1977–2002)*. Istanbul: Everest Yayınları, 2007.

———. *Toplu Yazılar (1978–2005)*. Istanbul: Everest Yayınları, 2007.

Yeats, W. B. *The Cat and the Moon and Certain Poems*. Dublin: Cuala, 1924.

———. *The Collected Poems of W. B. Yeats*. London: Macmillan, 1950.

———. *Discoveries: A Volume of Essays*. Dundrum: Dunn Emer Press, 1907.

———. *Essays and Introductions*. London: Macmillan, 1961.

———. *Mythologies*. London: Macmillan, 1959.

———. *Plays in Prose and Verse*. London: Macmillan, 1922.

———. *The Variorum Edition of the Poems of W. B. Yeats*. Ed. Russell K. Alspach. London and New York: Macmillan, 1966.

———. *A Vision*. London: Macmillan, 1937.

Zola, Emile. 'Naturalisme au théâtre'. In *Le Roman Experimental*. Paris: Charpentier, 1880, 107–156.

www.ingramcontent.com/pod-product-compliance
Lightning Source LLC
LaVergne TN
LVHW091044080826
845145LV00002B/617

9781783080731